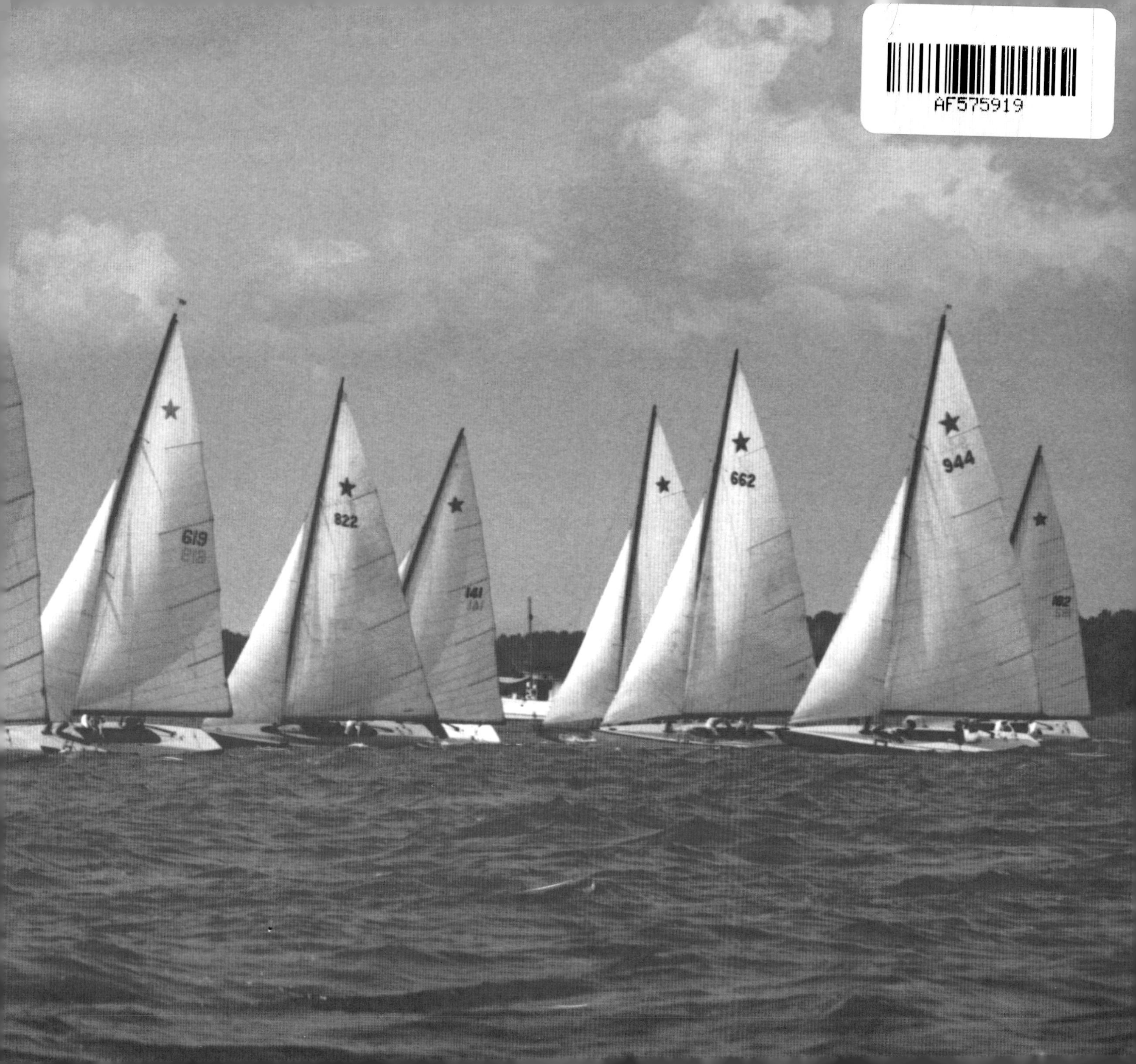
619
822
141
662
944

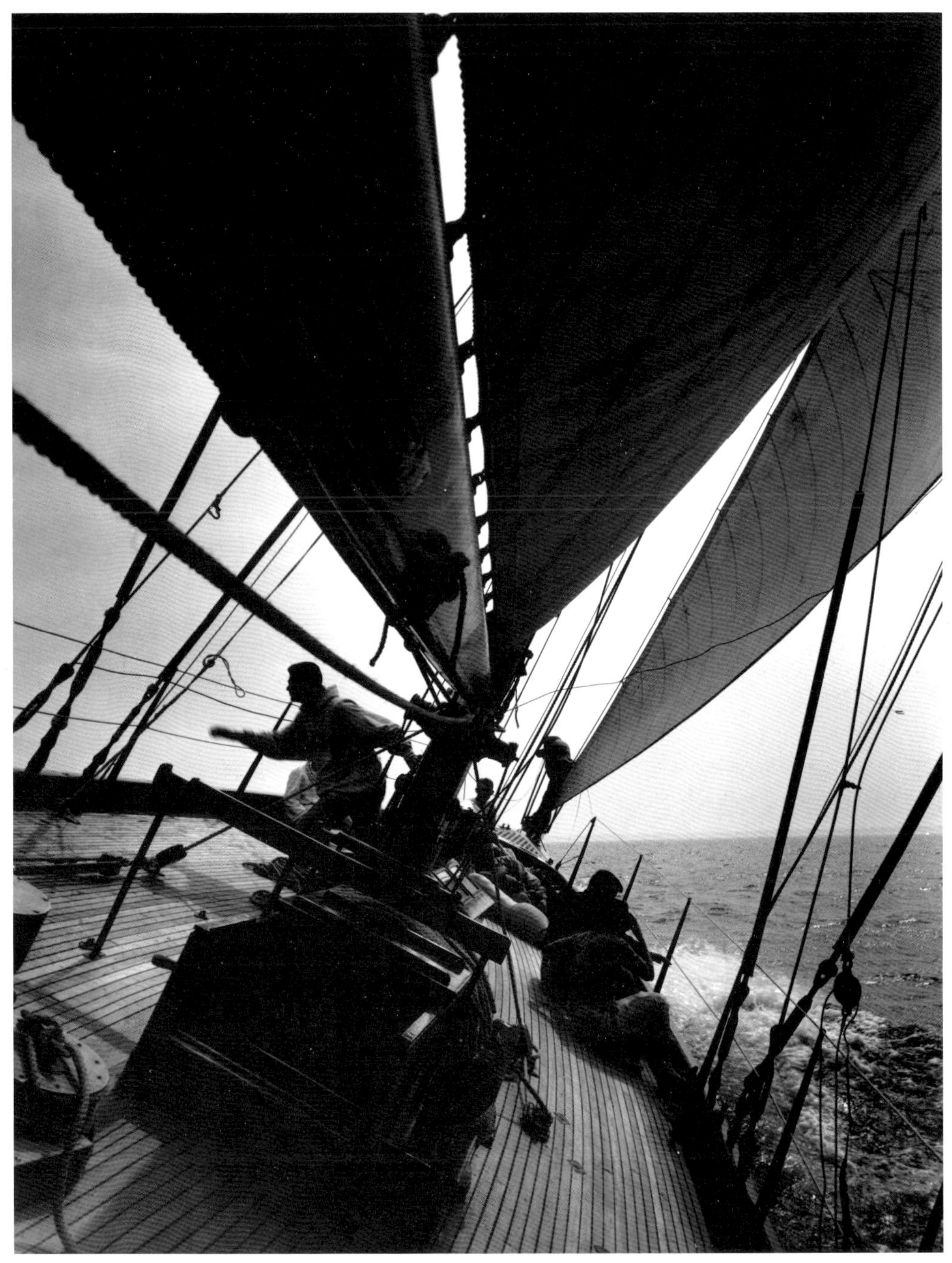

Jennifer B. Bodine

ANNAPOLIS

Photography of A. Aubrey Bodine

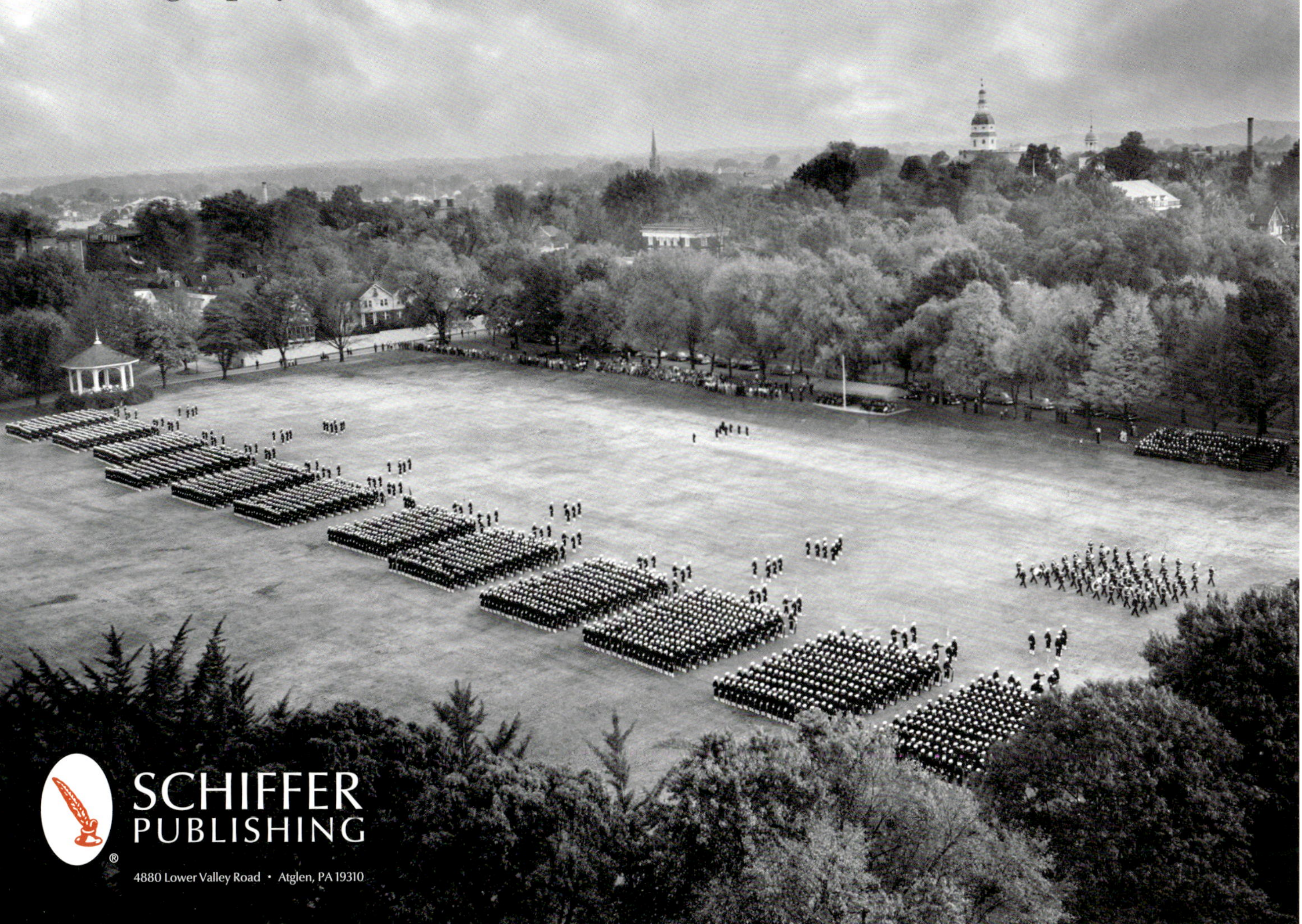

SCHIFFER PUBLISHING
4880 Lower Valley Road • Atglen, PA 19310

FRONT COVER: PLATE 001 Annapolis, City Dock (1946)
ENDSHEETS: PLATE 002 Shooting Stars (1953)
HALF TITLE PAGE: LEFT: PLATE 003 Chesapeake Bay Races (1961)
CENTER: PLATE 004 Maryland State House, Annapolis 1962
RIGHT: PLATE 005 June Week—Naval Academy, in Front of Bancroft Hall (1957)
OPPOSITE TITLE PAGE: PLATE 006 *Highland Light* (1956)
TITLE PAGE: PLATE 007 Annapolis, Brigade of Middies, Worden Field (1936)
OPPOSITE: PLATE 008 Chesapeake Days (ca. 1950)

OTHER SCHIFFER BOOKS BY THE AUTHOR:
Trains: Photography of A. Aubrey Bodine, ISBN 978-0-7643-5493-9
Bodine's City: The Photography of A. Aubrey Bodine, ISBN 978-0-7643-3844-1
Bodine's Chesapeake Bay Country, ISBN 978-0-87033-562-4
Bodine's Industry: The Dignity of Work, ISBN 978-0-7643-4285-1

Library of Congress Control Number: 2020930956

Cover design by Justin Watkinson
Type set in BauerBodni BT/Chaparral Pro

ISBN: 978-0-7643-6064-0
Printed in China

Published by Schiffer Publishing, Ltd.
4880 Lower Valley Road
Atglen, PA 19310
Phone: (610) 593-1777; Fax: (610) 593-2002
E-mail: Info@schifferbooks.com
Web: www.schifferbooks.com

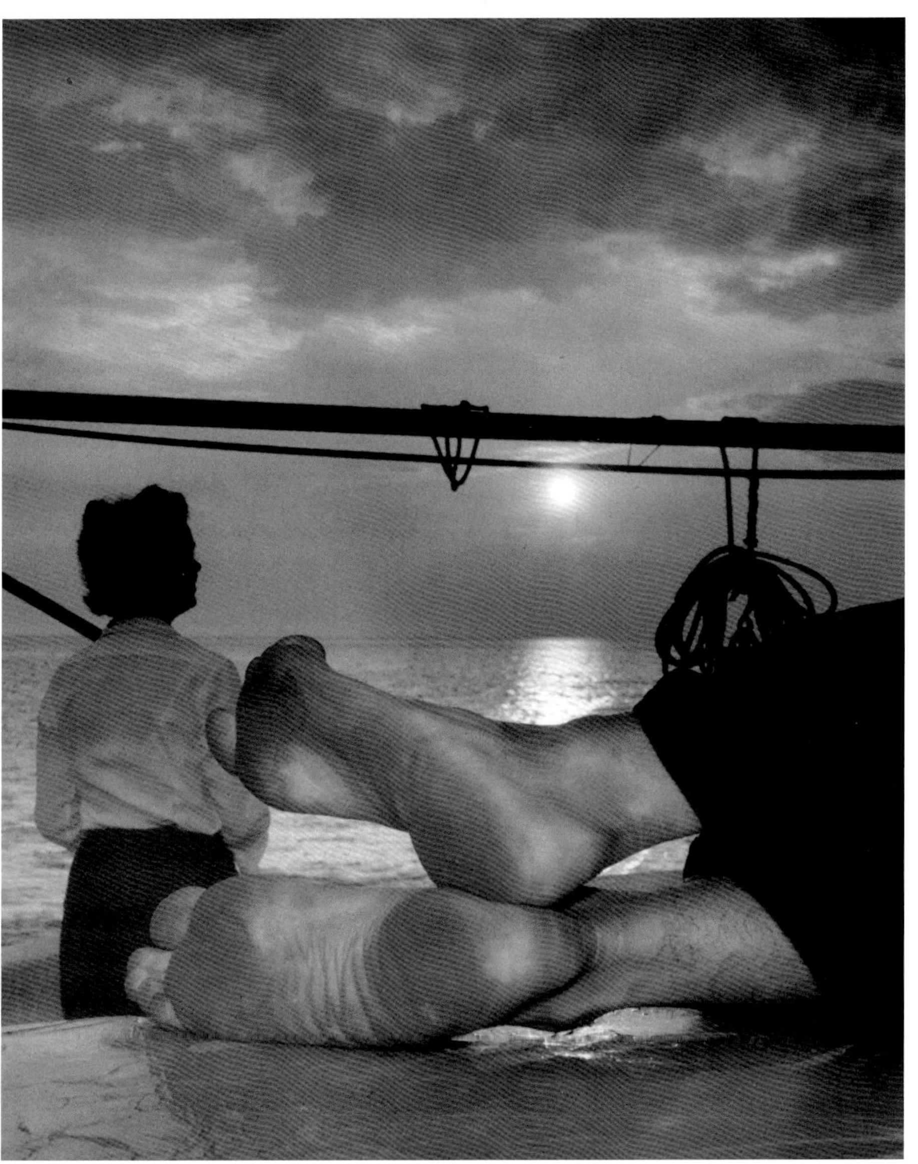

Annapolis is dedicated to the victims of the *The Capital* shooting. On June 28, 2018, an assassin murdered the following journalists at *The Capital*:

Gerald Fischman, columnist and editorial page editor

Rob Hiaasen, assistant editor and weekend columnist

John McNamara, sports reporter and editor, and primary reporter for the *Bowie Blade-News*

Rebecca Smith, sales assistant for Capital Gazette Communications

Wendi Winters, community beat reporter

One survivor stated that Wendi Winters charged the gunman with a trash can and recycling bin, screaming at him, distracting him long enough for survivors to escape.

The staff of *The Capital* and its parent company were subsequently chosen by *Time* magazine as Person of the Year 2018, as one of "The Guardians," a collection of journalists from around the world in their fight against the "War on Truth." On April 15, 2019, *The Capital* received a Pulitzer Prize Special Citation to "honor the journalists, staff, and editorial board of the *Capital Gazette*, Annapolis, Maryland, for their courageous response to the largest killing of journalists in US history in their newsroom on June 28, 2018, and for demonstrating unflagging commitment to covering the news and serving their community at a time of unspeakable grief."

THIS PAGE: PLATE 011 Government House, Annapolis (1967)

OPPOSITE PAGE: PLATE 012 Government House, Annapolis (1954)

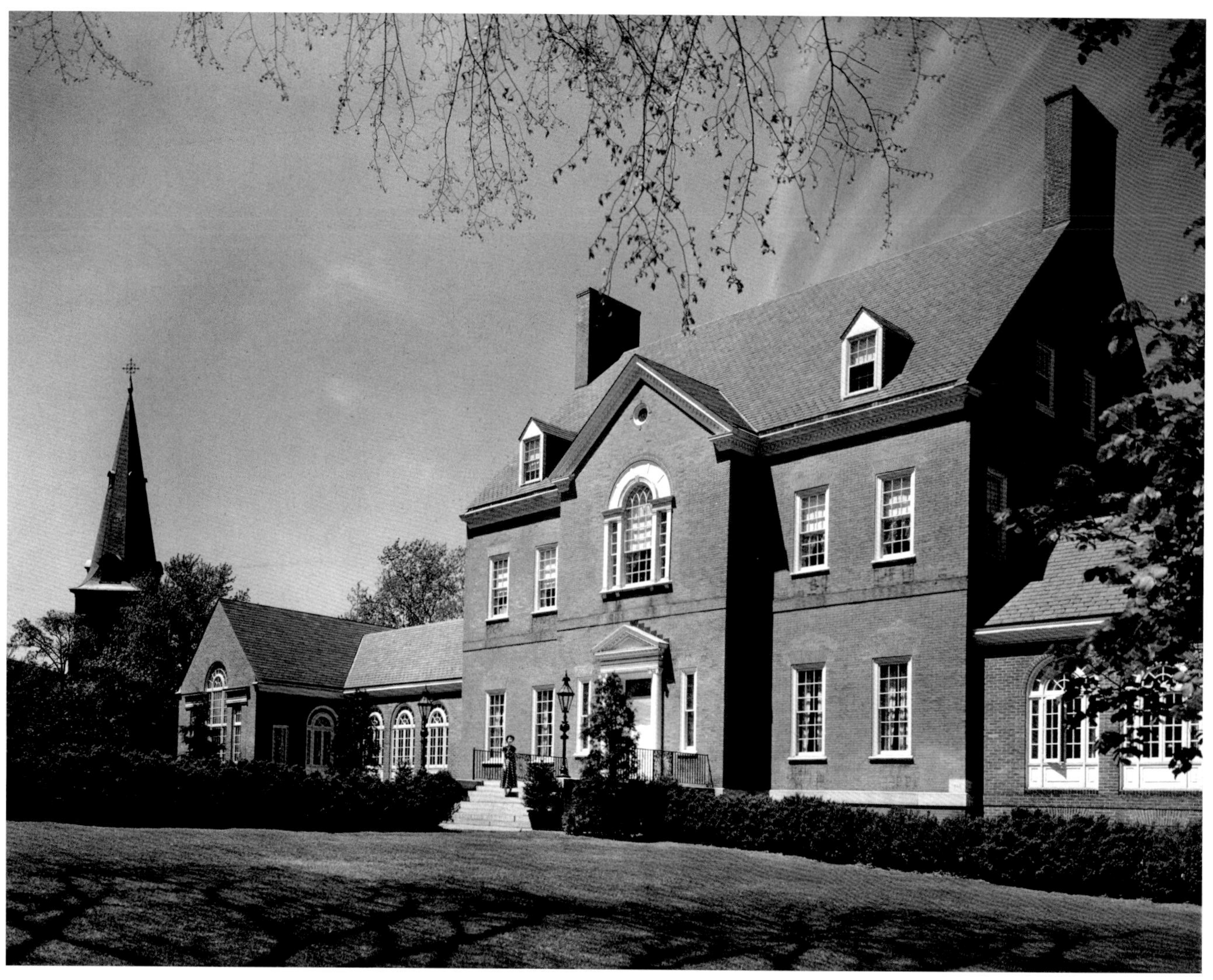

CONTENTS

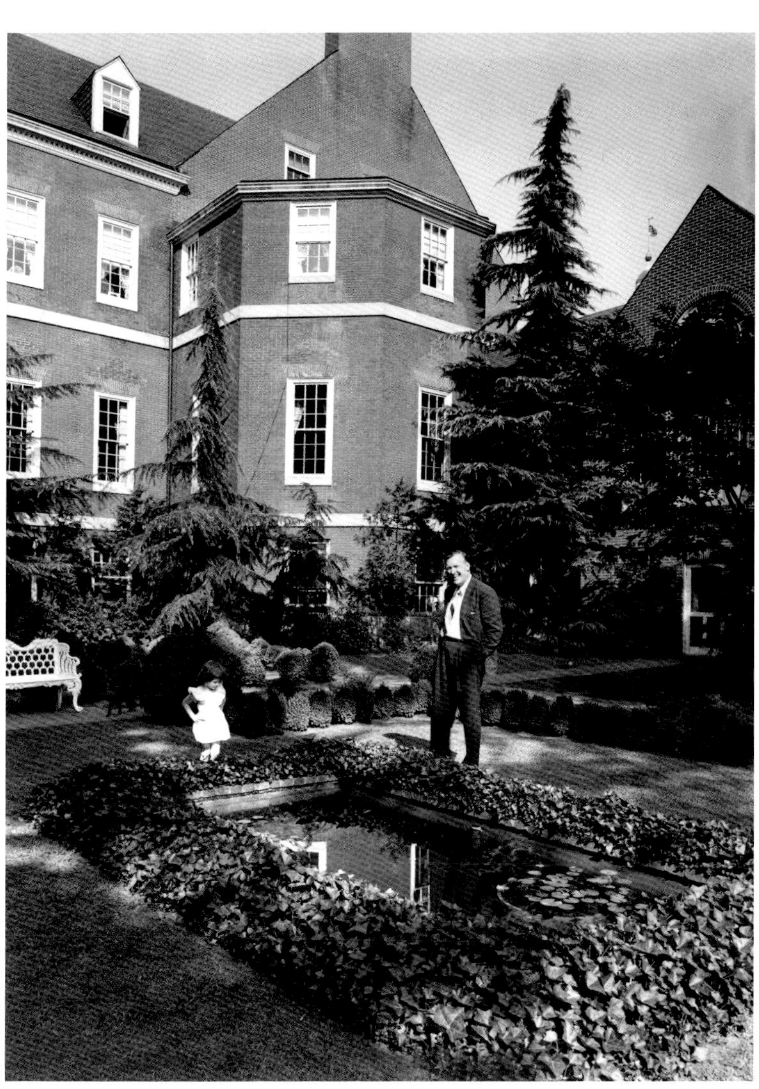

PREFACE

Annapolis is a marvelous city; it is colonial, with all the modern conveniences. My father, the late A. Aubrey Bodine (1906–1970)—newspaper photographer, pictorialist, modernist, and documentarian for the *Baltimore Sunday Sun*—photographed Annapolis for forty-six years. You will see in this volume his Annapolis feature work: colonial mansions and humbler abodes, charming streets, the US Naval Academy, government buildings, the Chesapeake Bay, and the sailing—*so much* sailing.

I am the custodian and curator of the A. Aubrey Bodine photography collection. I come to this privilege through genetic lottery. Coming to Bodine's story of Annapolis has been an interesting challenge, as I am neither a photographer nor a Maryland historian. From more than 10,000 images of mostly Maryland I have selected the pictures I found noteworthy, interesting, and examples of Bodine's unique artistic style. I had about 500 images from which to choose.

On a personal note, I sometimes traveled to Annapolis with my father on his assignments. On one occasion we went to the governor's home, Government House. We took his editor's daughter, who was my age, with us. We were compelled to write an essay about our educational experience—buzzkill. So why did my buddies willingly pass on the opportunity to experience a unique field trip with a master photographer of international stature? At an earlier time, he had a Naval Academy assignment and invited his stepdaughter—who was dating a midshipman—and me along for the ride. He was a no-show when we went to meet him at his appointed time; his car was gone—he finished early and returned to Baltimore. We had no money for bus fare and we could not locate the midshipman we were visiting. I do not recall the resolution, but two alternatives existed: panhandling bus fare, as we made for a pitiful sight, or a visit to the governor's house to borrow some cash for bus fare back to Baltimore. His stepdaughter went to school with the governor's niece. Bodine's wife, and mother of the abandoned children ages eighteen and four, was most displeased.

Bodine began his career in the 1920s, when photography as an art form was still in its infancy. His professional mission was to see newspaper photography regarded as a noble art form, not merely as documentary illustration. Bodine was most proud that his award-winning pictures came from his newspaper assignment work. He never considered any assignment beneath him. Bodine went on every job with the goal of coming back with a Salon-quality image; one worthy of competitive exhibition on the world stage. Salons were juried competitions and were one of the few avenues for showing photographs as art to the general public in his time. Every location had its own set of challenges requiring unique approaches. Bodine saw beauty everywhere he looked.

He was blessed with a lifetime of editors who nurtured his creativity, giving him the freedom to express his art *in his own way*. How he chose to present an image was his call. He was always a features guy who never shot spot news—pictures taken under rapidly changing circumstances beyond his control. He was an artist with a regular paycheck and an expense account permitting the rental of airplanes, helicopters, and boats. This book is replete with pictures requiring boats and helicopters. Bodine covered his state of Maryland from one end to the other until the day he died.

A marching brigade or a sailing ship each presented an array of artistic choices. He said he found pictures everywhere he went; it was just a matter of walking around and finding the best angle.

There is one best spot from which to shoot the subject and it is the photographer's job to find that best spot . . . and *do the common thing uncommonly*. His varied treatments of subject matter demonstrated the versatility and individuality of Bodine the artist and documentarian.

In 1920, Bodine left home and school at age fourteen and went to work for the *Baltimore Sunday Sun* as an office boy. Here began a career that rocketed to the mountaintop of twentieth-century photography: a newspaper man who showed the world that photography is an art and not just a documentary trade. The essence of Bodine's work was his astounding knowledge and sense of light, and how he controlled it to communicate beauty and mood. He authored magazine articles and books, judged photography competitions, and lectured along the East Coast while holding a full-time job at a major metropolitan newspaper. He was awarded Honorary Fellowships in the Photographic Society of America and the National Press Photographers Association, the first photographer to be dually honored.

The *Sun* photographers and darkroom were near his workstation. These early colleagues were not interested in photography; to Bodine it was artistic expression. He started "making" pictures when he was fifteen, and he had access to all the toys in a commercial darkroom. It was here where his development into a darkroom master began. Bodine was promoted to Commercial Art Department photographer at eighteen; he made commercial pictures for the *Sunday Sun* and Salon competition pictures for himself. While in his late teens, Bodine provided "arty" photographs to his editor for publication in the rotogravure section—a part of the *Sunday Sun* devoted to feature stories that included artistic images. It was the local *People* magazine of the time. His byline was "Sun Staff Photo."

By misfortune of another photographer, the position of *Sunday Sun* feature photographer opened up and Bodine applied for the job; it was his. He was twenty-one. And so began a career that spanned forty-three years, until the day he died in 1970, felled by a stroke in his darkroom. In these years he competed in Salons all over the world up until his end. His acceptance rate into these juried Salons was 1.999 out of 2.000. That is an impressive record.

Bodine was a pictorialist, for which he had no apologies:

> One of the most pleasant accomplishments a photographer can achieve is to be able to change or inject an idea into a photograph which will lift the scene above the run of the mill. There is much pleasure to be derived from such an attainment.

Describing the essence of the pictorial method, he wrote:

> The most striking and simple method is the use of Combination Negative Printing. This technique is old and goes way back to 1855, when two Scotchmen, [*sic*] Berwick and Annan, introduced a figure from one negative into a landscape. They really started something, because two years later Rajlander used thirty negatives to produce a single picture. This, of course, was a stunt, and was widely heralded, but the idea was born and was greatly simplified. In the following year H. P. Robinson perfected and successfully finished the first of a long series of combination prints. Robinson, being a fine craftsman and artist, soon gained prominence, thus combination work became a craze, but was far from being a stunt.

Bodine used large-format cameras. His gear was high quality, but not fancy. His favorite camera was a 5 × 7 Linhof that he used with a heavy wooden tripod and an old black oil cloth. Big cameras provided large negatives, allowing special treatment. He painted and scratched his negatives. In Bodine's lifetime, changes to any photograph happened in the darkroom, and all were done by hand one picture at a time. He was particularly adept at combination negative printing, the seminal technique of pictorialists. He said that he had as much right to make additions to his pictures as writers have to use adjectives. He maintained a large file of cloud negatives; he shot many of his cloud formations in Maine and Nova Scotia.

The Bodine family always kept a current Hagerstown *Farmer's Almanac* to reference times for sunrises, sunsets, tides, and moon phases. Bodine had an alarm clock to get him out of bed. He said his alarm clock was his most important tool. All his camera gear and peripherals were stored in the trunk of his car. Trunk and ashtray size drove the car purchase decision. He smoked pipes.

Bodine published four books in his lifetime: *My Maryland*, *Face of Maryland*, *Chesapeake Bay*, and *Tidewater and Face of Virginia*. After he died, two biographies were written: *Bodine, A Legend in His Time* by Harold A. Williams, his last editor and close friend, and *A. Aubrey Bodine, Baltimore Pictorialist, 1906–1970* by Kathleen M. E. Ewing—the Bodine family agent—before her retirement. Since 2006 I have published four collections of Bodine images: *Bodine's Chesapeake Bay Country* (2006), *Bodine's City* (2011), *Bodine's Industry* (2013), and *Trains: Photography of A. Aubrey Bodine* (2018).

Bodine mostly disappeared from public awareness after his death in 1970. In 2000, Maryland Public Television made a documentary about six Maryland photographers, including Bodine. This event inspired my husband, Richard Orban—a software engineer—to bring Bodine's work back to life. To this end he designed a website and launched the business of AAubreyBodine.com. I scanned more than 13,000 Bodine photographs and digitally restored almost 6,000 images. The entire A. Aubrey Bodine archive of photographs has been posted to our website, www.aaubreybodine.com. The pictures are indexed and are searchable online. Bodine left quite a legacy, and it has been my honor to be the custodian of this great man's body of work and to make it available for the entire world to see and purchase.

PLATE 013 Annapolis Main Street (1965)

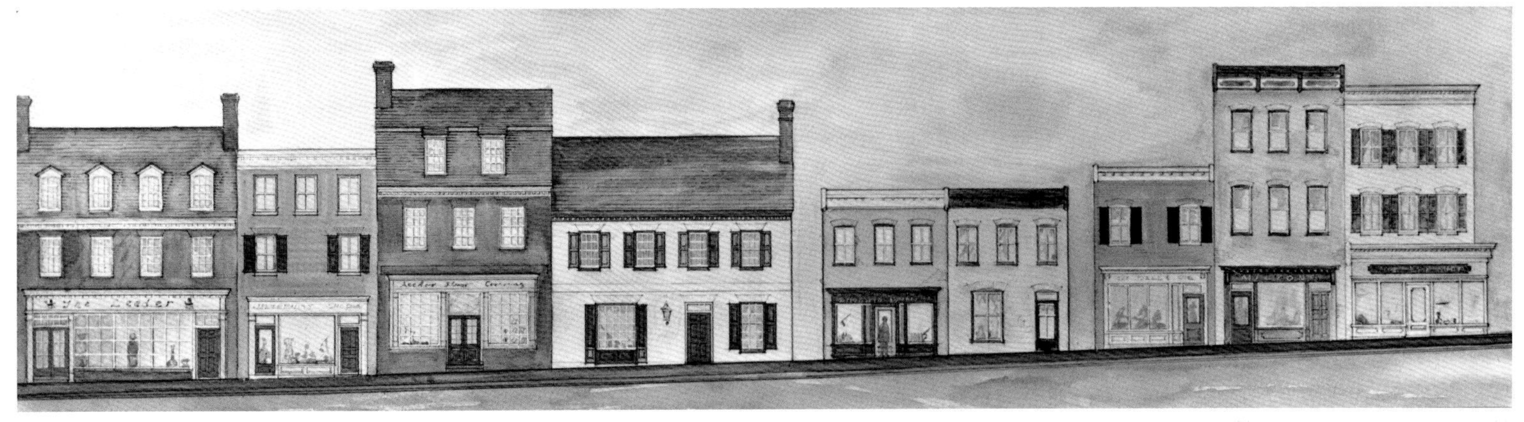

INTRODUCTION

"Queen city of this country is Annapolis, named in honor of a princess who became Queen Anne. Annapolis, which is almost surrounded by water, is many things: county seat, trading center, college town, pleasure boat port, state capital, home of the Naval Academy, and, in the words of one authority, the most perfect example of a Colonial city extant in America today," wrote A. Aubrey Bodine. The following pages contain Bodine's exquisite pictorial documentarian presentation of Annapolis, the capital of his beloved Maryland. It spans a forty-five-year period in the mid-twentieth century. As feature photographer for the *Baltimore Sunday Sun* he made many trips to Annapolis. The topics are varied, as you shall see. City Dock, off Spa Creek, forms one boundary of Annapolis, with College Creek and the Severn River forming the other sides. Annapolis is the only state capital deliberately laid out in colonial times primarily as the home of state government. All four of Maryland's signers of the Declaration of Independence had homes in Annapolis, and all four have survived.

Annapolis is home to public and government buildings. I accompanied my father on a shoot with then governor Theodore McKeldin. We stood by the reflecting pool of Government House, the official residence of Maryland's governor. I am the little girl in the picture. In 1964 Bodine shot the interior of Government House when J. Millard Tawes of Crisfield was governor. I wonder if this is how the office really looked, or did Bodine move things around to make a more balanced image; he was not beyond such behavior. On December 23, 1783, George Washington resigned his commission in the Old Senate Chamber. The Old Treasury building at State Circle is the oldest public building in Maryland. It is currently undergoing historical preservation. It is to be open to the public with interpretive exhibits relating to the history of the building and seventeenth-century Maryland history. These exhibits create a historical link with Historic St. Mary's City, capital of the Maryland colony until it was moved to Annapolis in 1695.

Joy, USN, at the time superintendent of the Naval Academy, had ordered the helicopter away. It made so much noise that no commands could be heard on the field. I couldn't hear either for four days until I got some hospital treatment. The weekly dress parade almost ended disastrously that day because of my picture. But I was forgiven when the admiral saw the picture. He asked for a large print for his office.

Tecumseh—the statue—is positioned on a base of Vermont marble immediately in front of Bancroft Hall. The Naval Academy Chapel is where the midshipmen attended nondenominational services every Sunday. Attendance was required until 1972. The chapel dome towers more than 200 feet. In a crypt beneath the chapel is the sarcophagus of John Paul Jones.

My decision as to whom I would dedicate this book revealed itself on June 10, 2018, when *The Capital Gazette* newspaper—descendant of the *Maryland Gazette* founded in 1727—was attacked. Five journalists were slaughtered; others were injured.

As karma would have it, the only pictures I have in the Bodine archive that show both Annapolis and journalism happens to be a picture of Jonas Green's home. Jonas Green, publisher of the *Maryland Gazette*, was an American newspaper publisher during the colonial era and a strong opponent of the Stamp Act; he loathed it, as it directly taxed his newspaper. When lawyers and printers were singled out for a tax, no one in England thought there was danger in targeting the very people who have barrels of ink and the wherewithal to use them? Resisting payment, he stated that the newspaper would cease publication. Reason persuaded Green to return to publishing as part of the struggle against tyranny. Publication resumed.

These folks were *Sun* people, as the *Capital Gazette* was acquired by Baltimore Sun Media Group in 2014. Bodine was a *Sun* man first, last, and always, and he would share the outrage of working journalists being gunned down in their offices doing the sainted job of delivering the news to their community. It is only appropriate that a *Sun* man respectfully acknowledge the passing of his colleagues.

PLATE 014 Chesapeake Bay Bridge (1955)

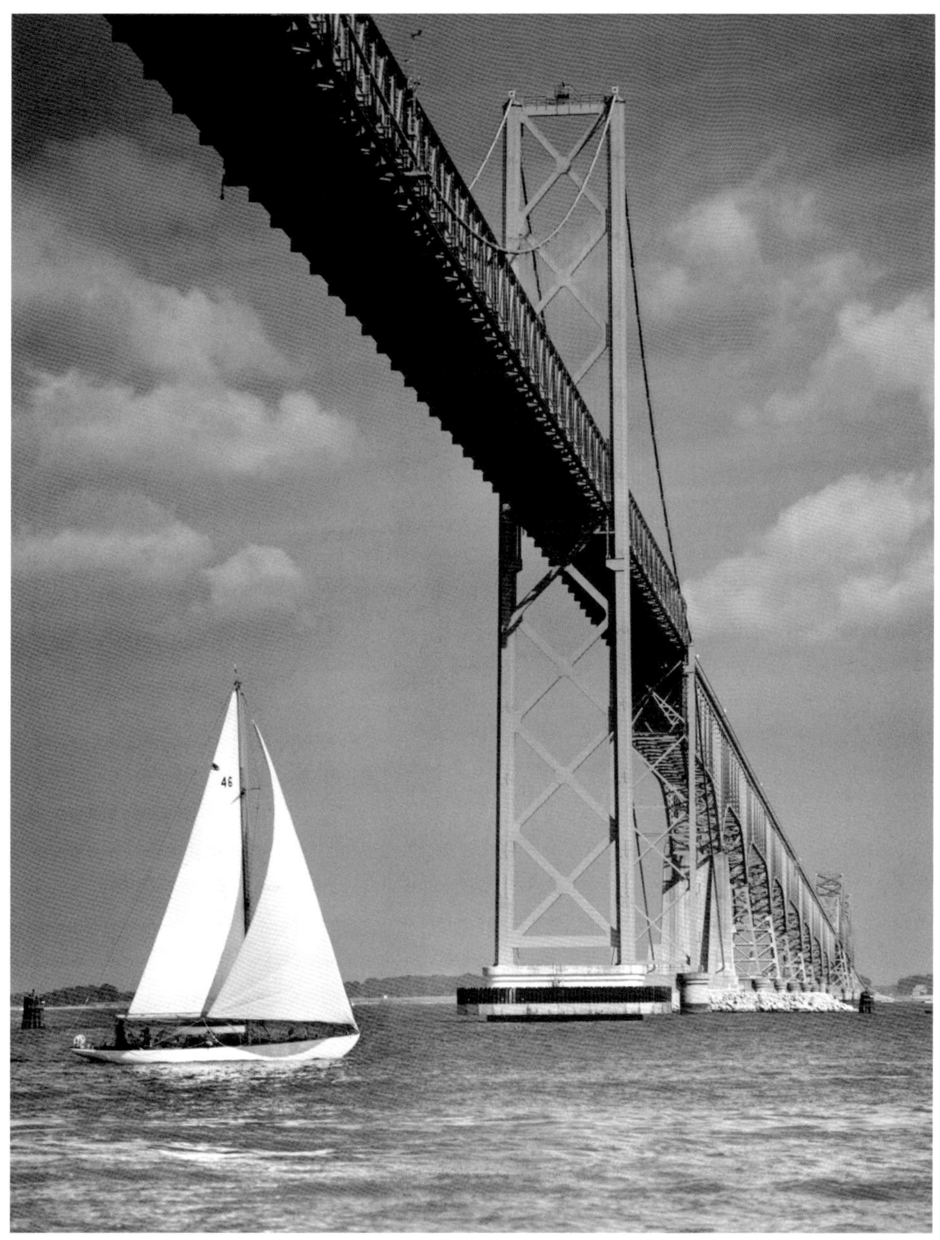

IMAGES

LEFT: PLATE 015 City Dock, Annapolis Harbor (1950)
RIGHT: PLATE 016 Annapolis Harbor (1957)

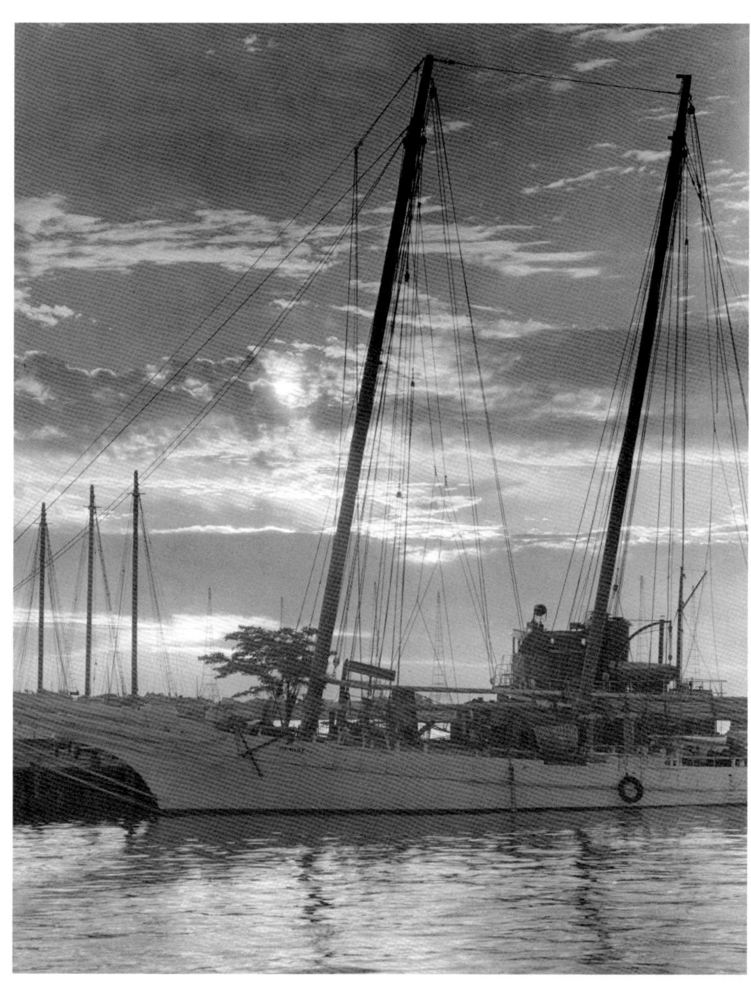

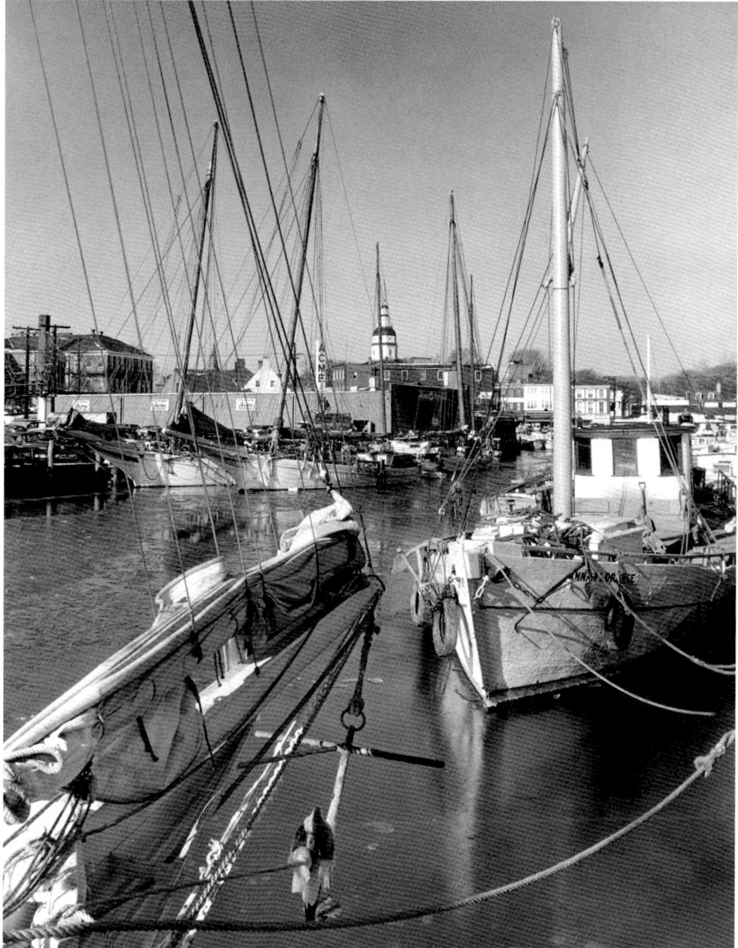

PLATE 017 Reflections of City Dock (1946)

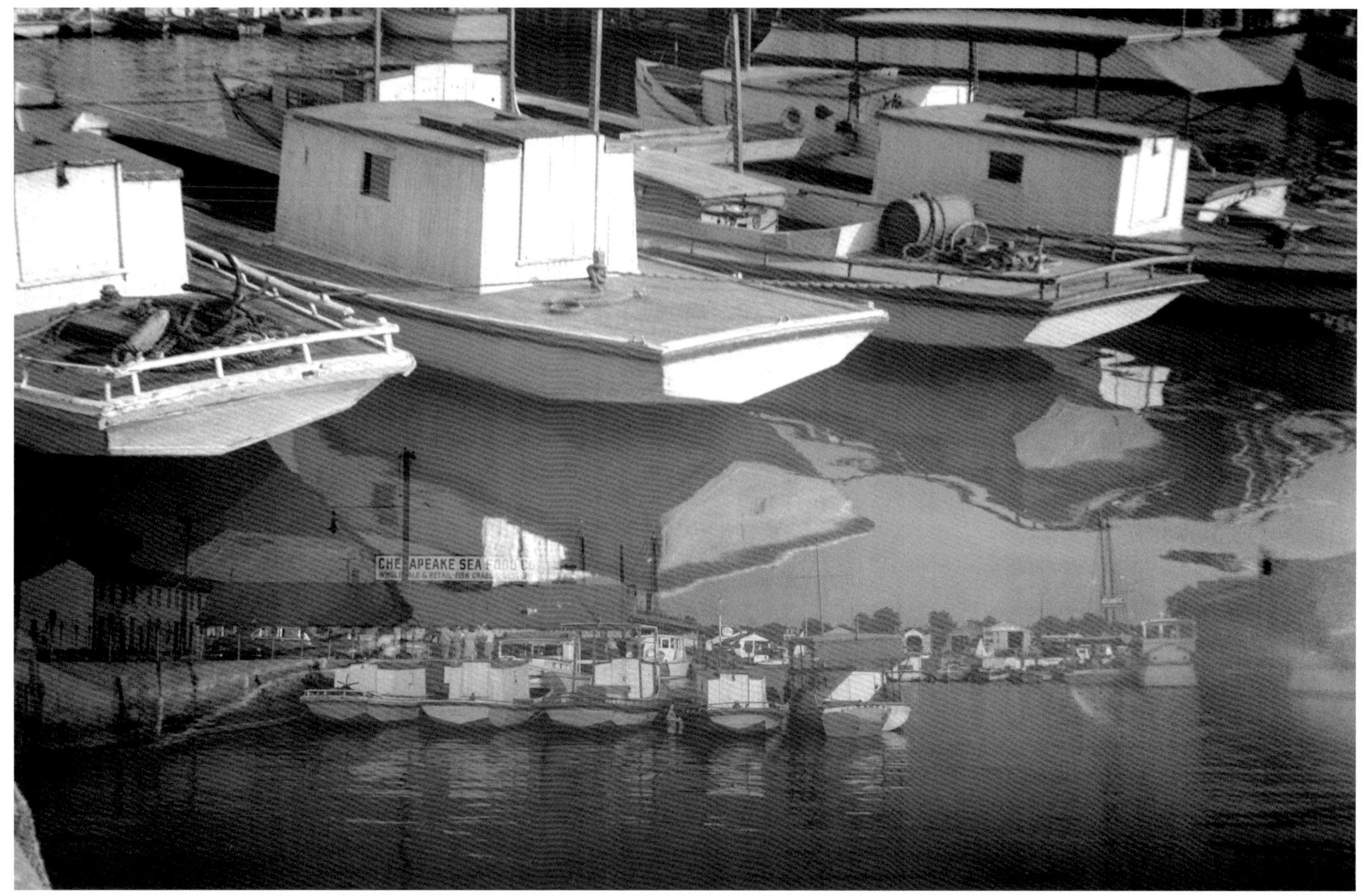

PLATE 018 City Dock, Annapolis (1946)

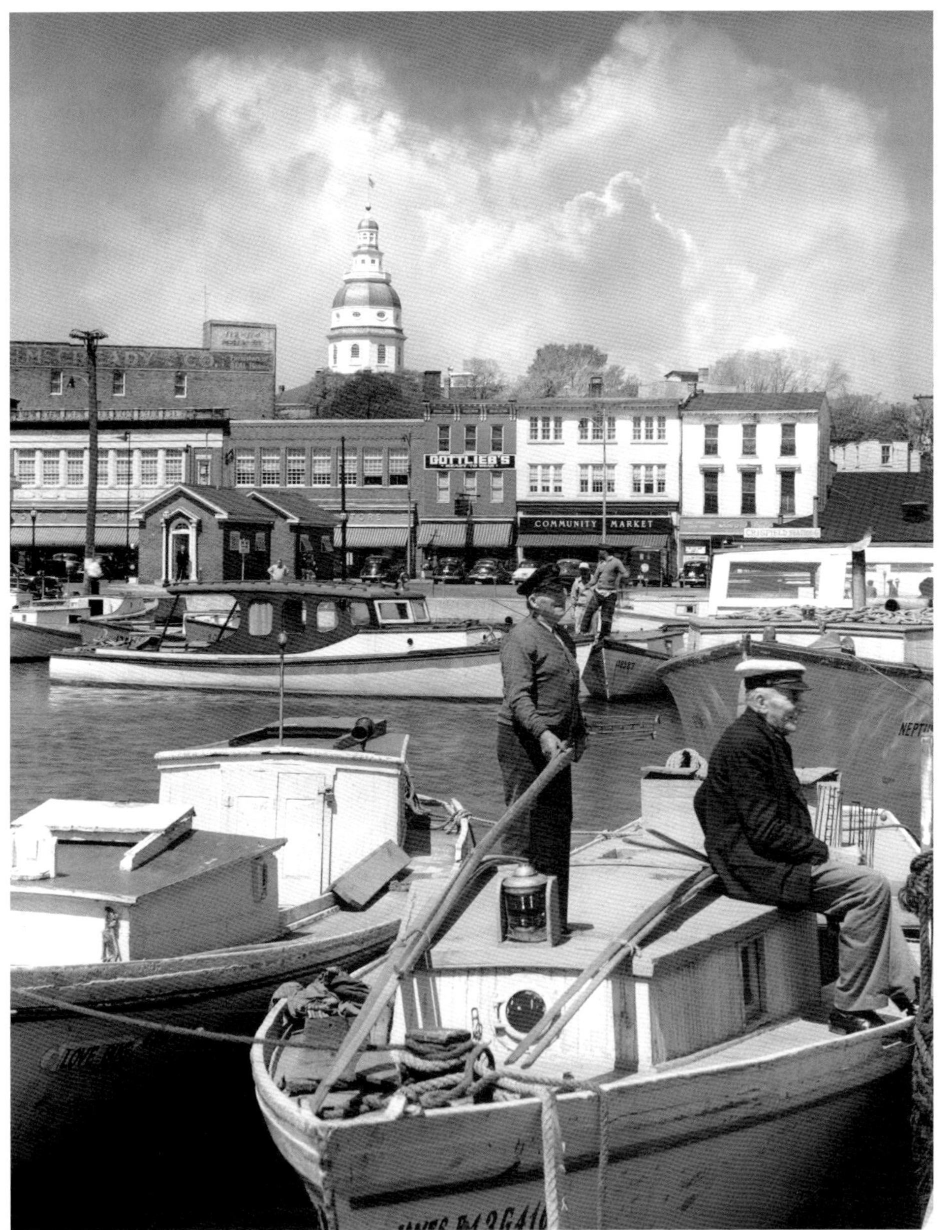

PLATE 019 City Dock, Annapolis (1946)

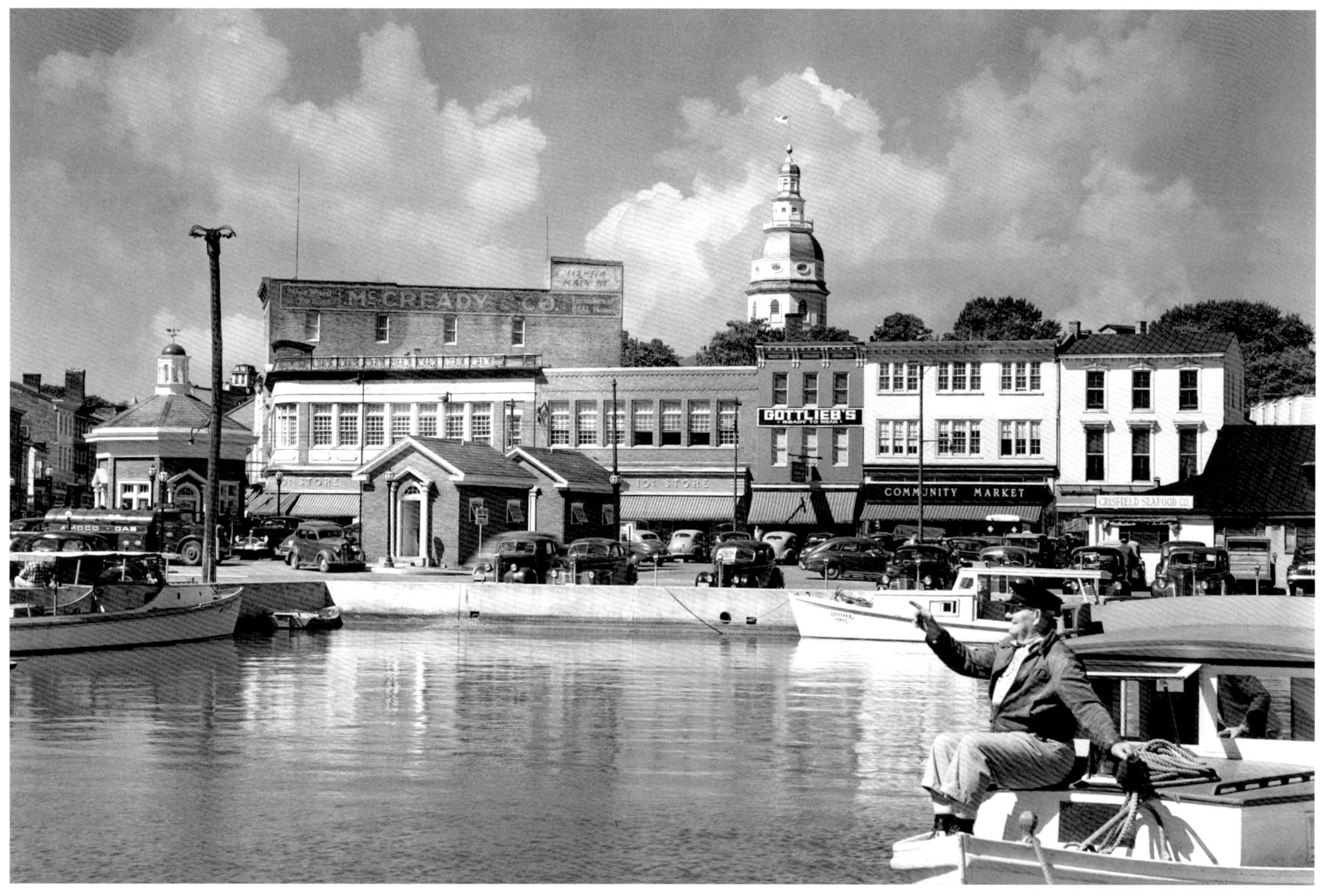

PLATE 020 City Dock, Annapolis (1946)

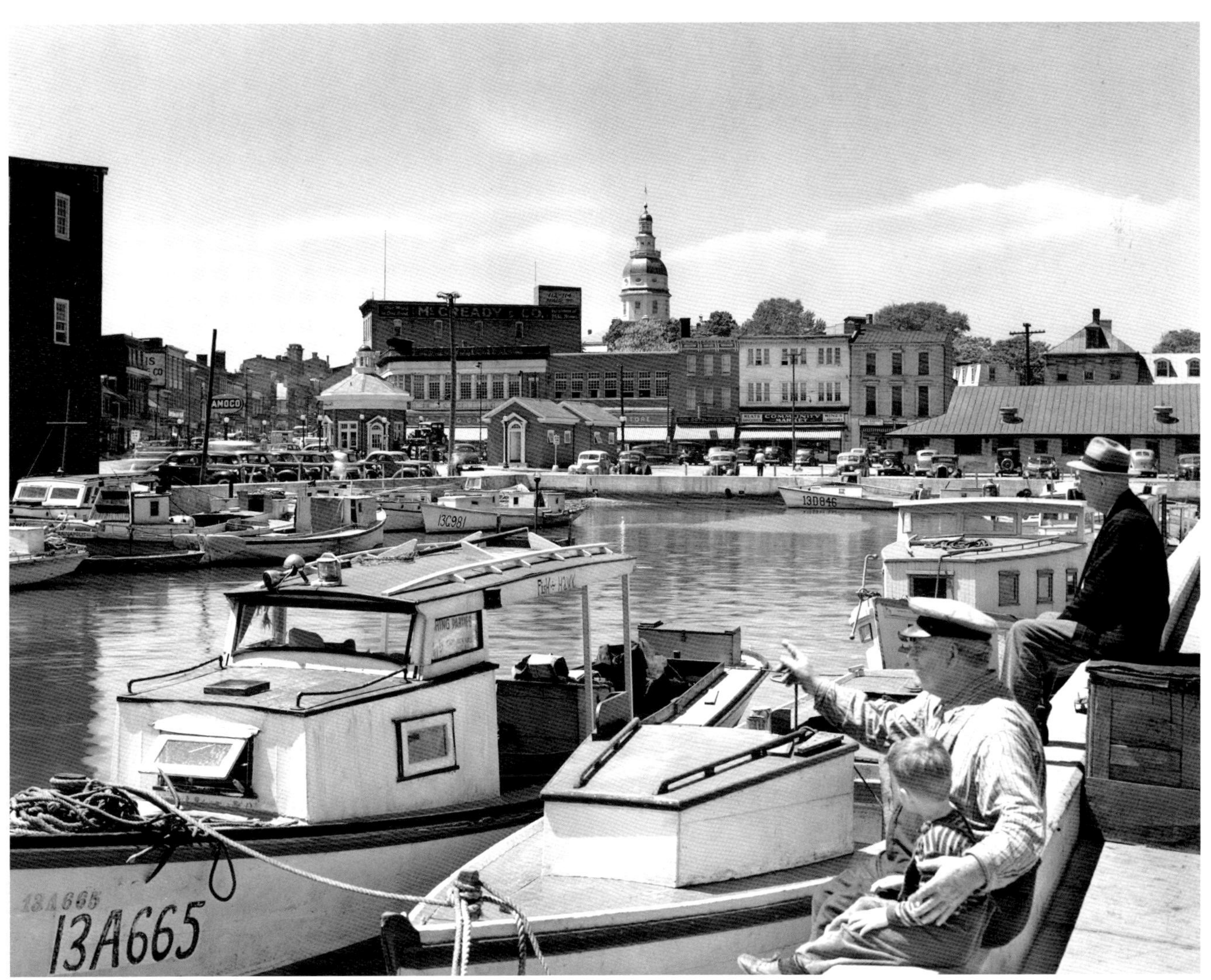

PLATE 021 City Dock, Annapolis (1957)

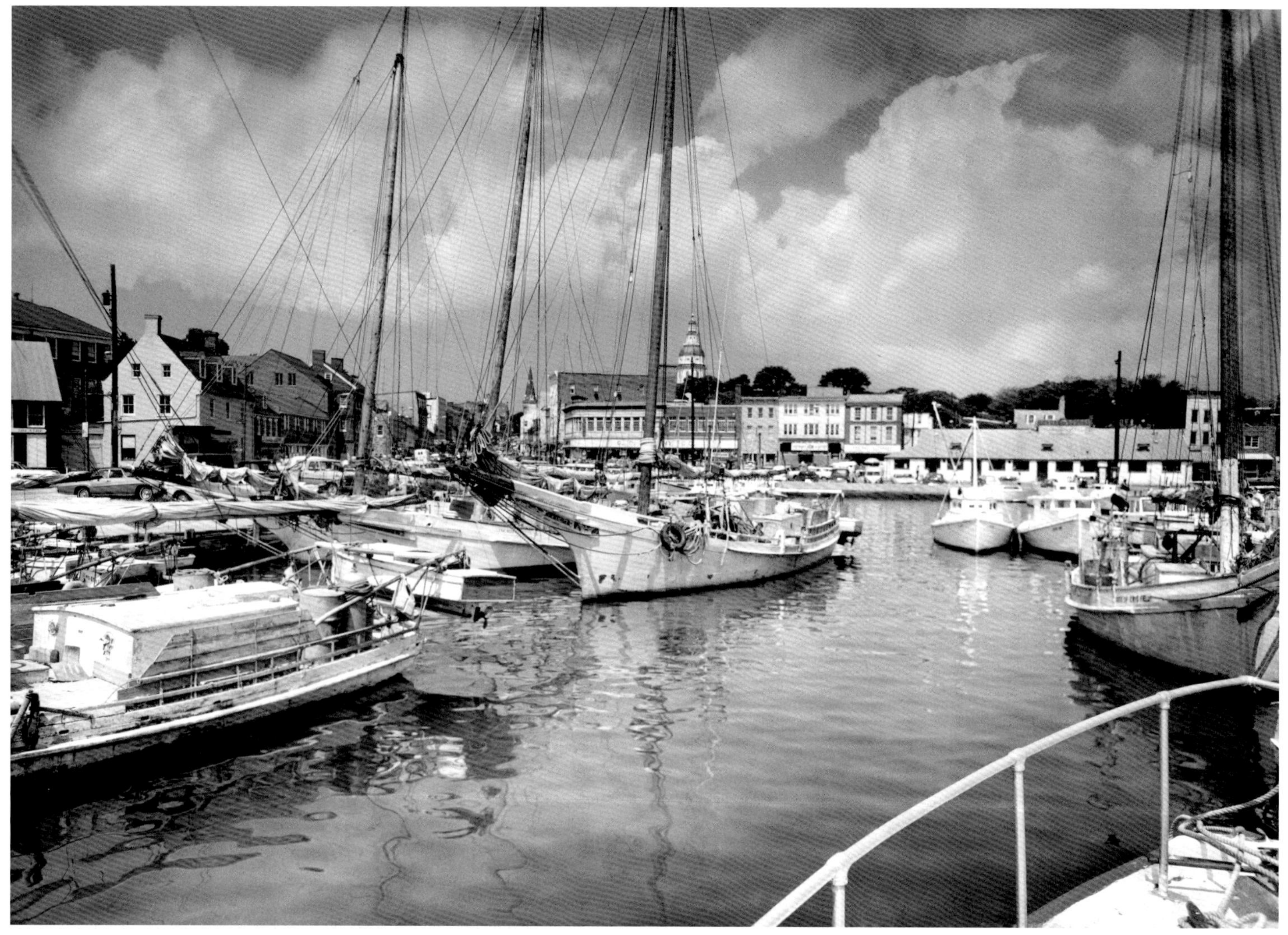

PLATE 022 City Dock, Annapolis (1959)

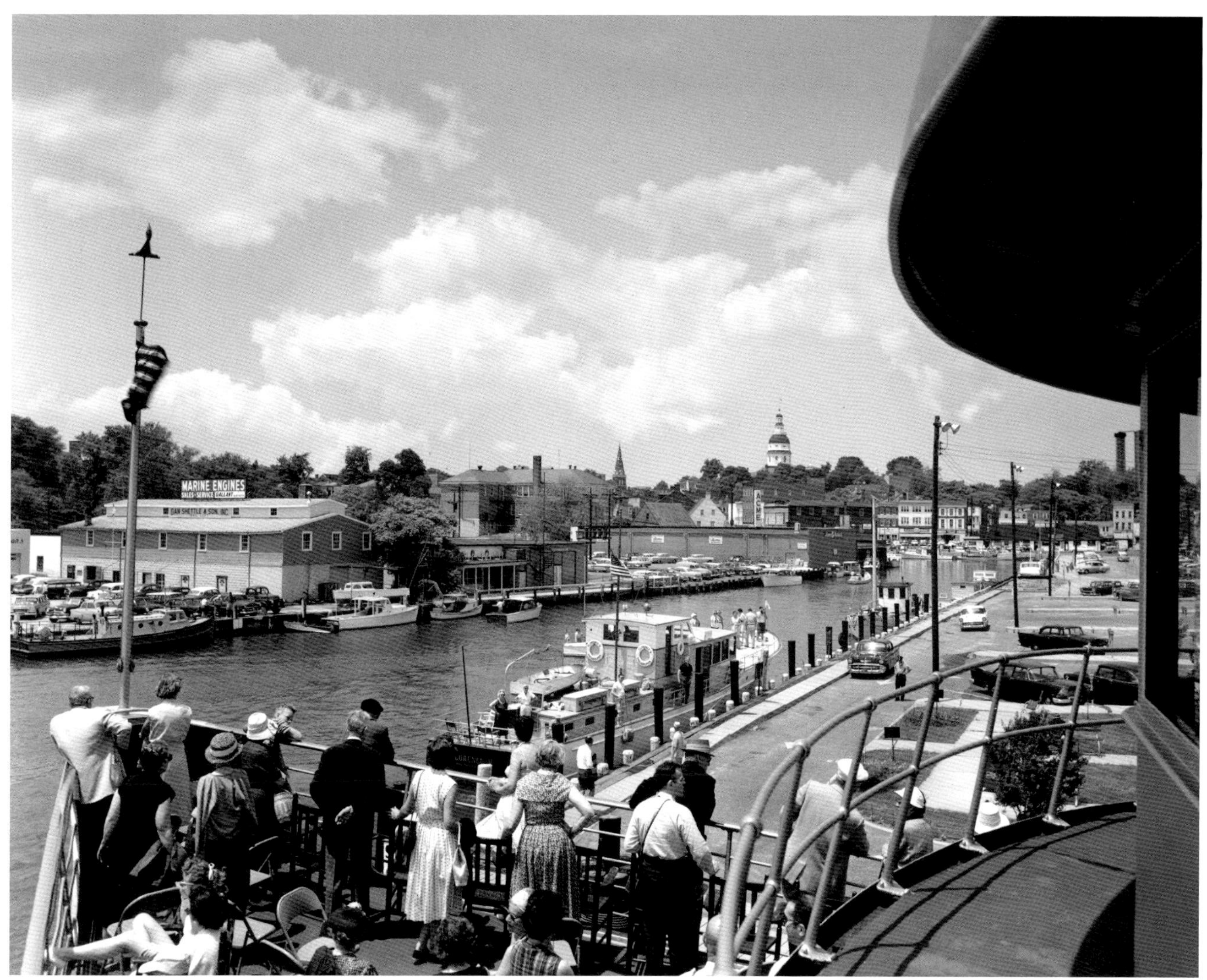

LEFT: PLATE 023 Annapolis Harbor (1947)
RIGHT: PLATE 024 Annapolis Harbor (1942)

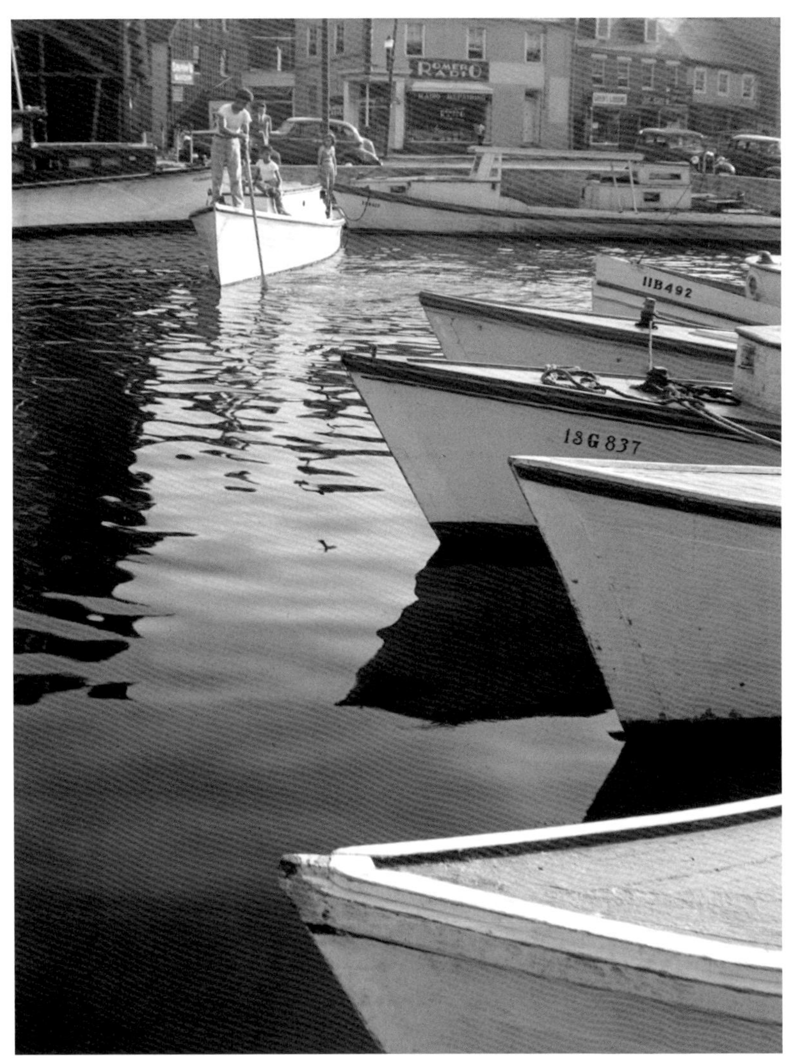

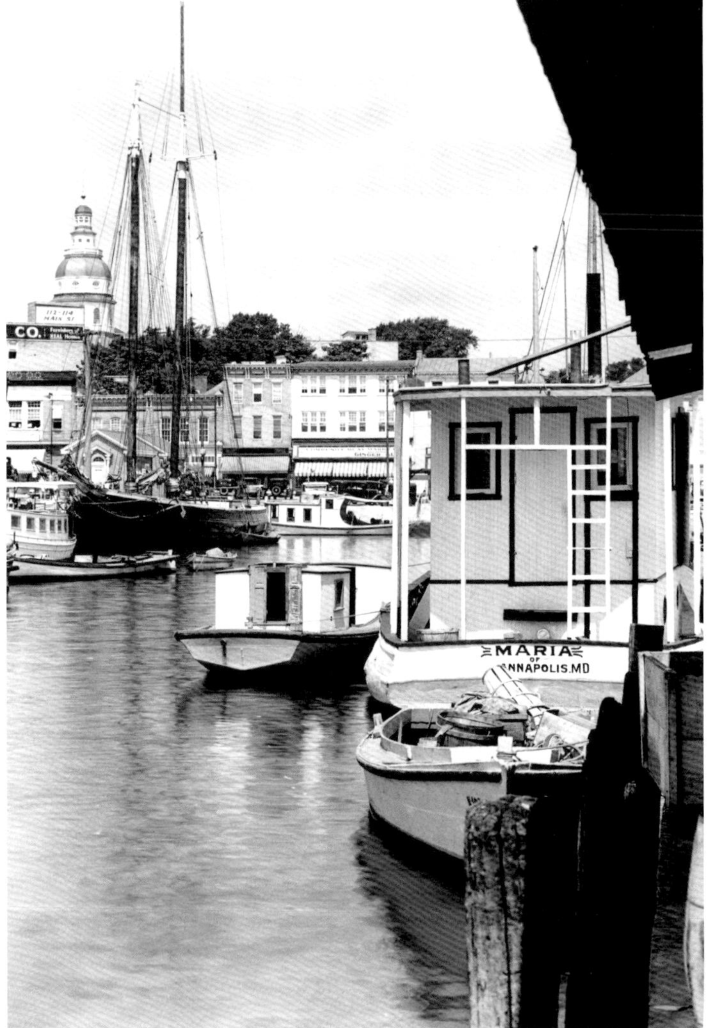

PLATE 025 St. Mary's and the Carroll House, Annapolis (1959)

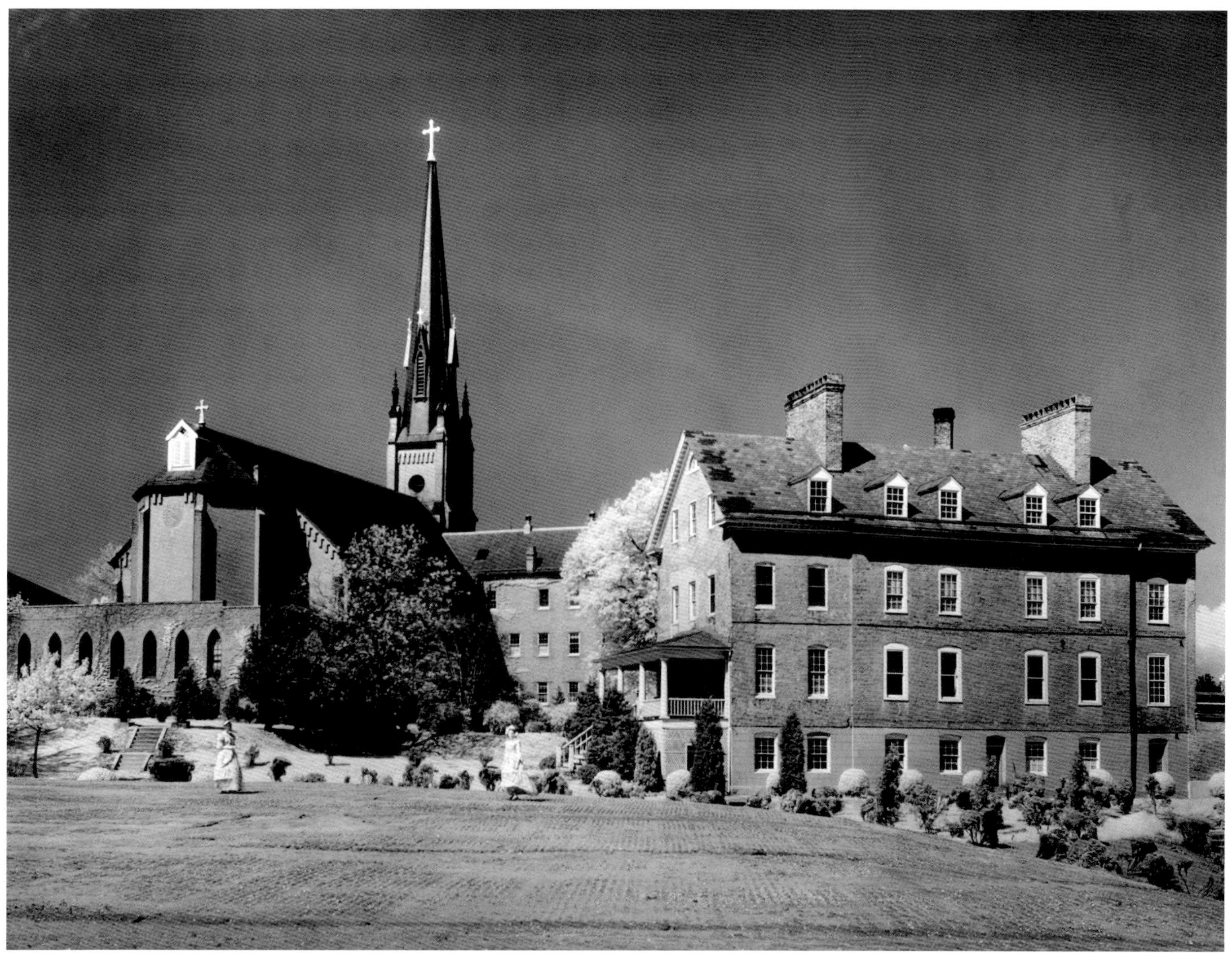

PLATE 026 St. Mary's and the Carroll House, Annapolis (1943)

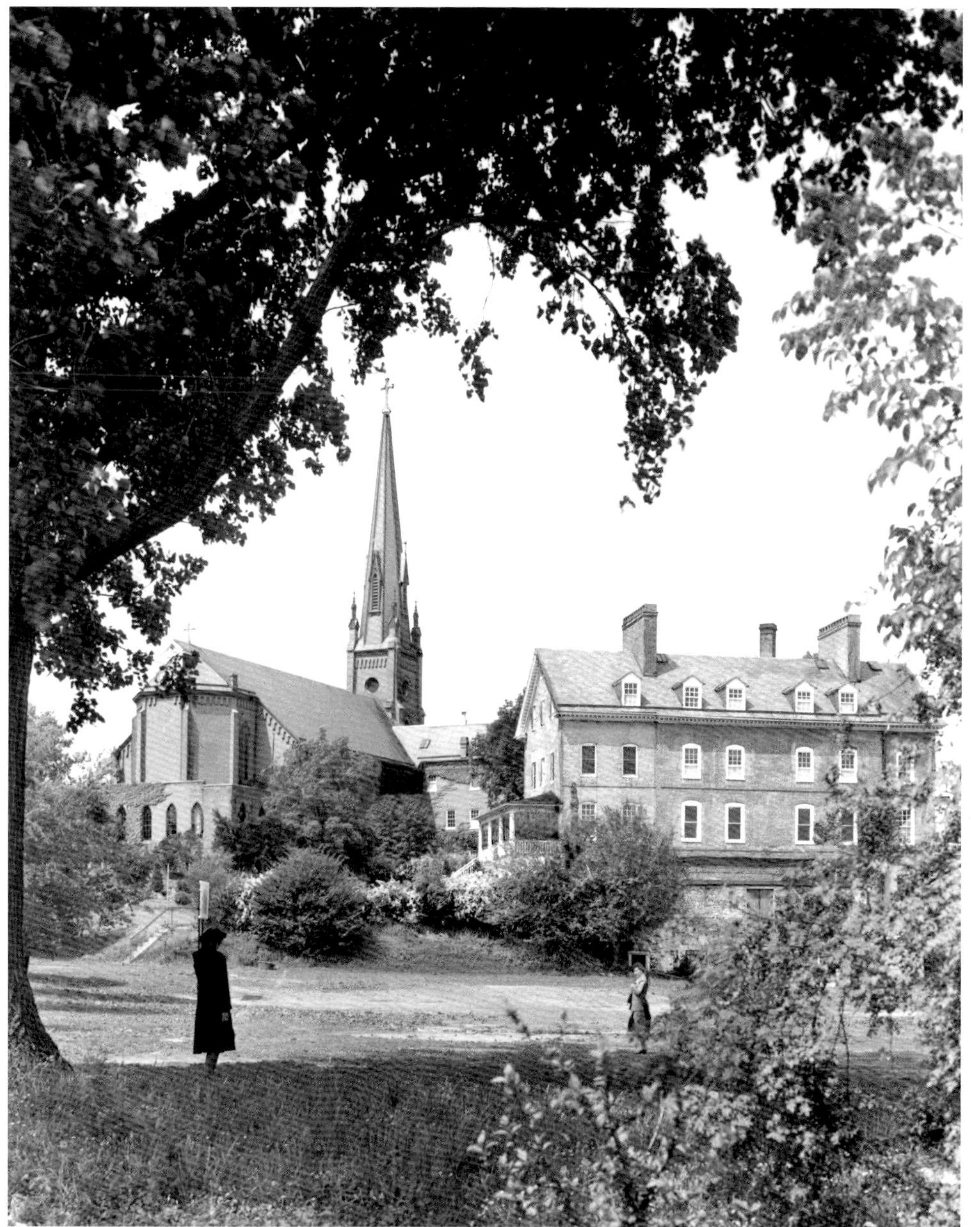

TOP: PLATE 027 Aerial View of Annapolis (1945)
BOTTOM: PLATE 028 Aerial View of Annapolis (1945)

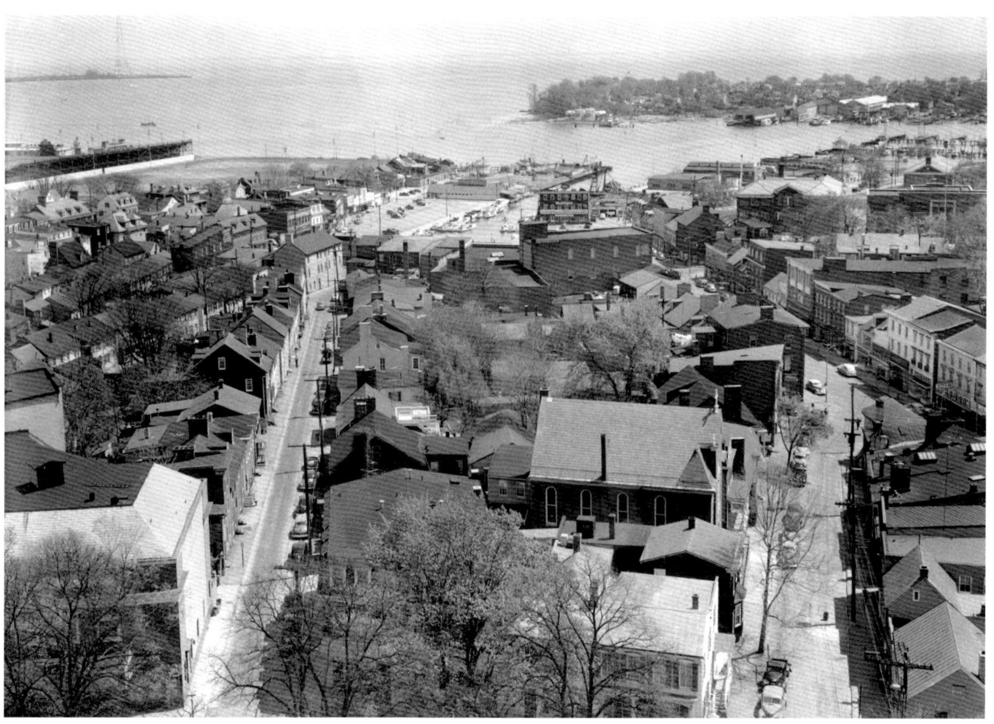

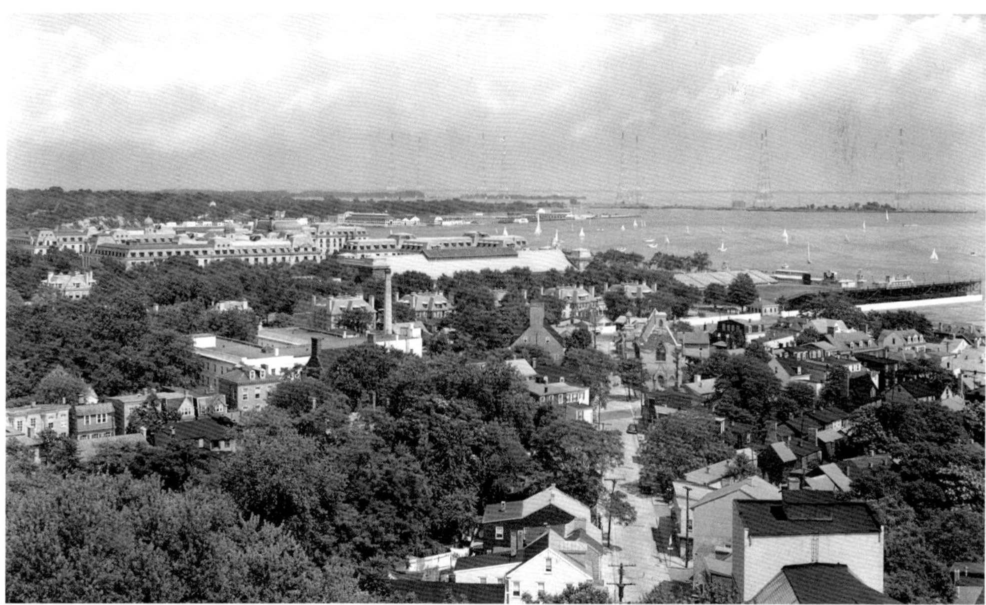

PLATE 031 Government House, Governor and Mrs. Spiro T. Agnew (1967)

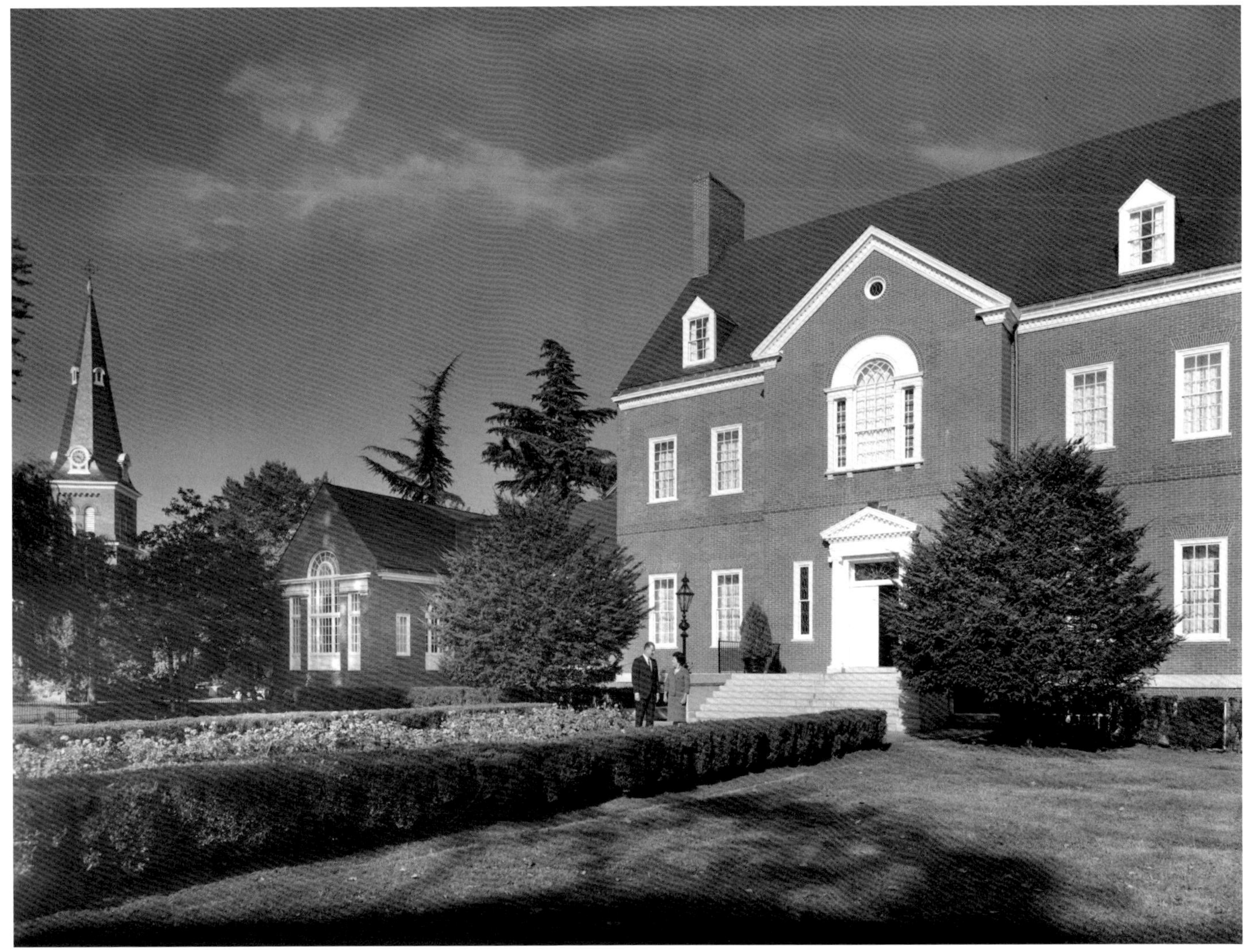

LEFT: PLATE 032 Government House (1967)
RIGHT: PLATE 033 Government House (1936)

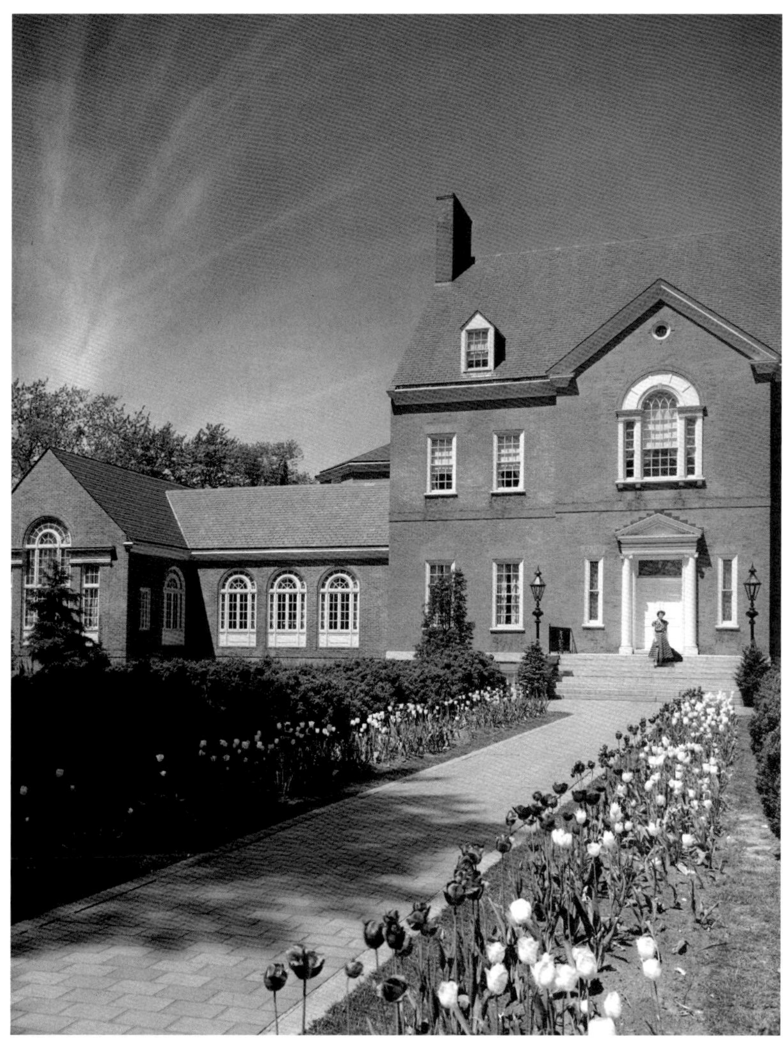

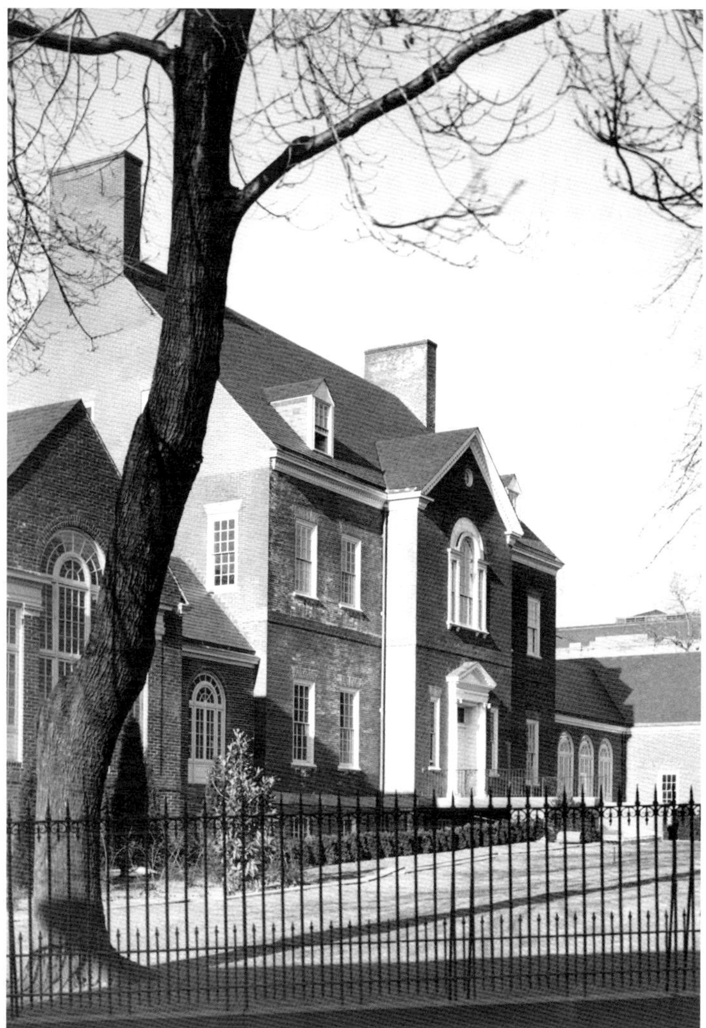

PLATE 034 Government House Entrance Hall (1964)

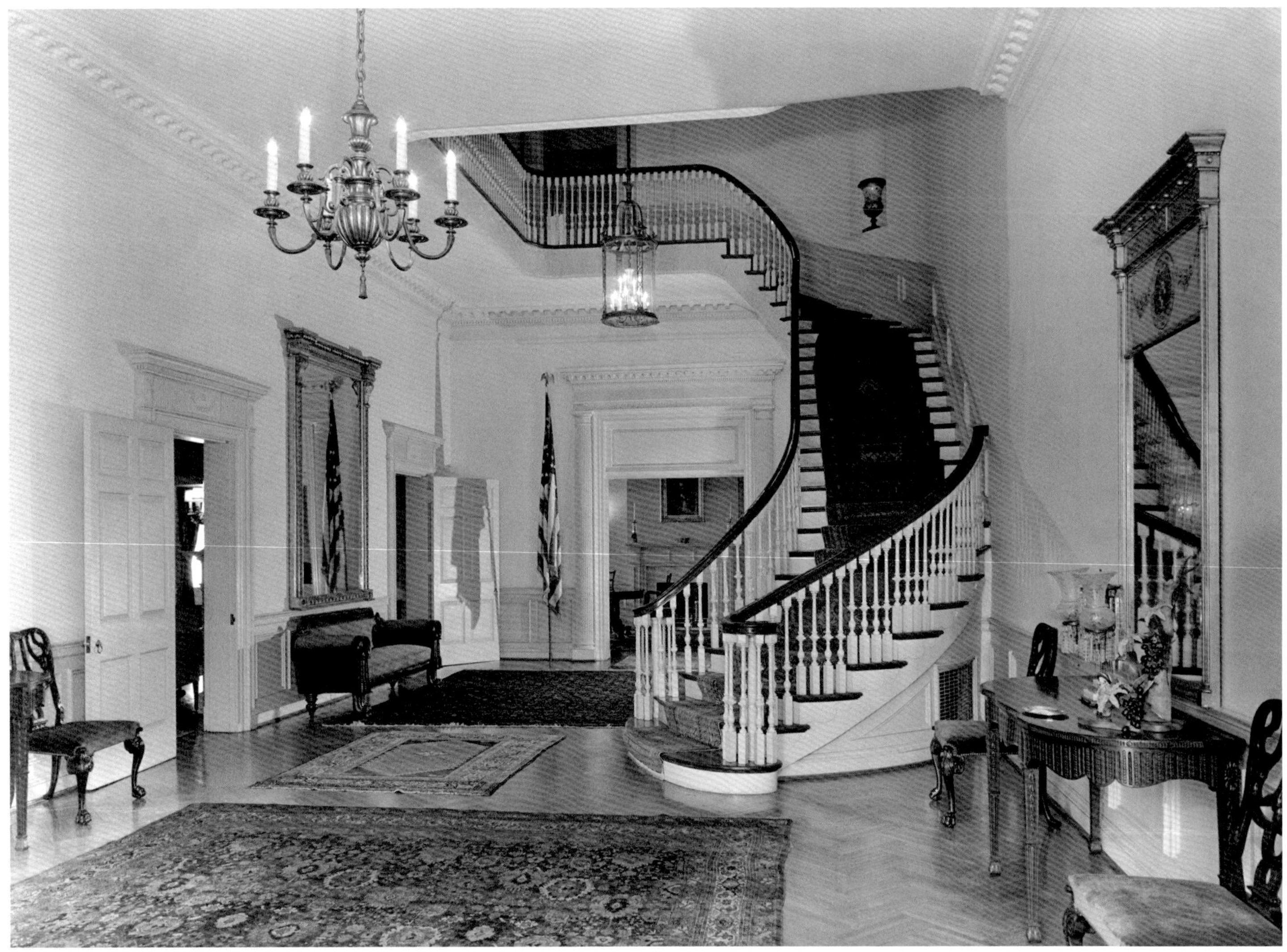

PLATE 035 Government House Drawing Room (1964)

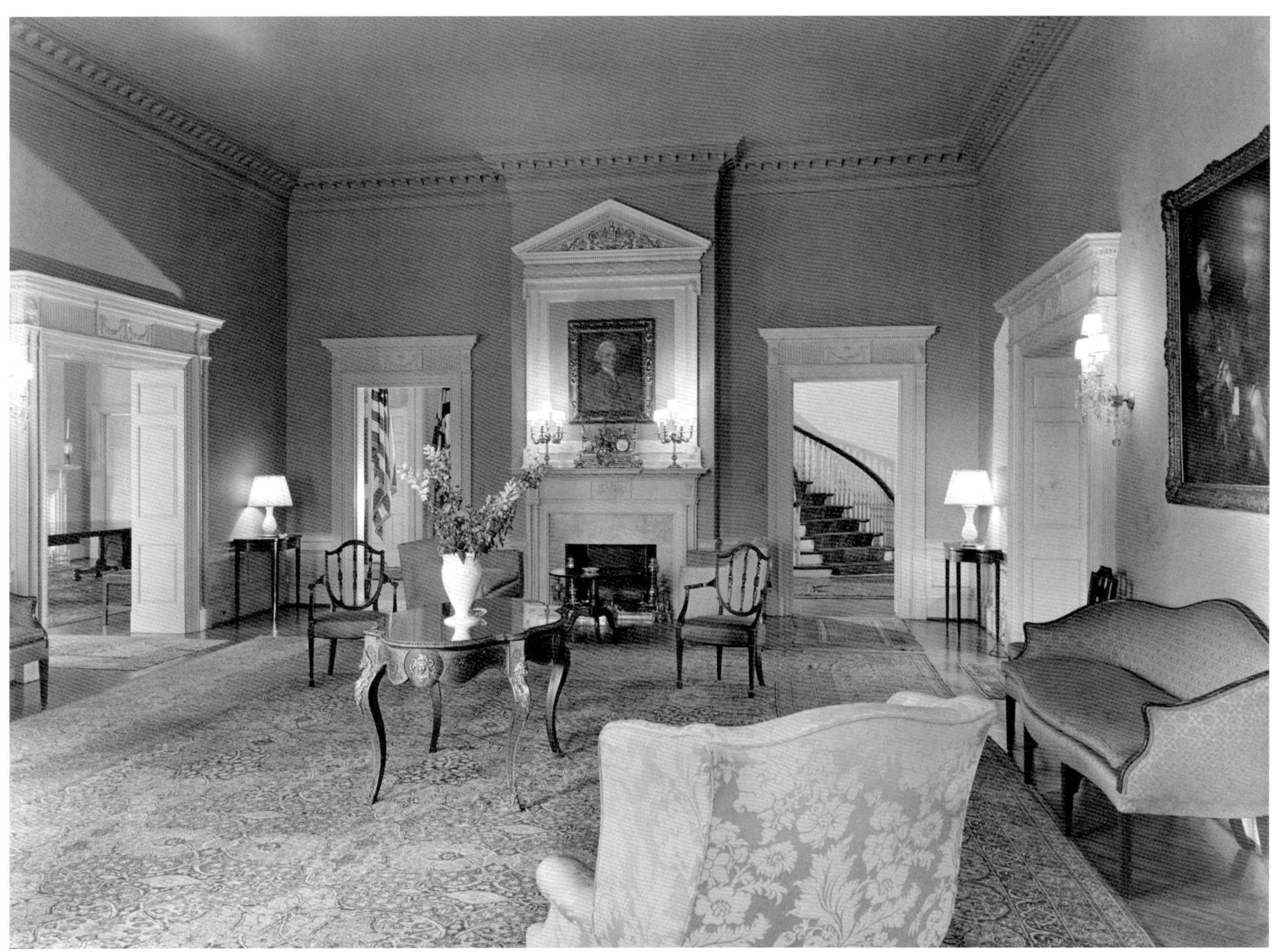

PLATE 038 State House, Annapolis (ca. 1950)

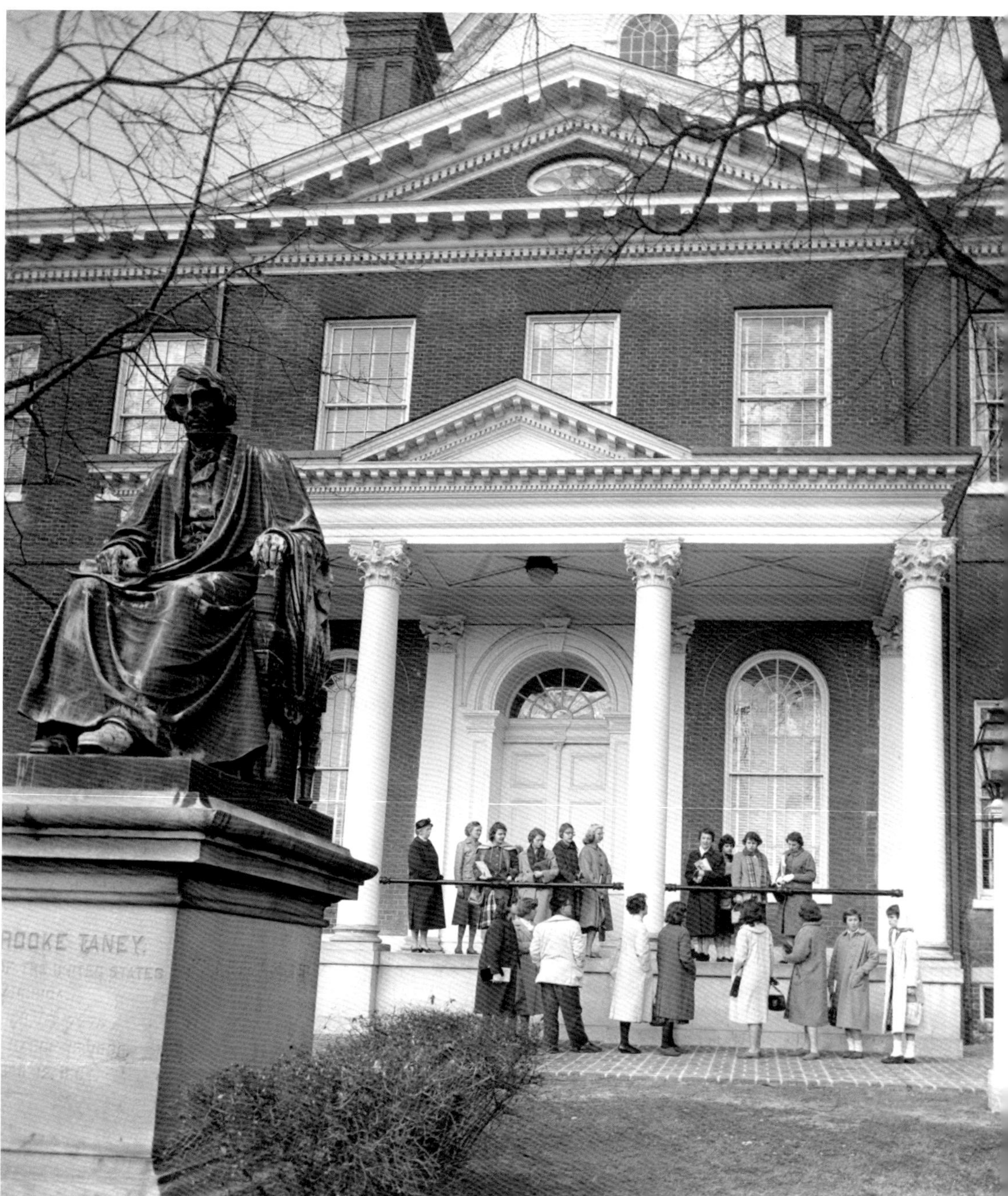

LEFT: PLATE 039 Maryland State House Capitol Dome at Night (1962)
RIGHT: PLATE 040 Maryland State House Capitol Dome in Daytime (1962)

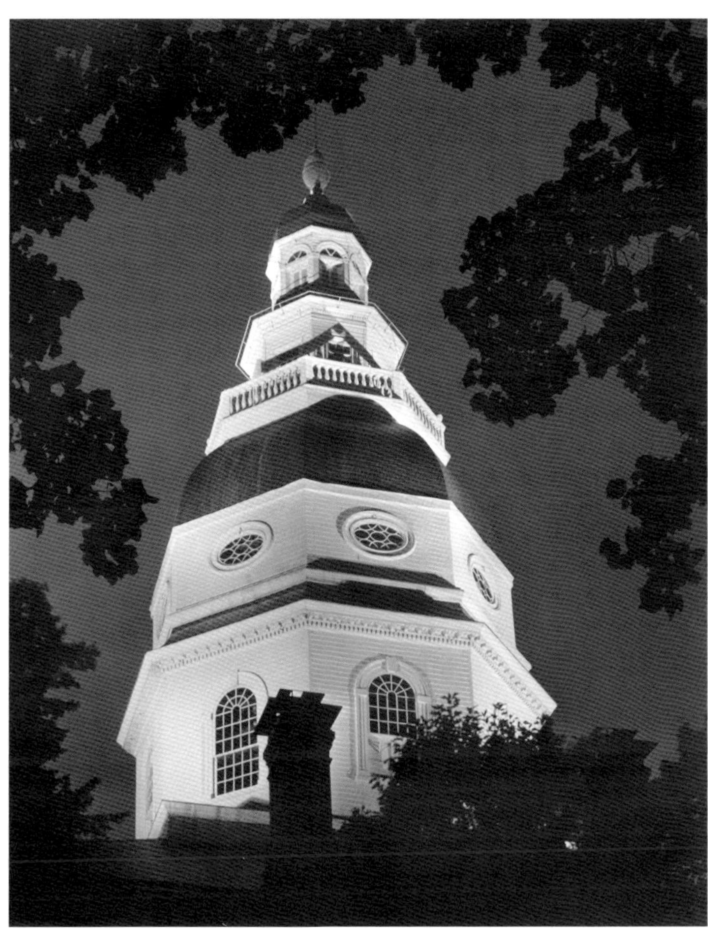

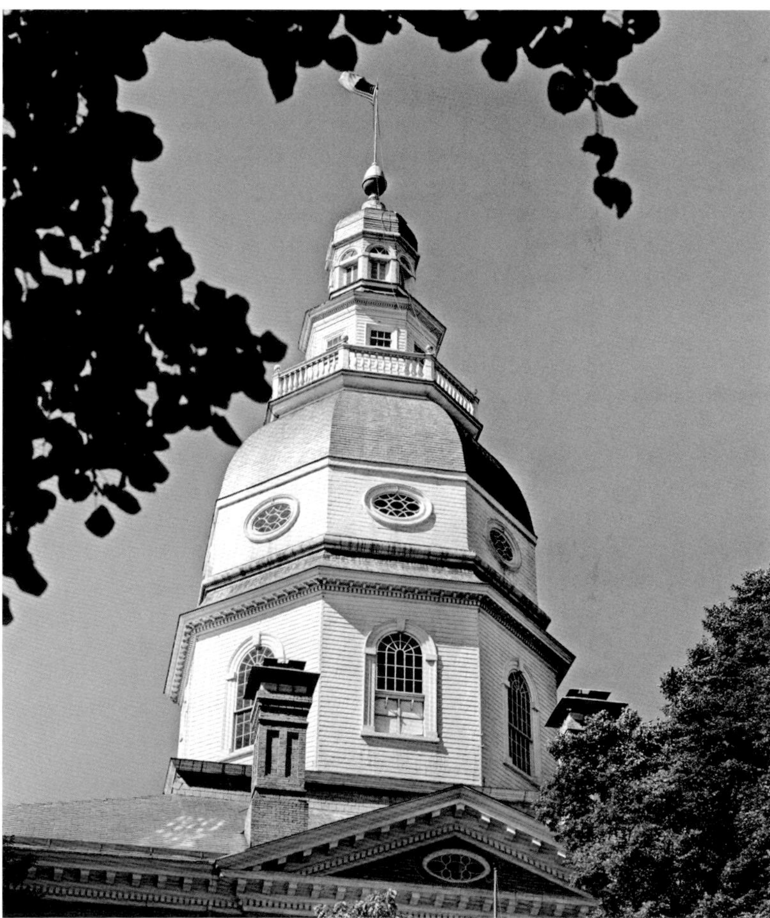

PLATE 041 Annapolis State House Dome Interior (1962)

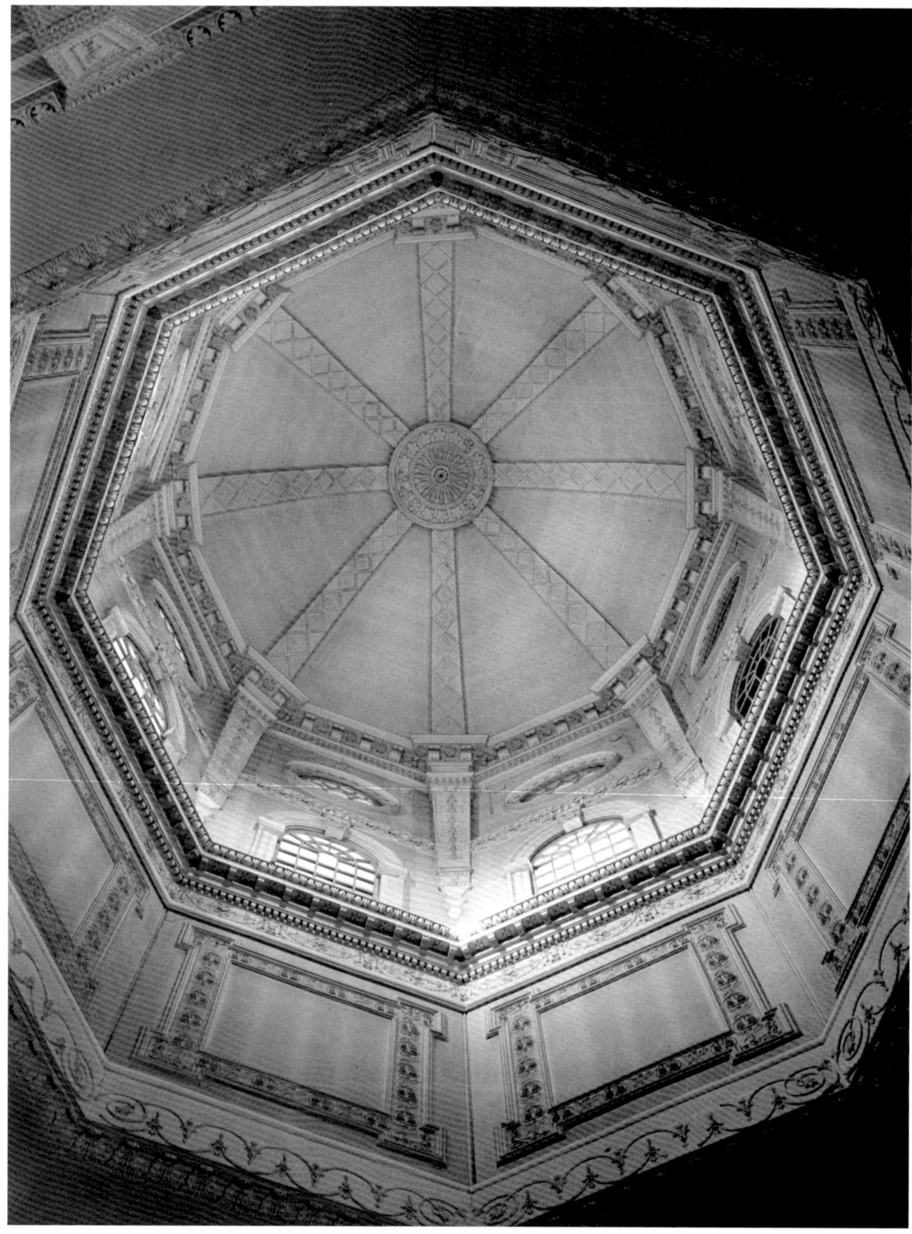

PLATE 042 Annapolis State House, Where Washington Resigned His Commission (1948)

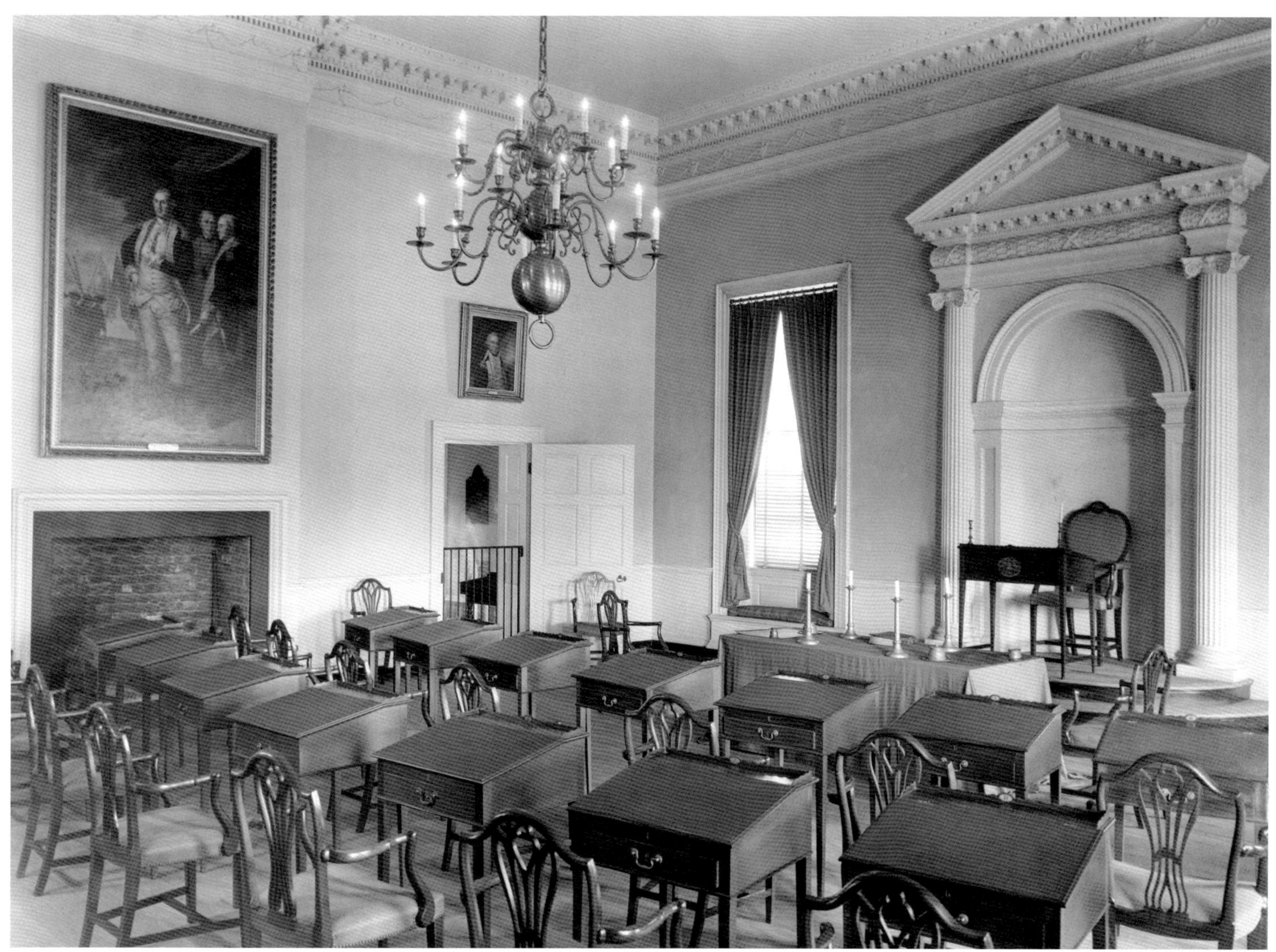

LEFT: PLATE 043 Ridout House, 120 Duke of Gloucester Street *(1959)*
RIGHT: PLATE 044 Ridout House, 120 Duke of Gloucester Street (1959)

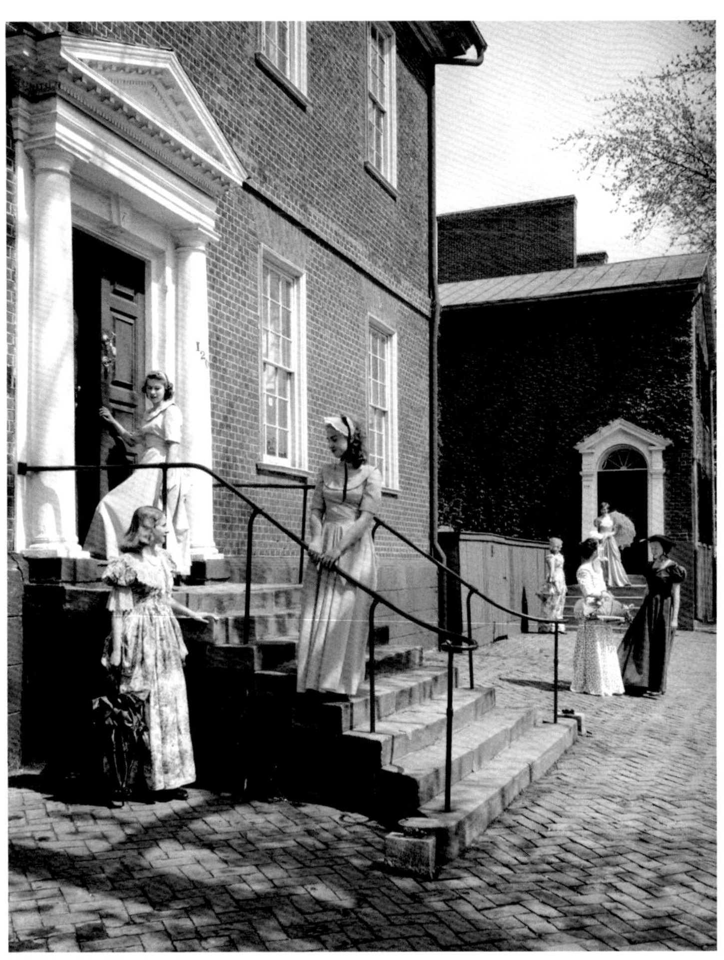

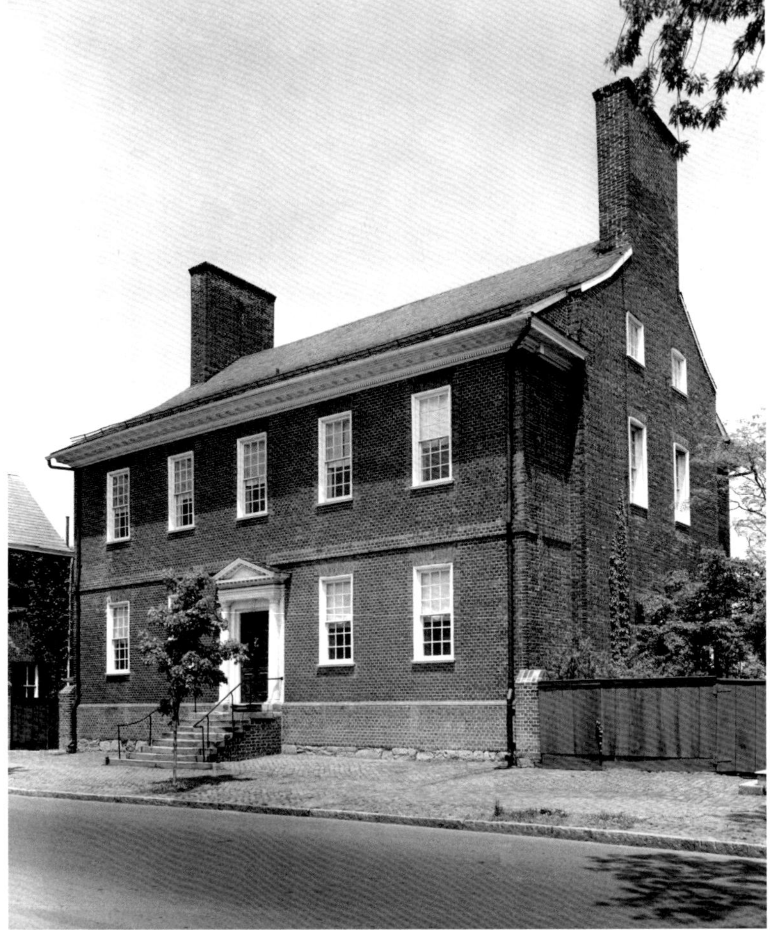

LEFT: PLATE 045 Shiplap House (1960)
RIGHT: PLATE 046 Carvel Hall (1970)

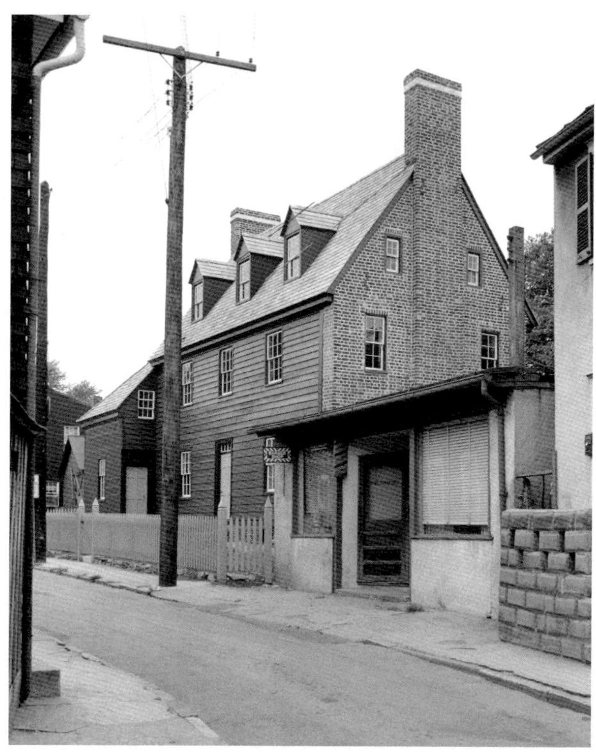

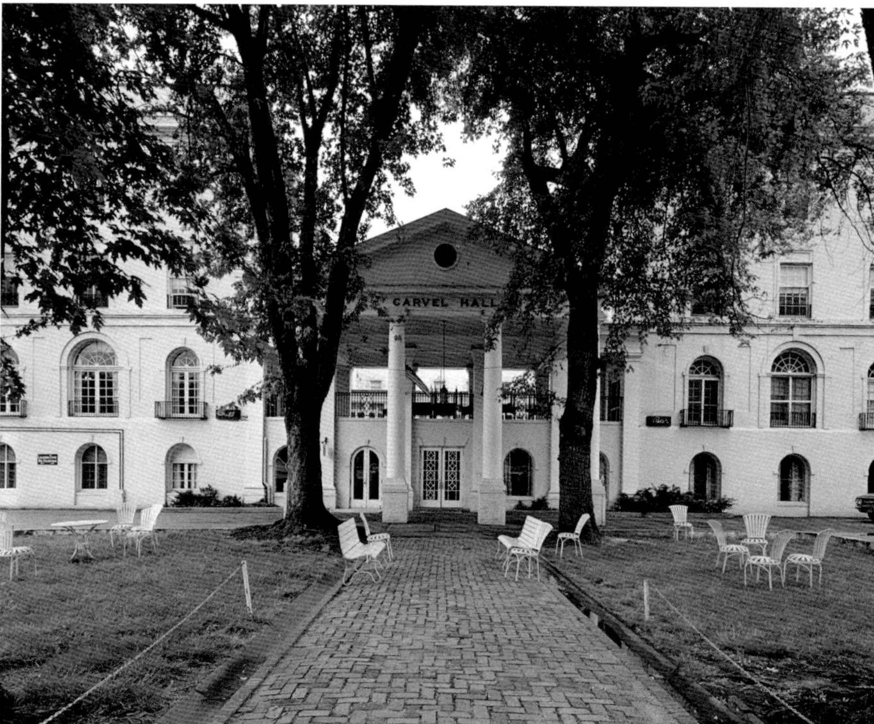

TOP LEFT: PLATE 047 Brice House (1937)

TOP RIGHT: PLATE 048 Brice House (1937)

BOTTOM: PLATE 049 Brice House (1937)

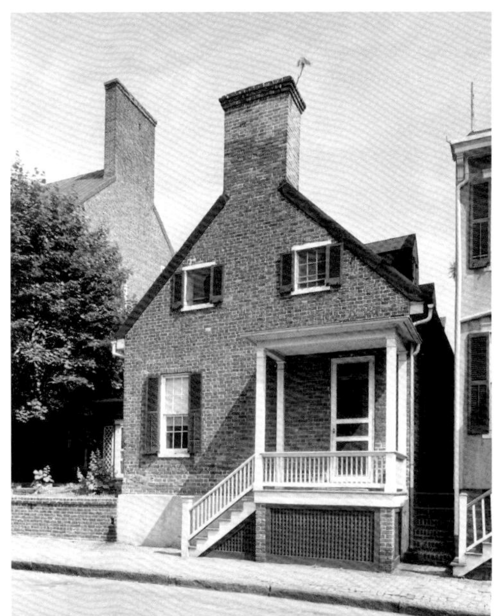

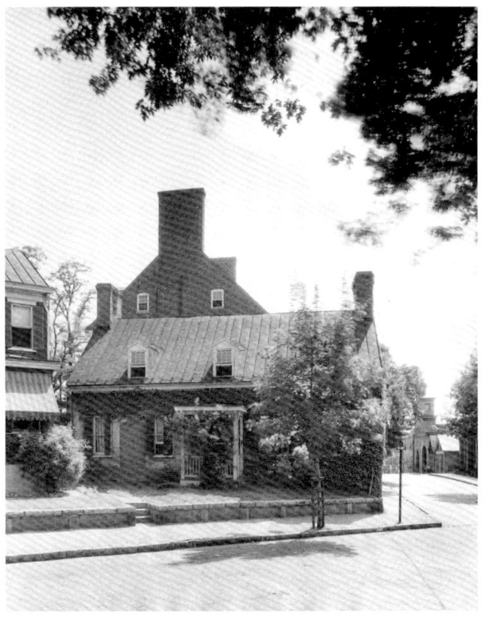

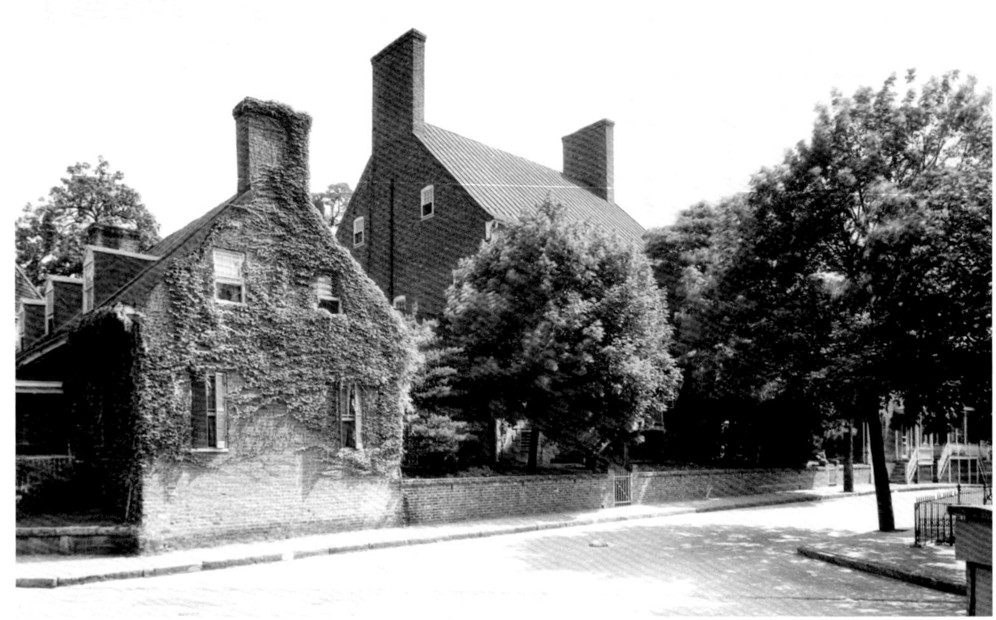

PLATE 050 Brice House (1956)

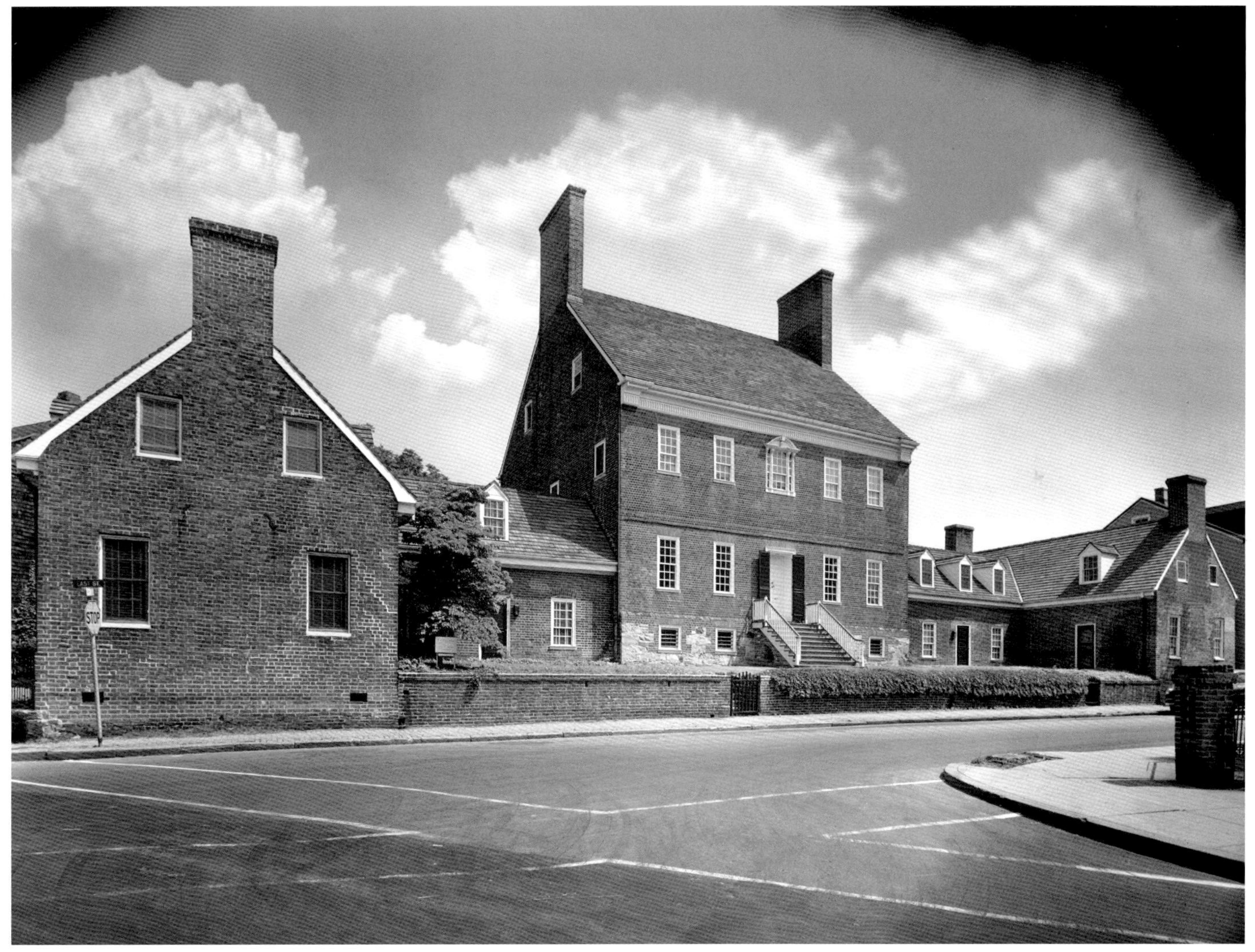

PLATE 051 Brice House (1944)

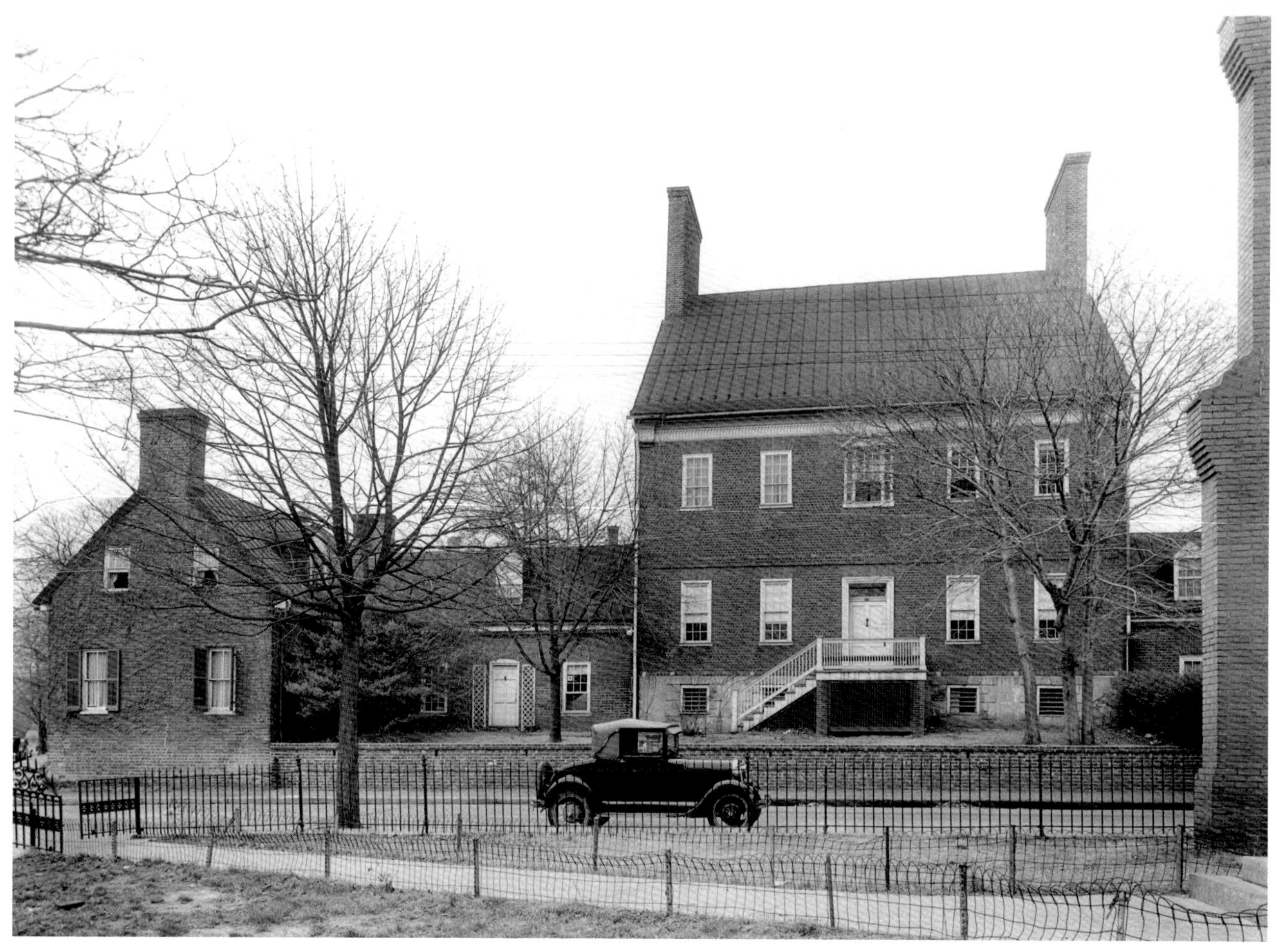

LEFT: PLATE 052 Hammond Harwood House (1950)
RIGHT: PLATE 053 Hammond Harwood House (1952)

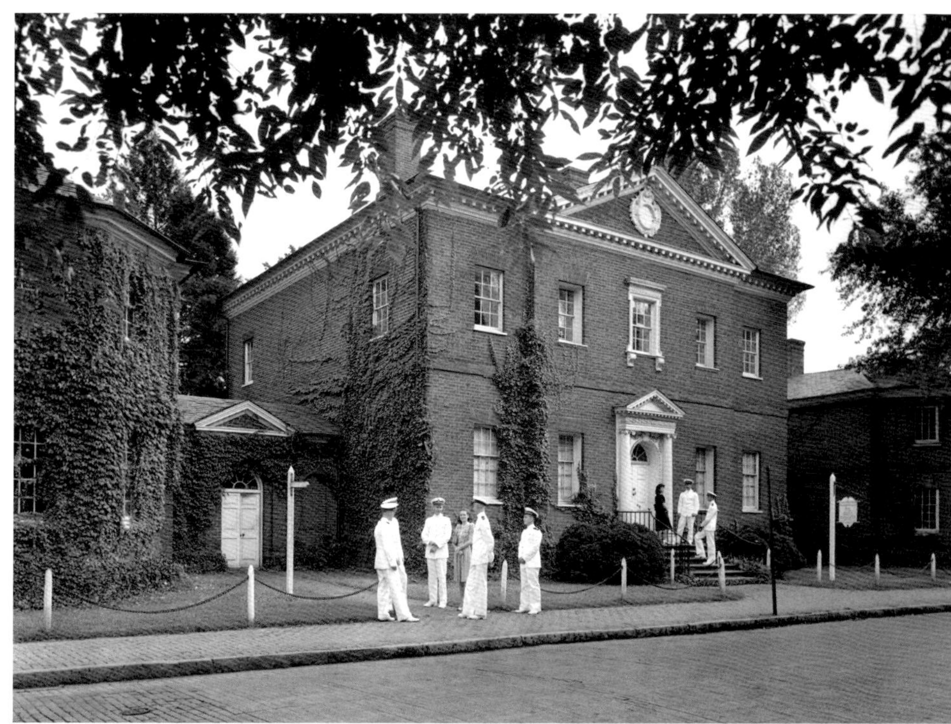

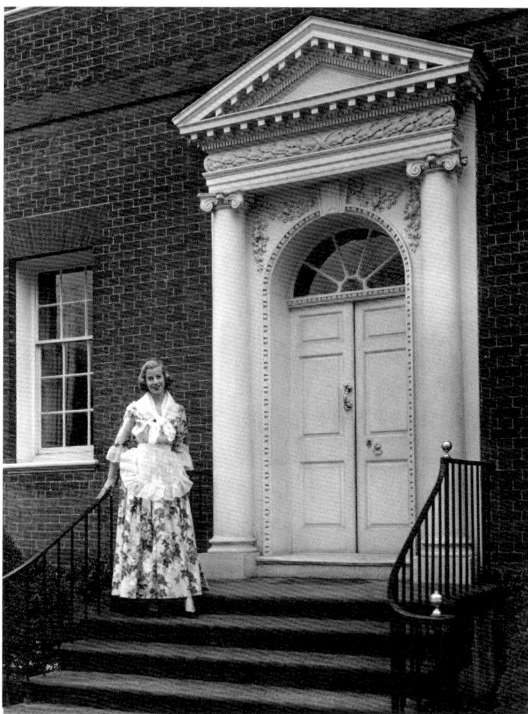

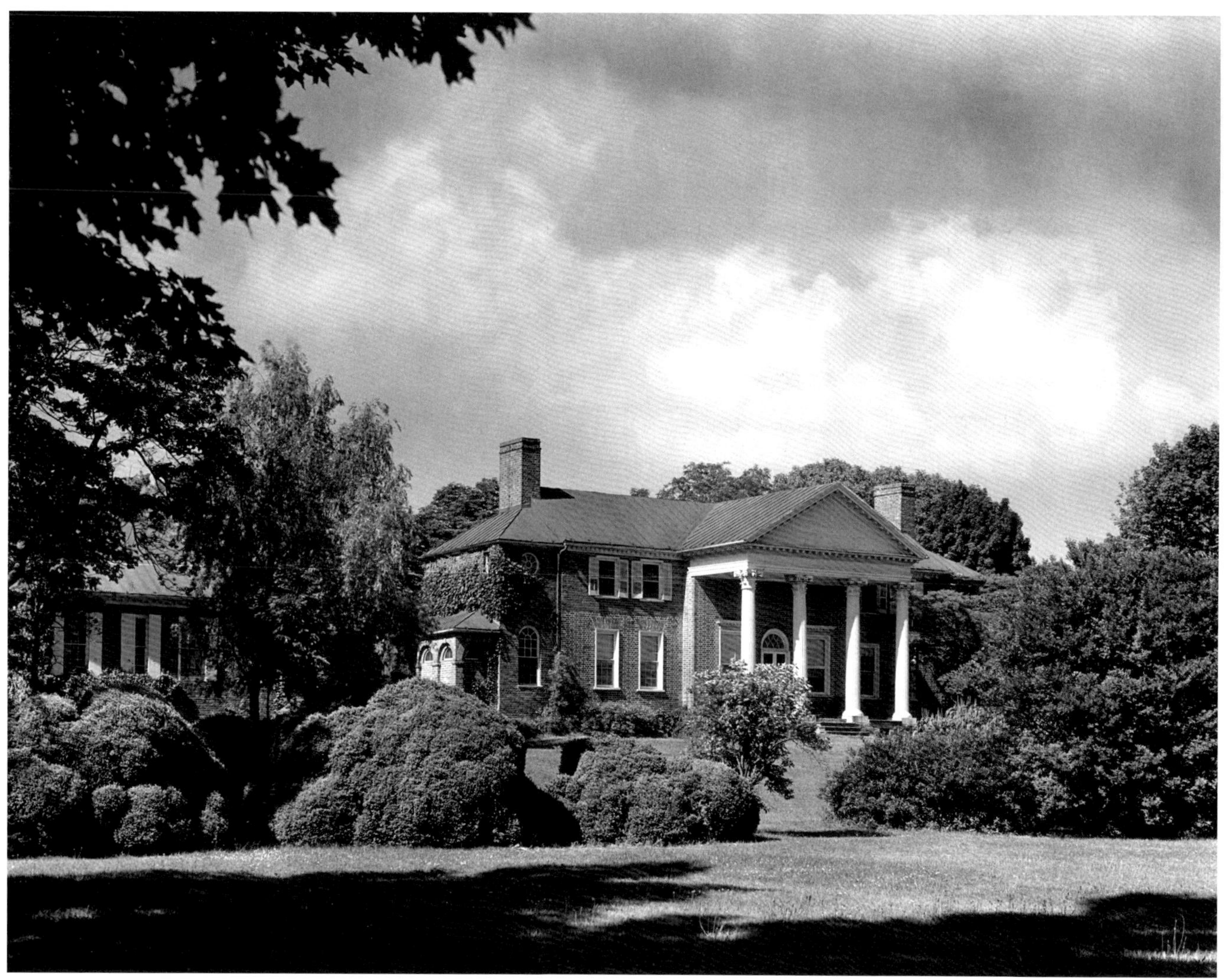

PLATE 059 Tulip Hill (ca. 1950)

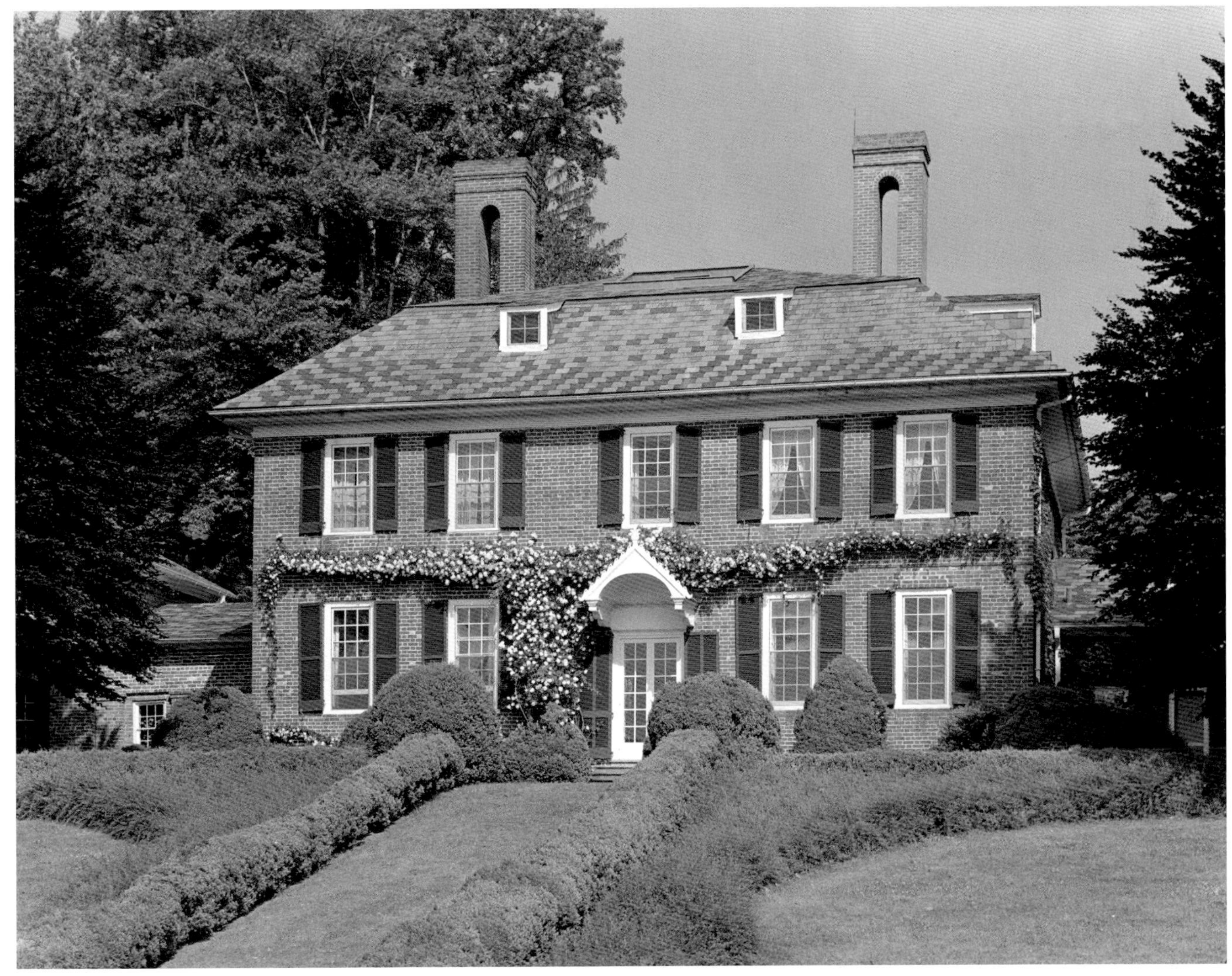

PLATE 060 Oyster Tongers (1958)

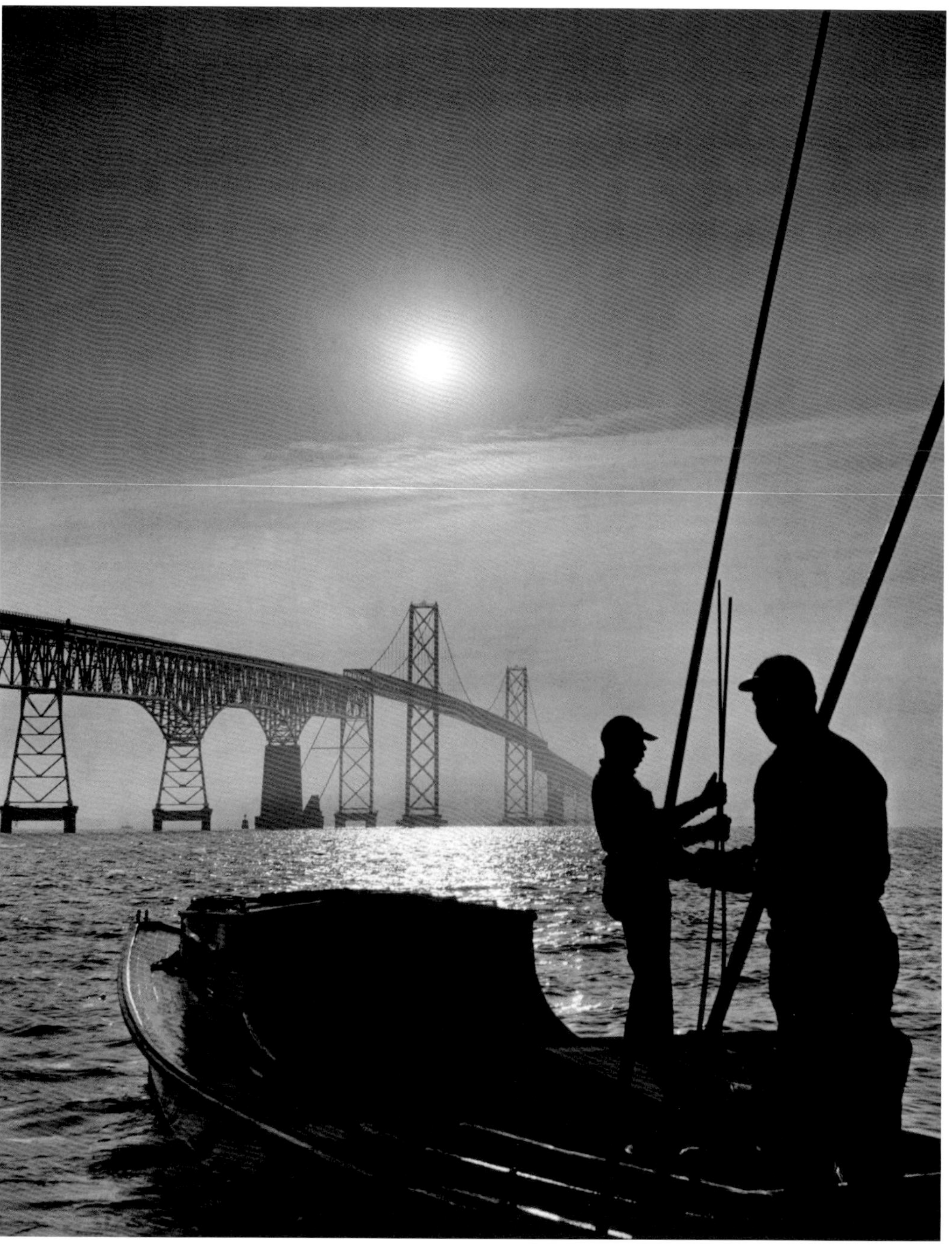

PLATE 061 Bay Bridge Rising (1951)

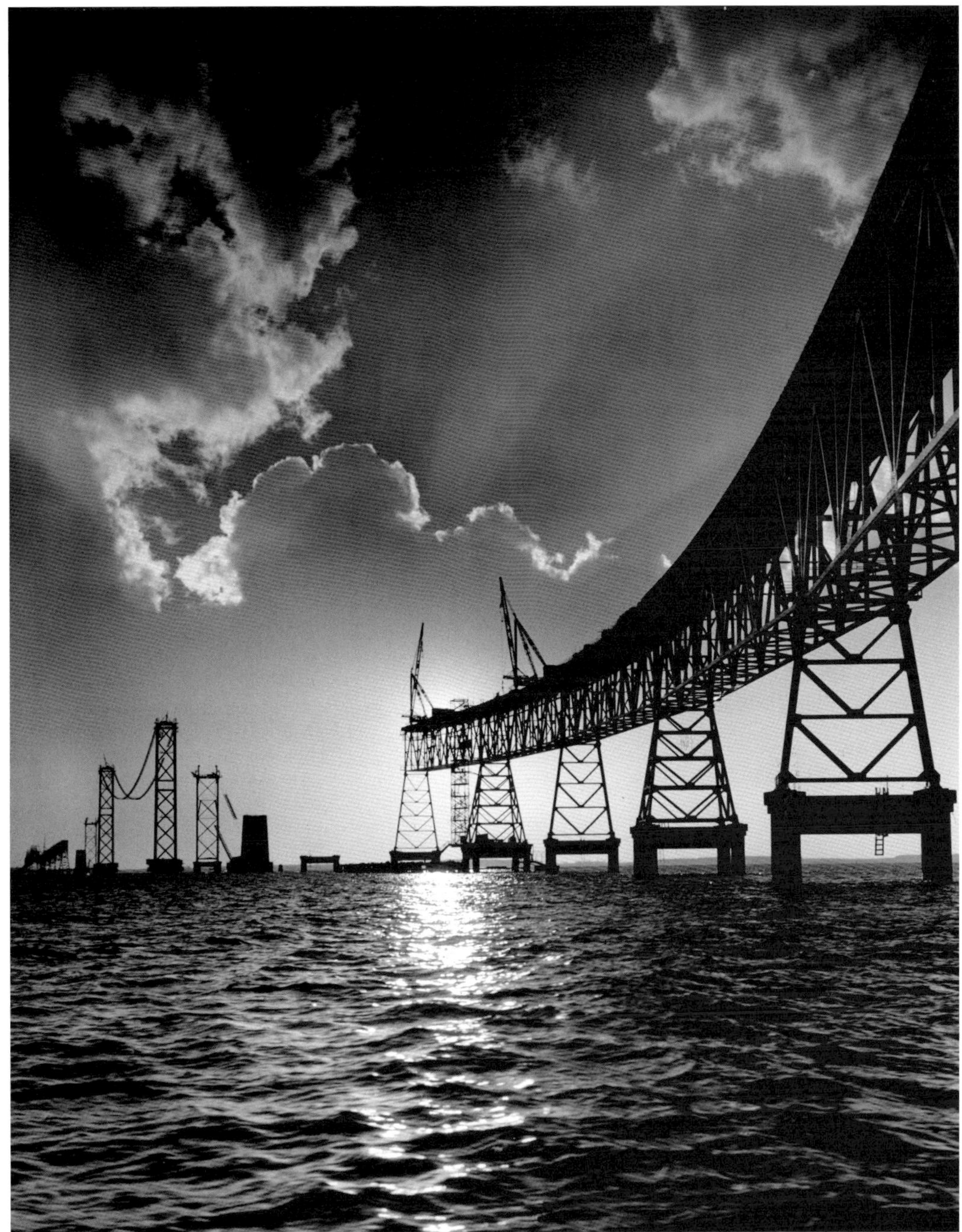

LEFT: PLATE 062 Chesapeake Bay Bridge Construction (1951)
RIGHT: PLATE 063 Chesapeake Bay Bridge Construction (1951)

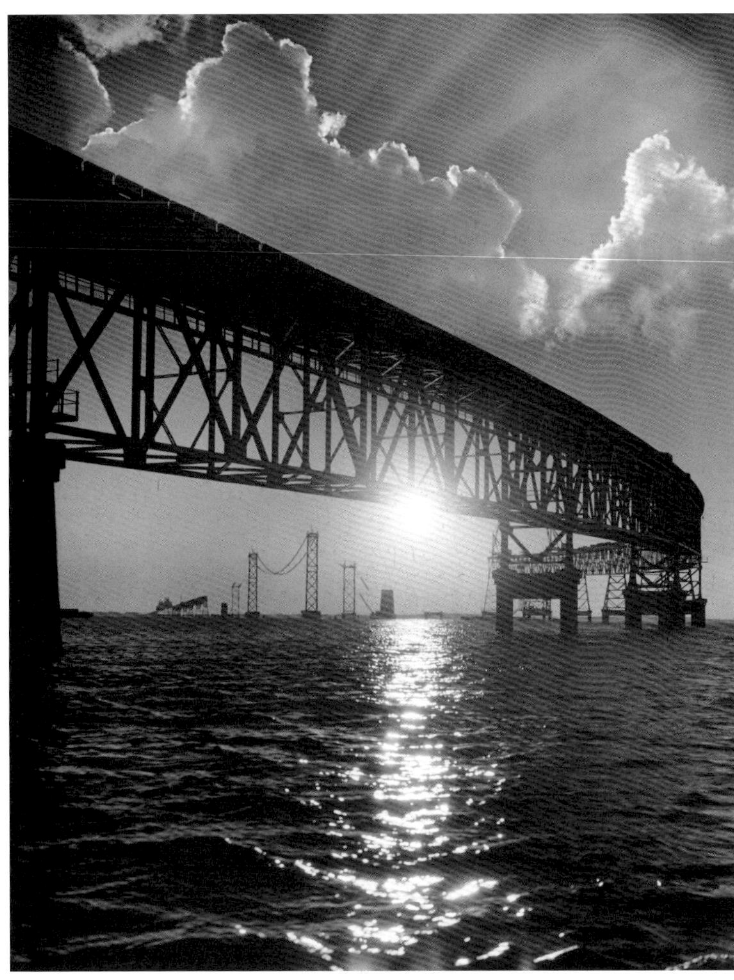

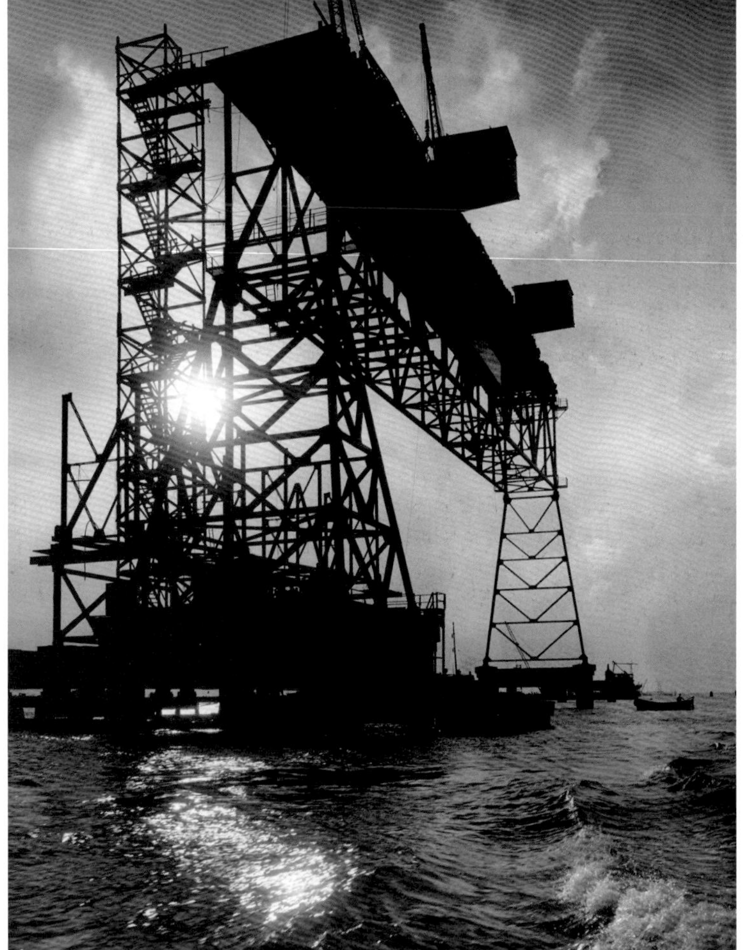

PLATE 064 Moon Light Bay (1955)

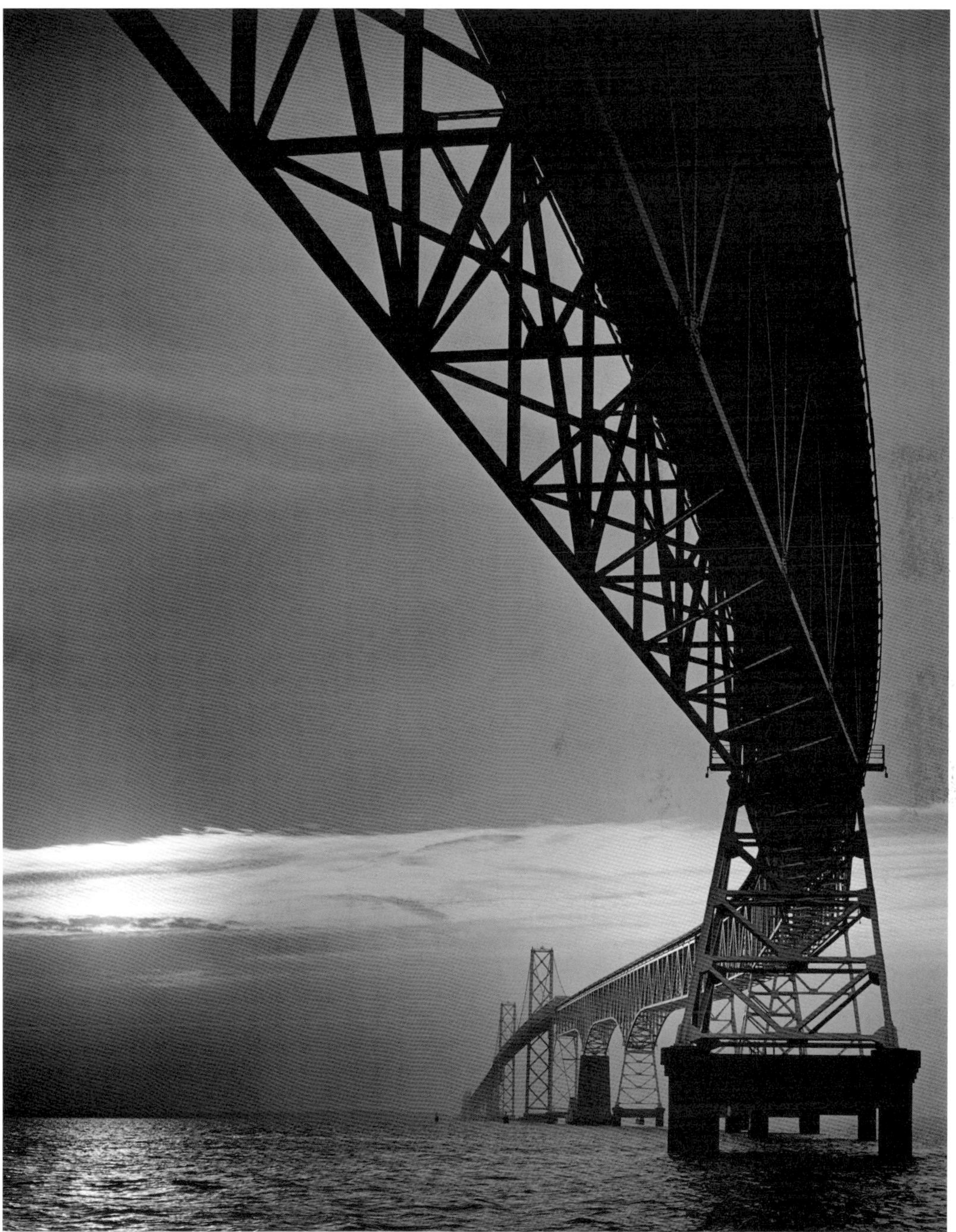

PLATE 065 Ribbon of Light (1953)

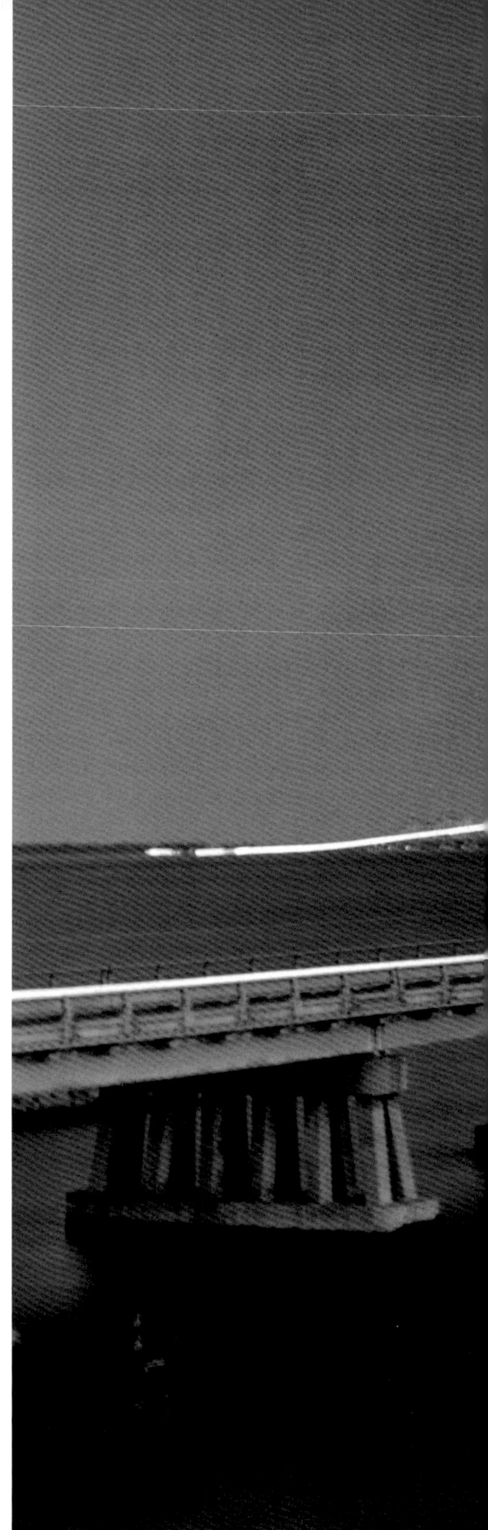

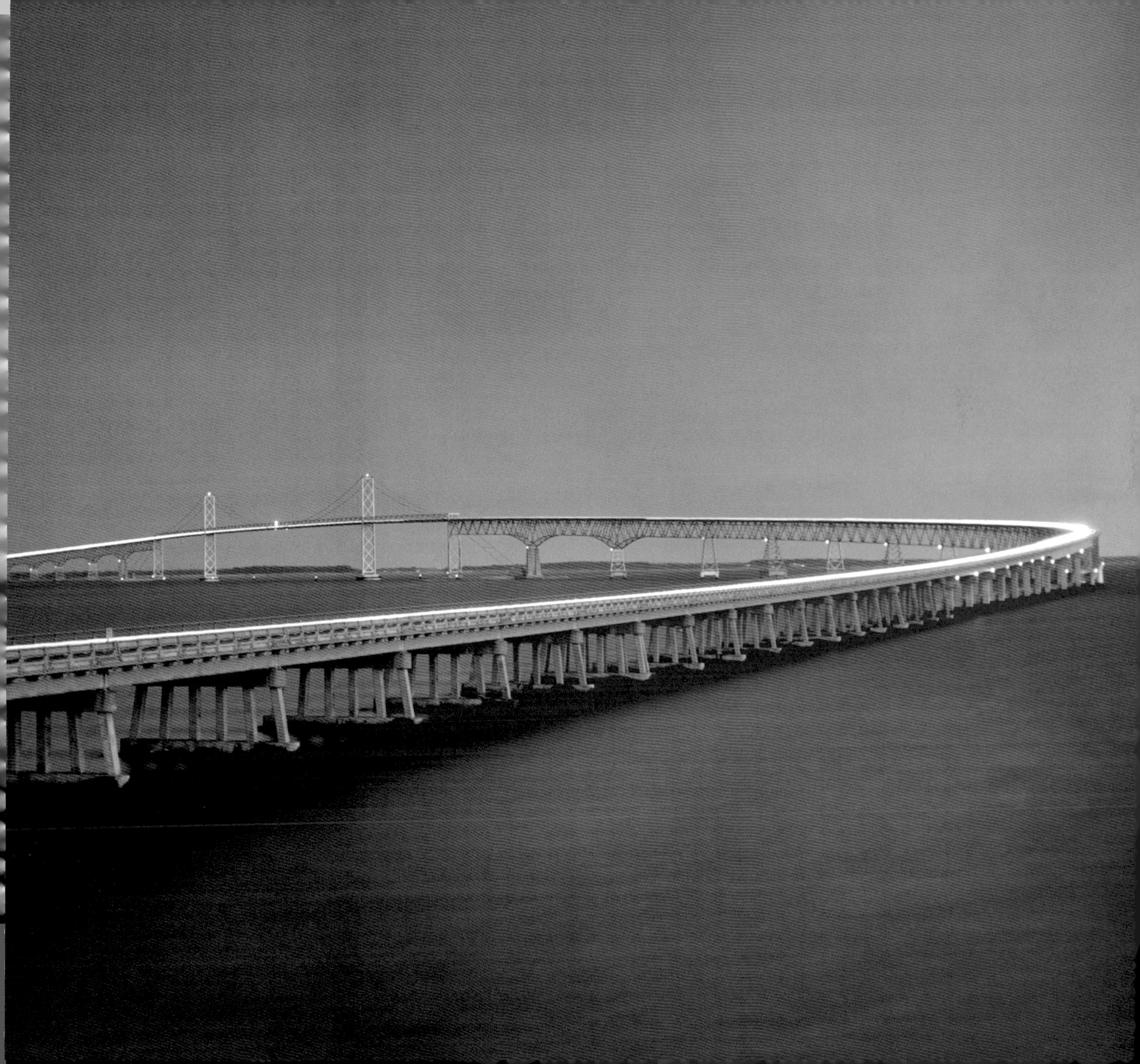

LEFT: PLATE 069 Cornhill Street, Annapolis (1953)
RIGHT: PLATE 070 State House from Chancellor Court (1959)

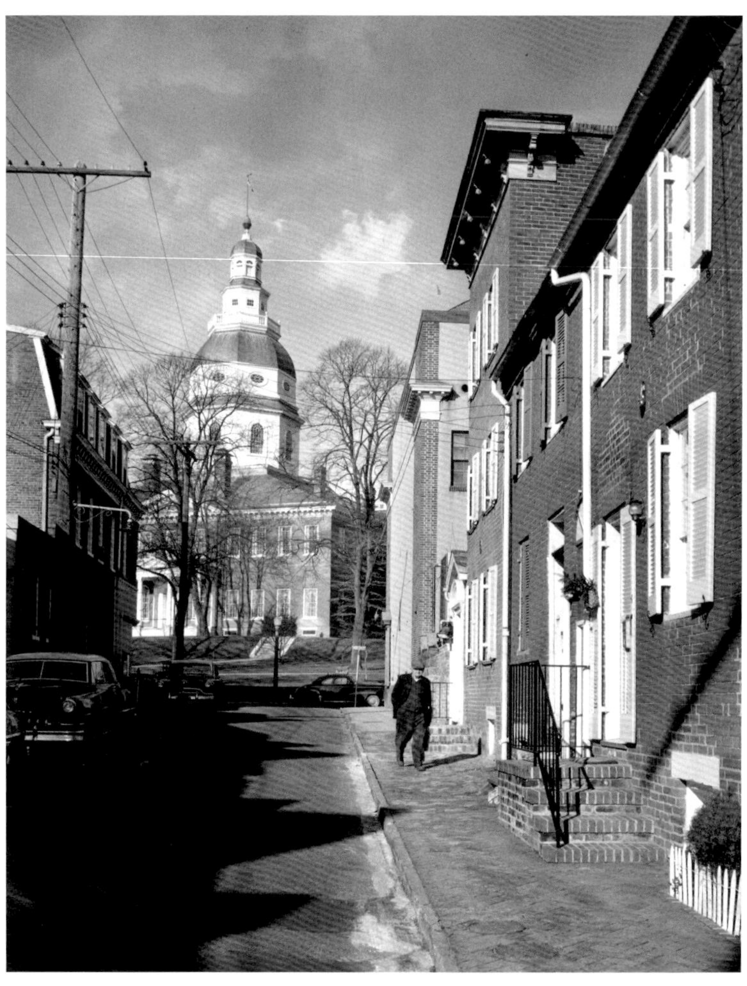

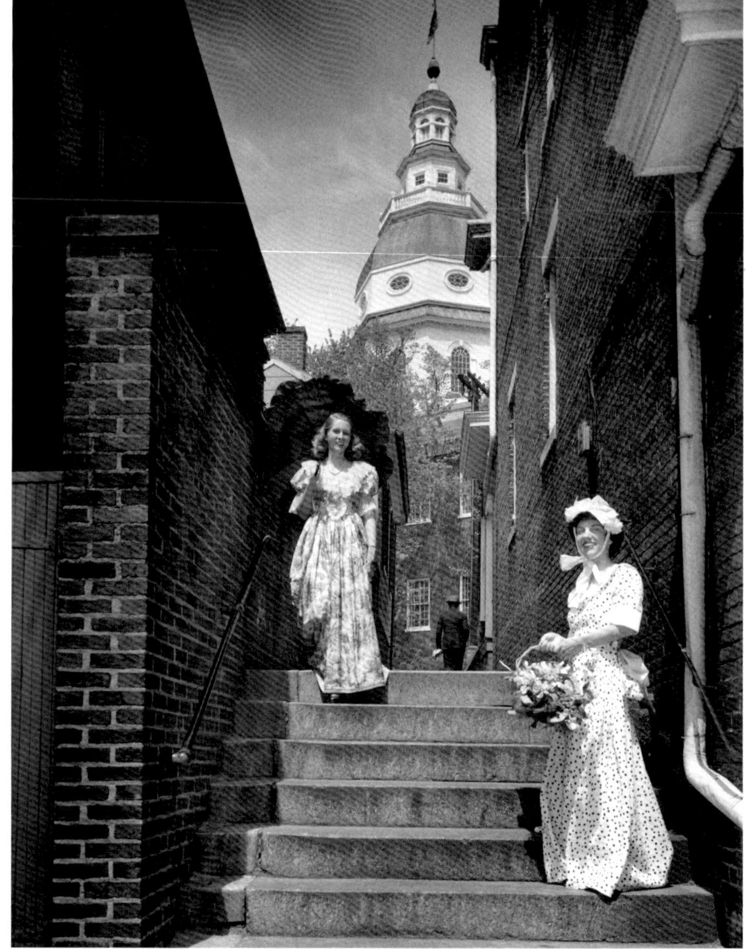

LEFT: PLATE 071 Cornhill Street, Annapolis (1959)
RIGHT: PLATE 072 Reynolds Tavern, St. Anne's Church (1940)

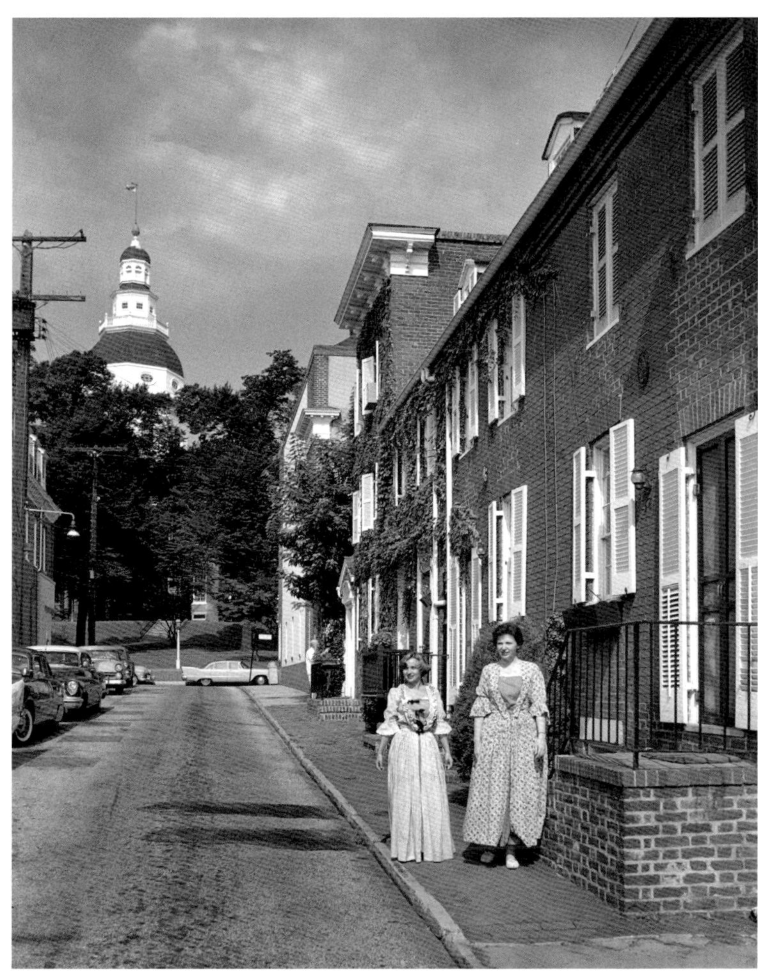

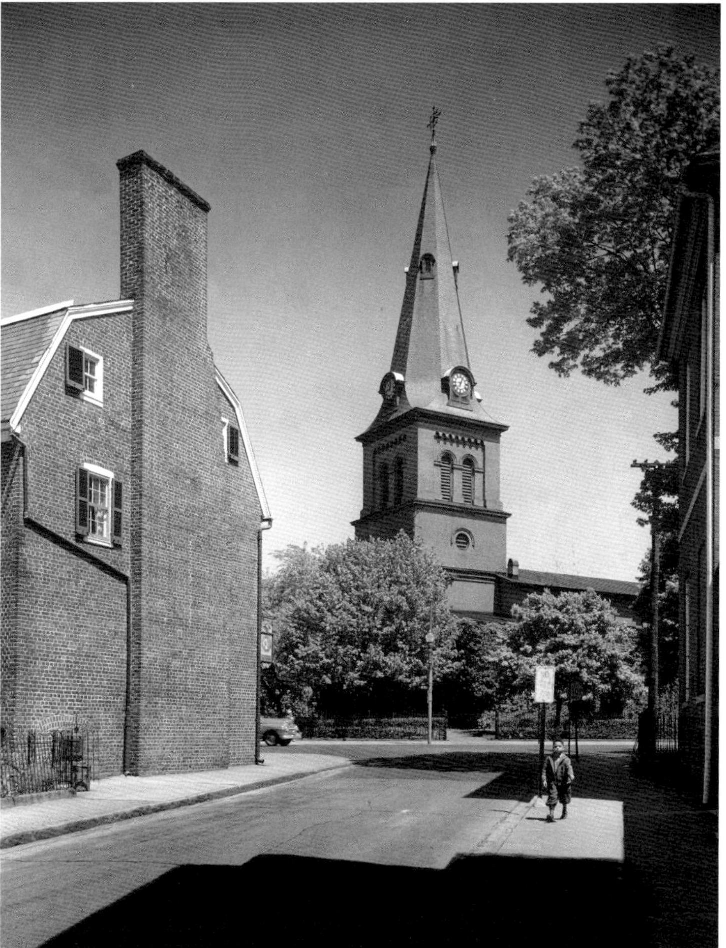

LEFT: PLATE 073 Taylor Street, Helen's Lunchroom (1950)
RIGHT: PLATE 074 Taylor Street, Annapolis (ca. 1950)

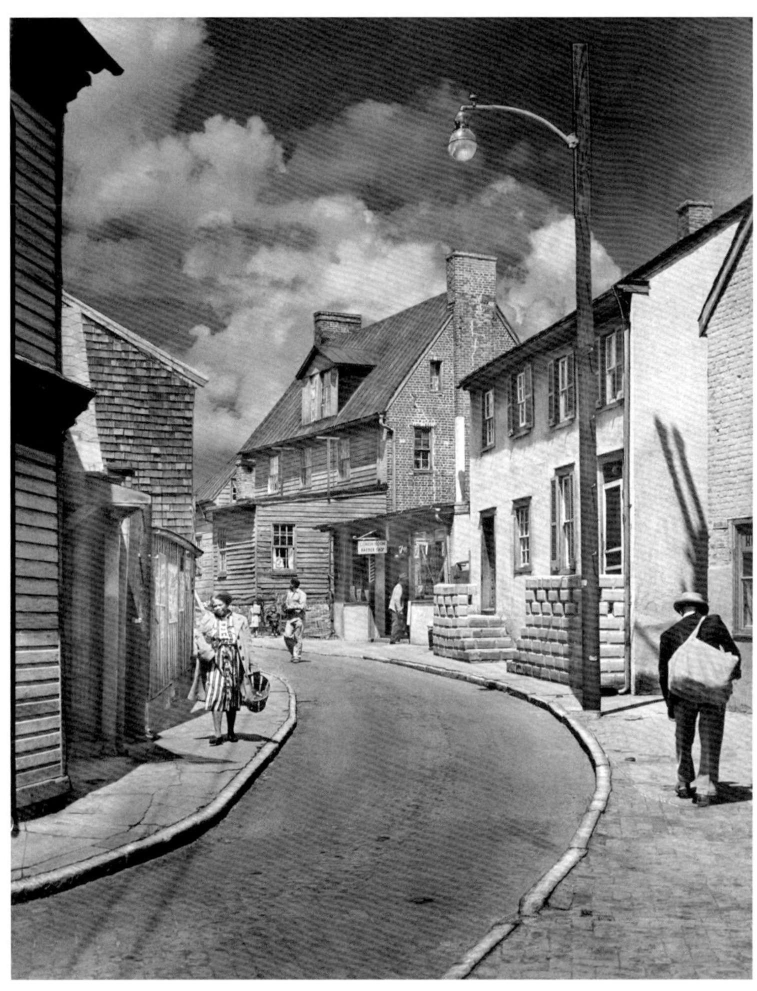

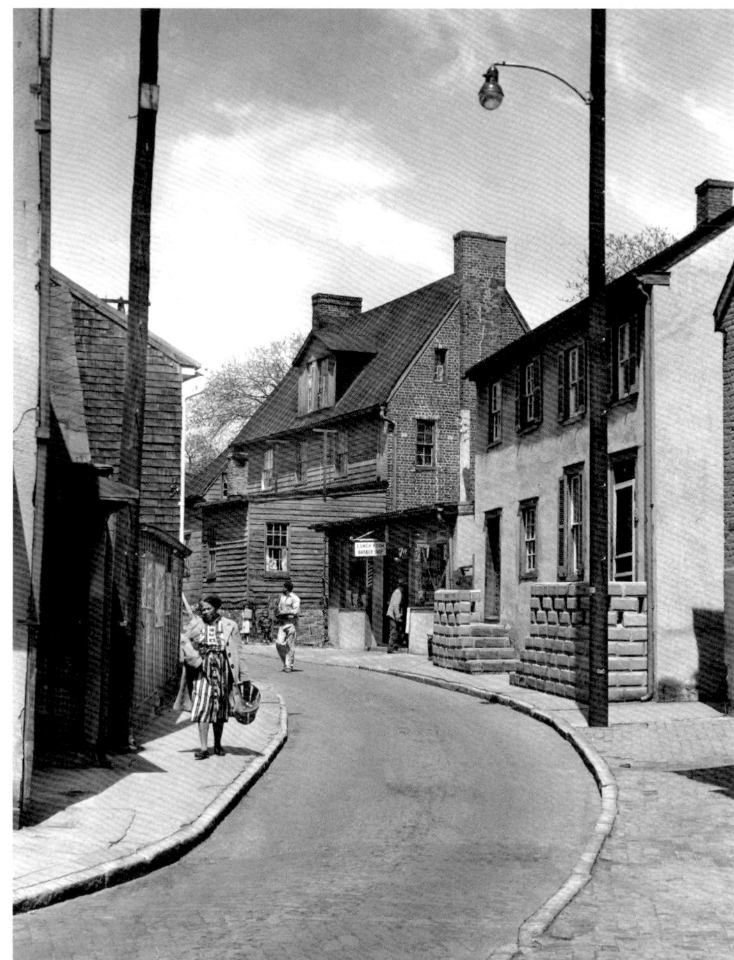

LEFT: PLATE 075 Taylor Street, Annapolis (1952)

RIGHT: PLATE 076 Taylor Street, Annapolis (1952)

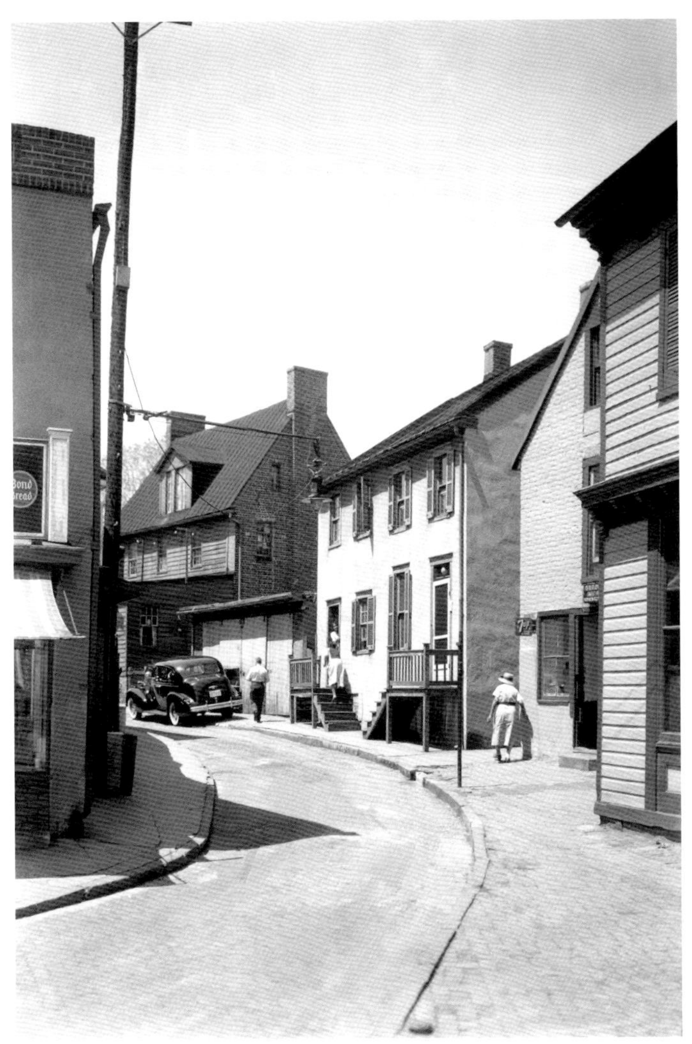

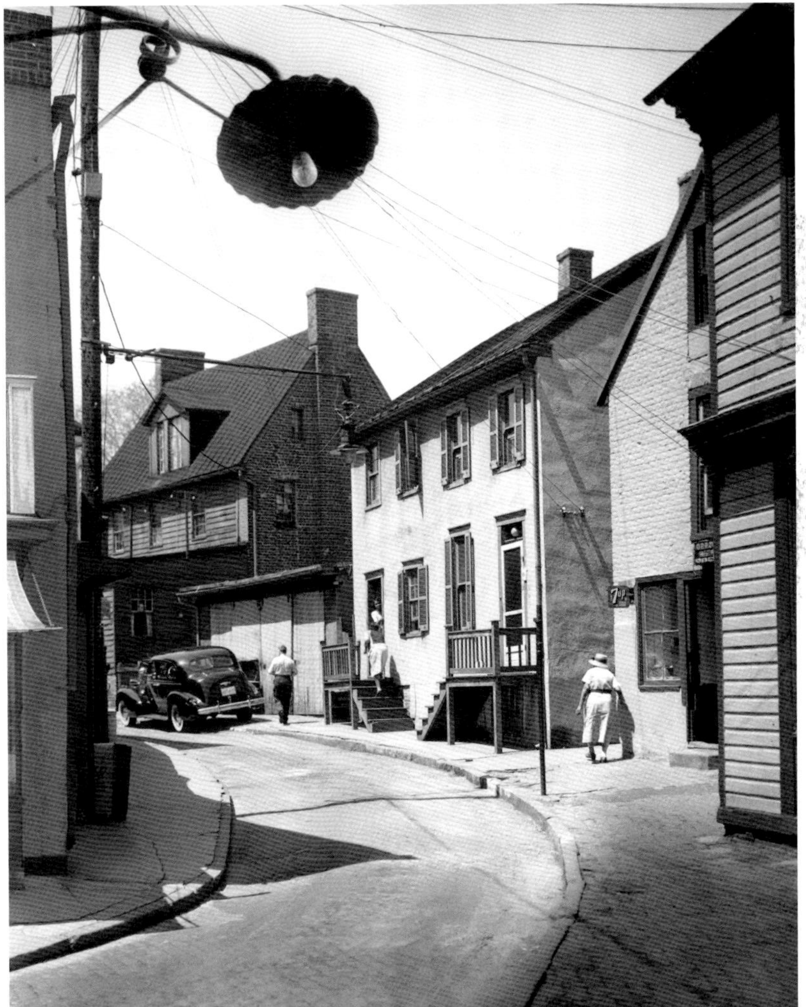

LEFT: PLATE 077 Cornhill Street (1953)
RIGHT: PLATE 078 Cornhill Street (1953)

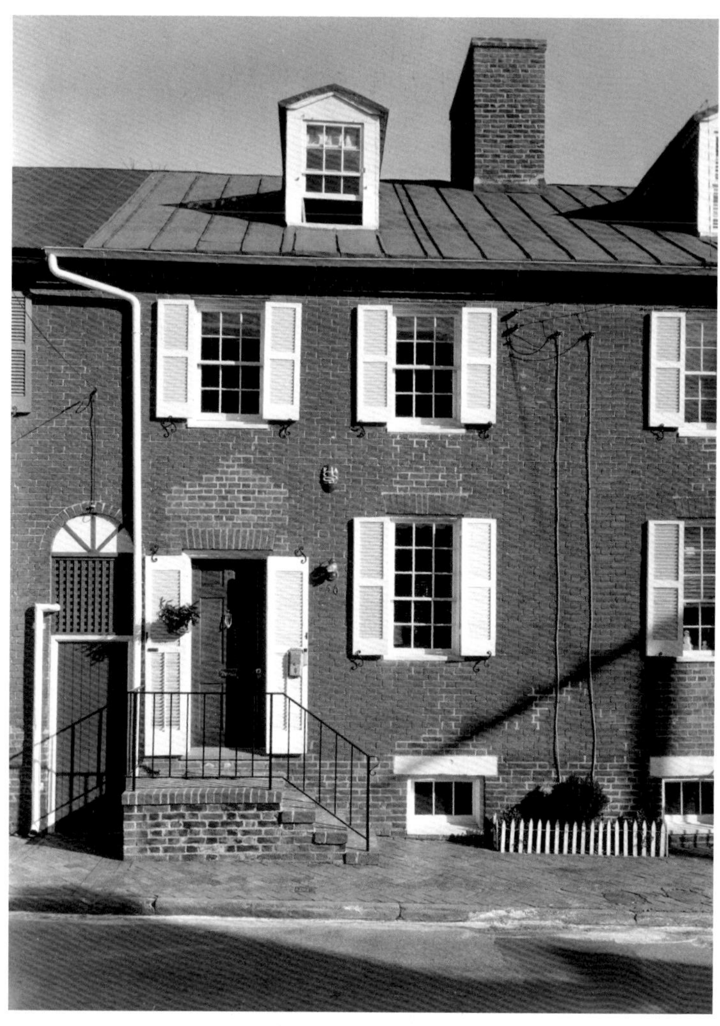

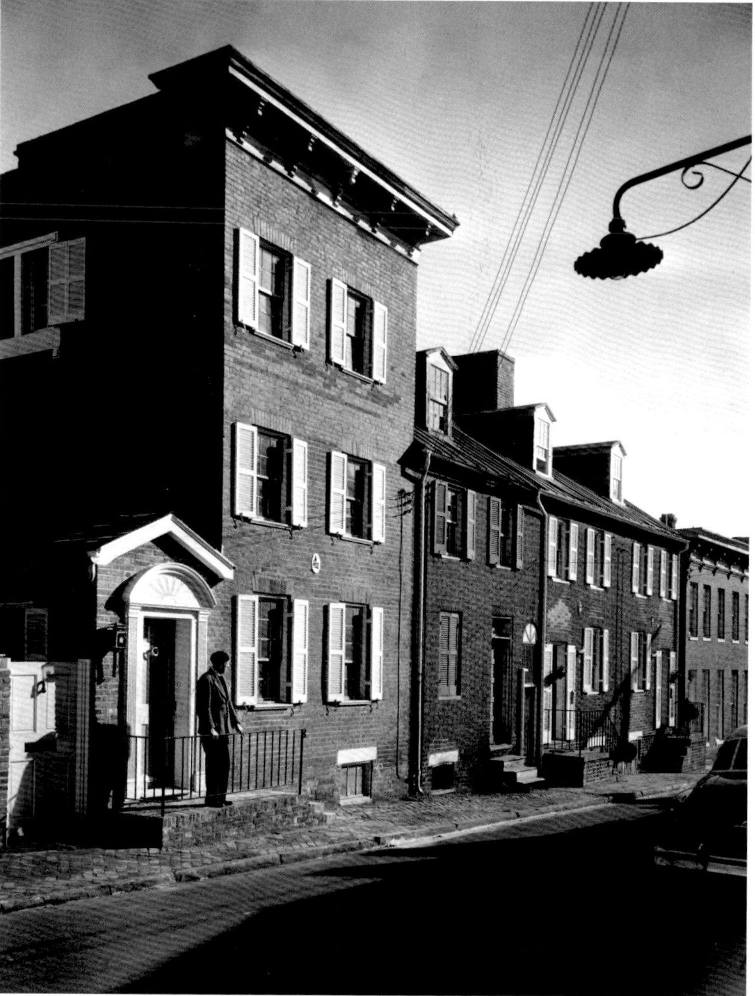

PLATE 079 Rock Fishing on the Ice, Spa Creek Annapolis (1945)

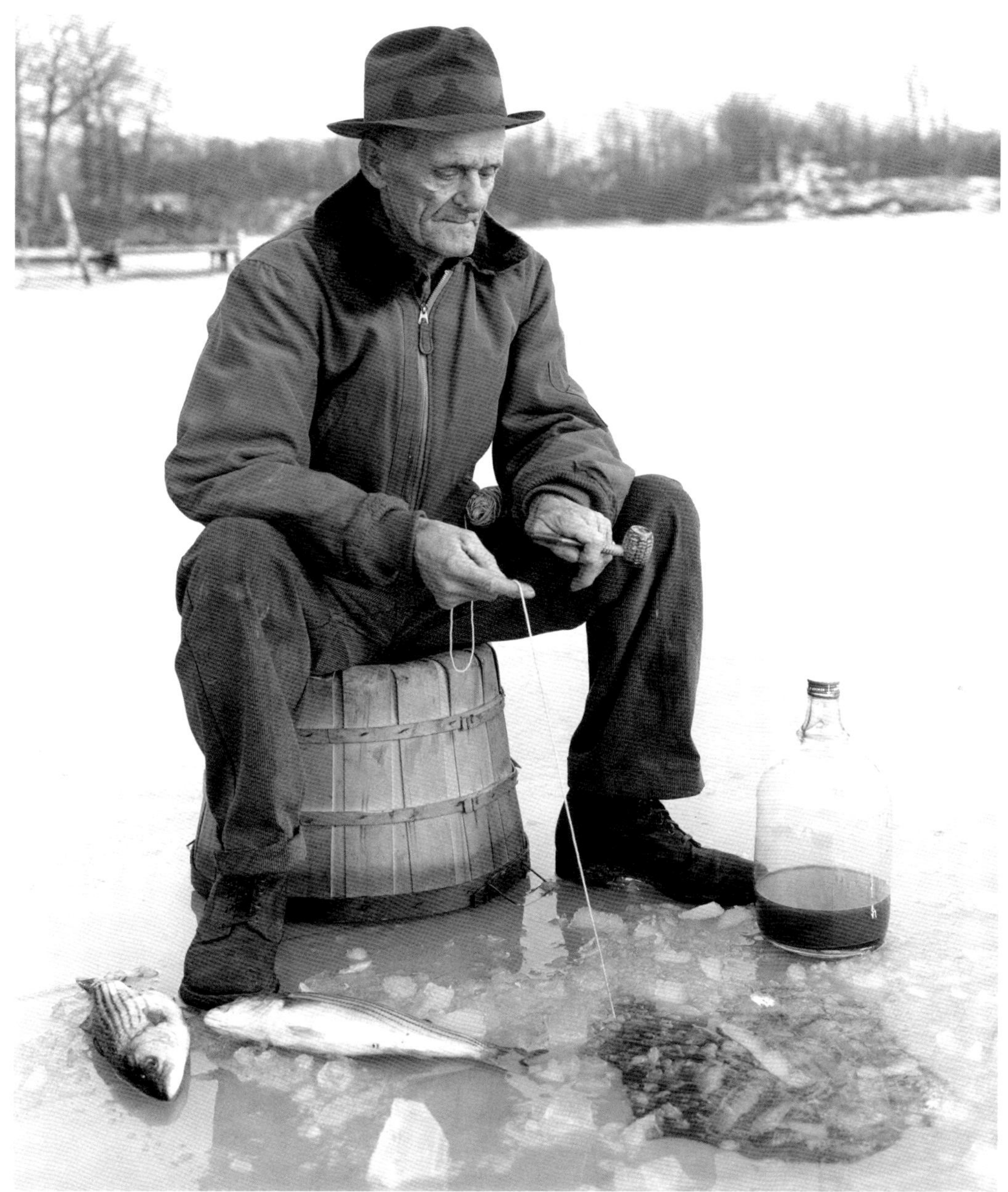

LEFT: PLATE 080 St. John's College (1952)
RIGHT: PLATE 081 St. John's, McDowell Hall (1952)

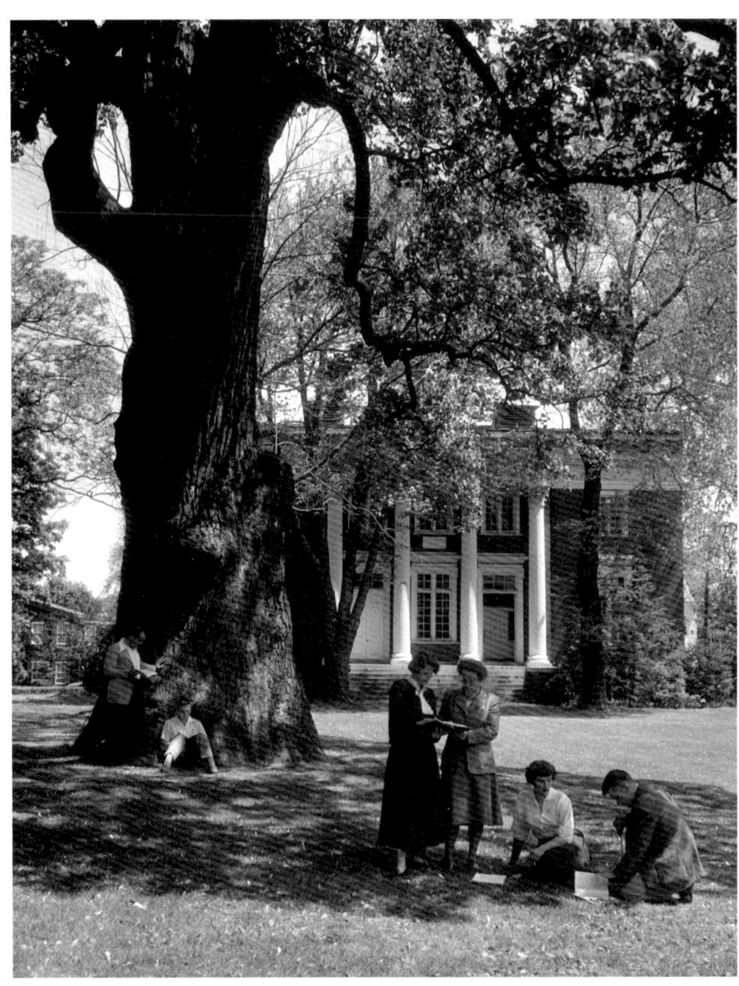

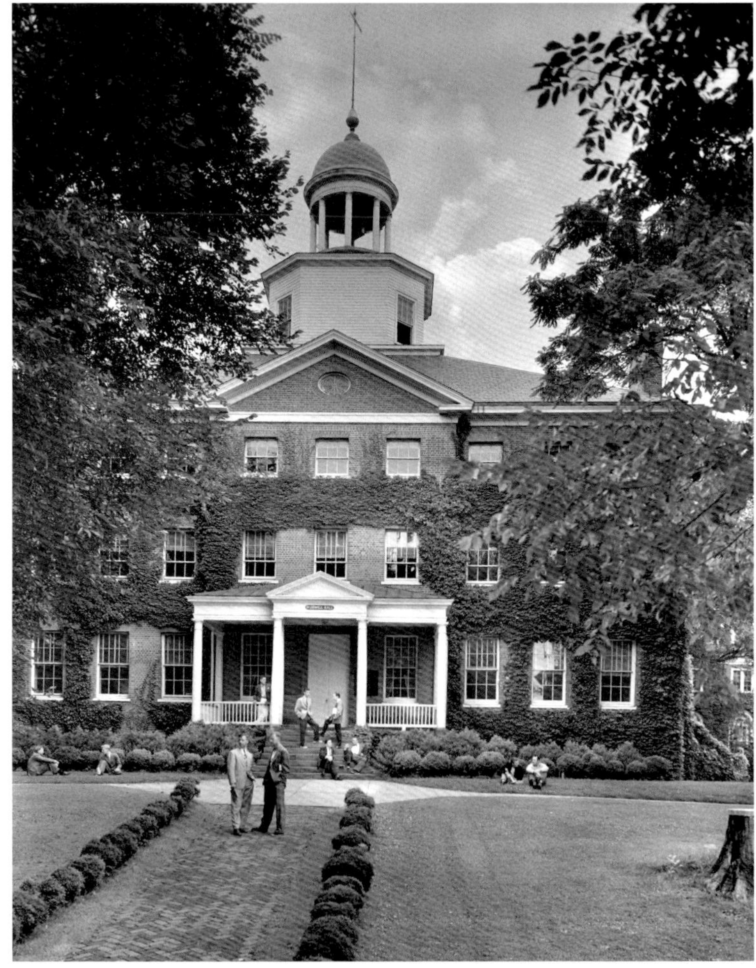

PLATE 082 Liberty Tree, St. John's, Woodward Hall (1952)

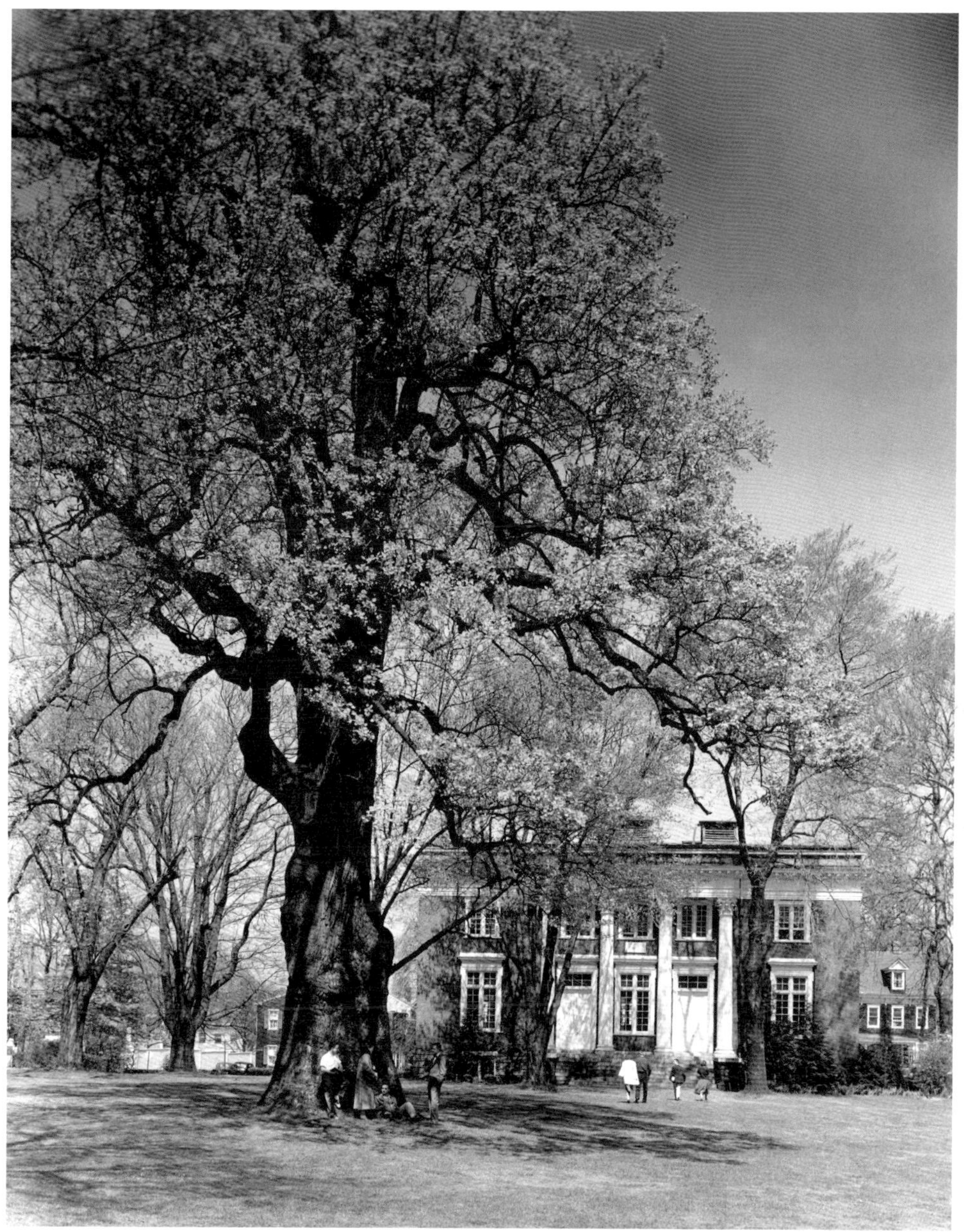

PLATE 085 Old Treasury Building (1956)

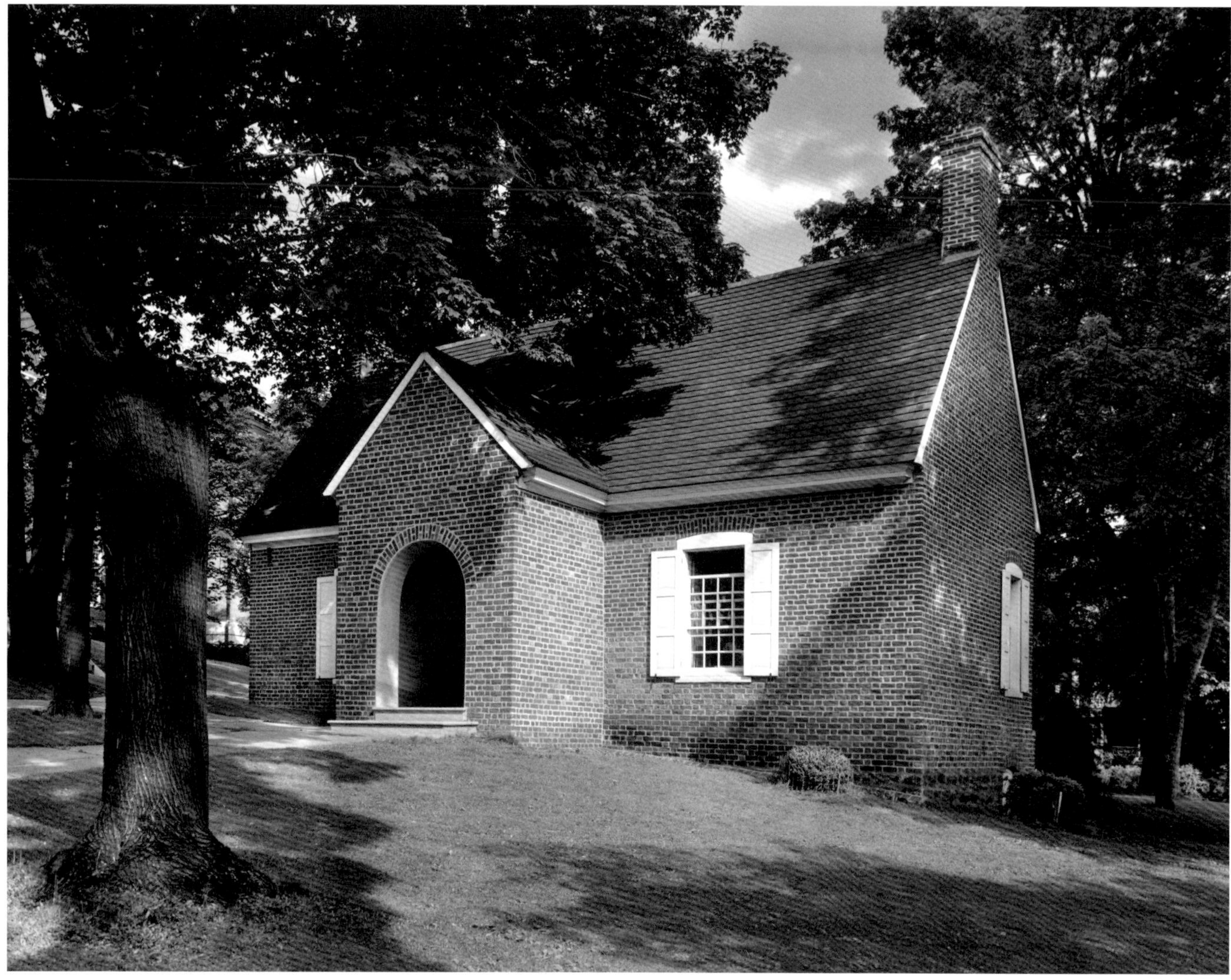

PLATE 086 Sandy Point Light (ca. 1950)

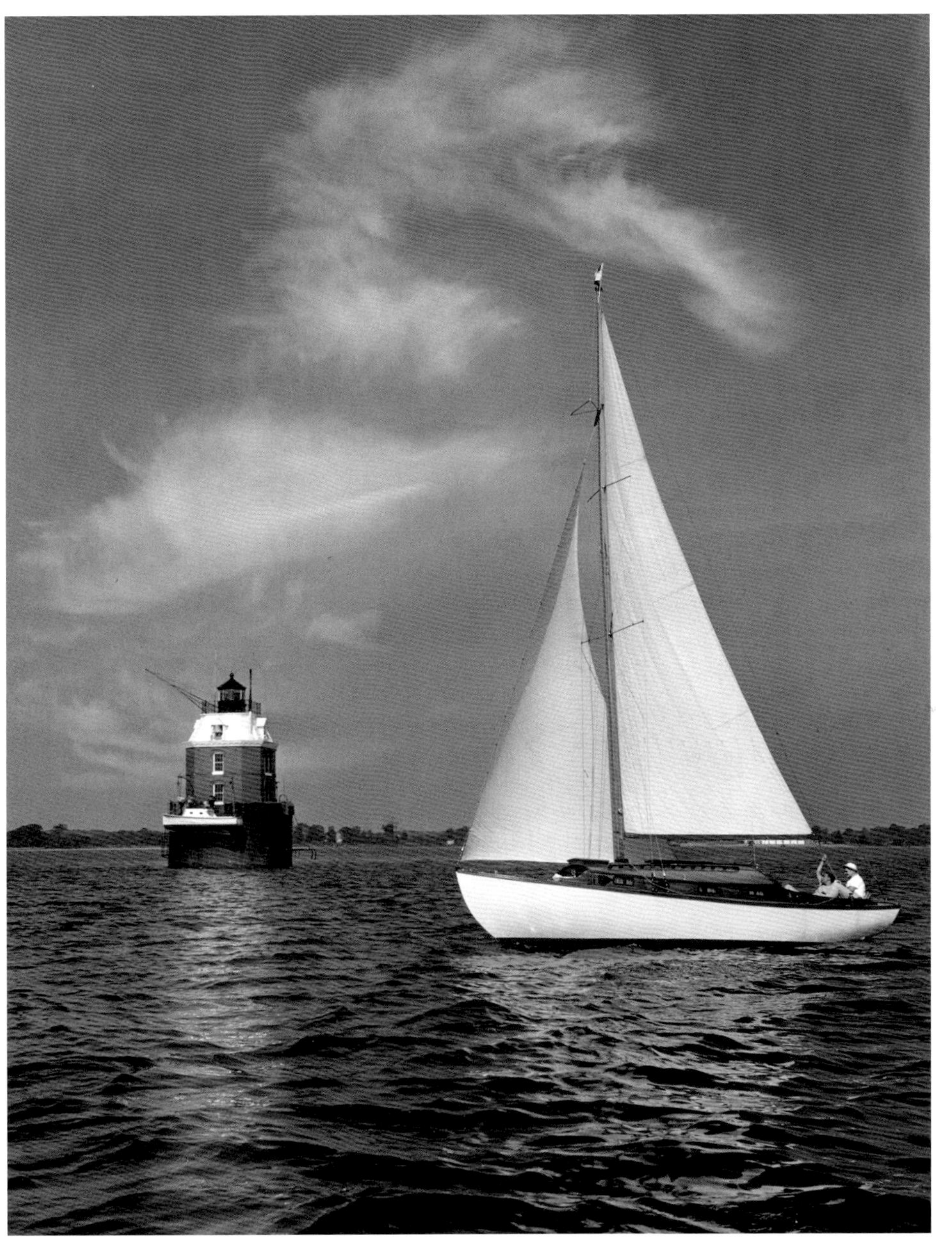

PLATE 089 *Danmark*, "The Old and the New" (1958)

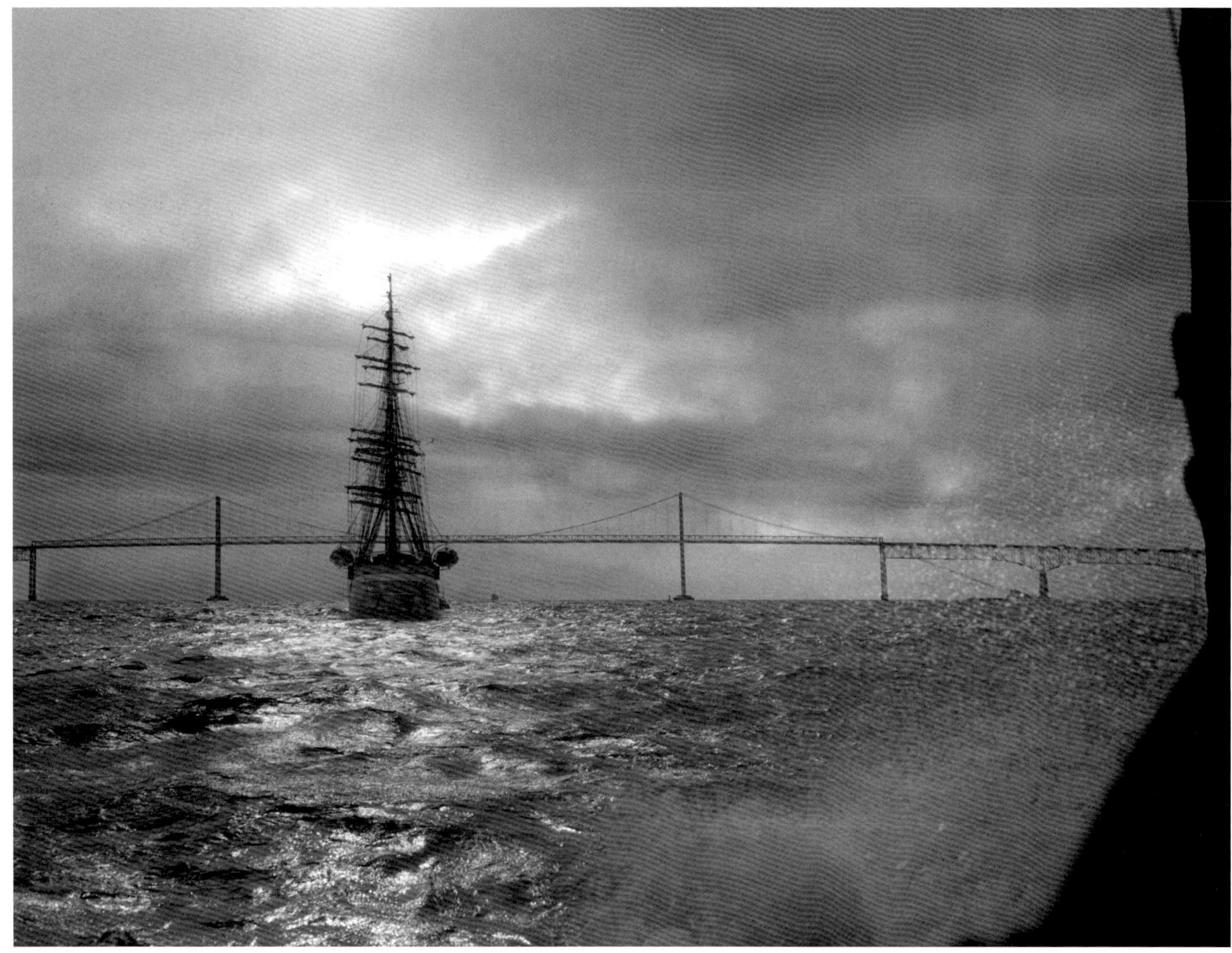

PLATE 090 Galesville (1952)

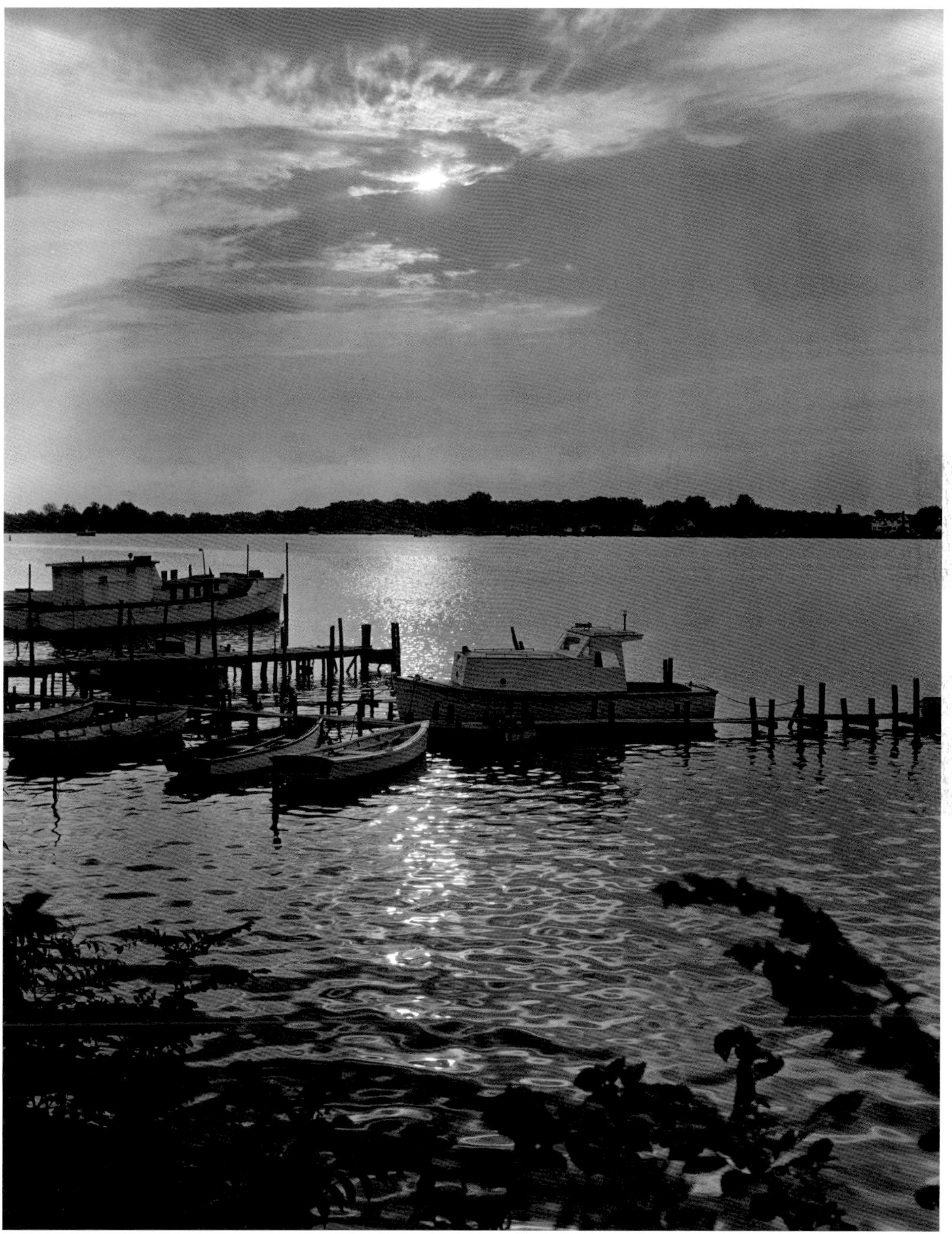

LEFT: PLATE 091 Oyster Boat and Buy Boat (1936)
RIGHT: PLATE 092 Oyster Boats (1936)

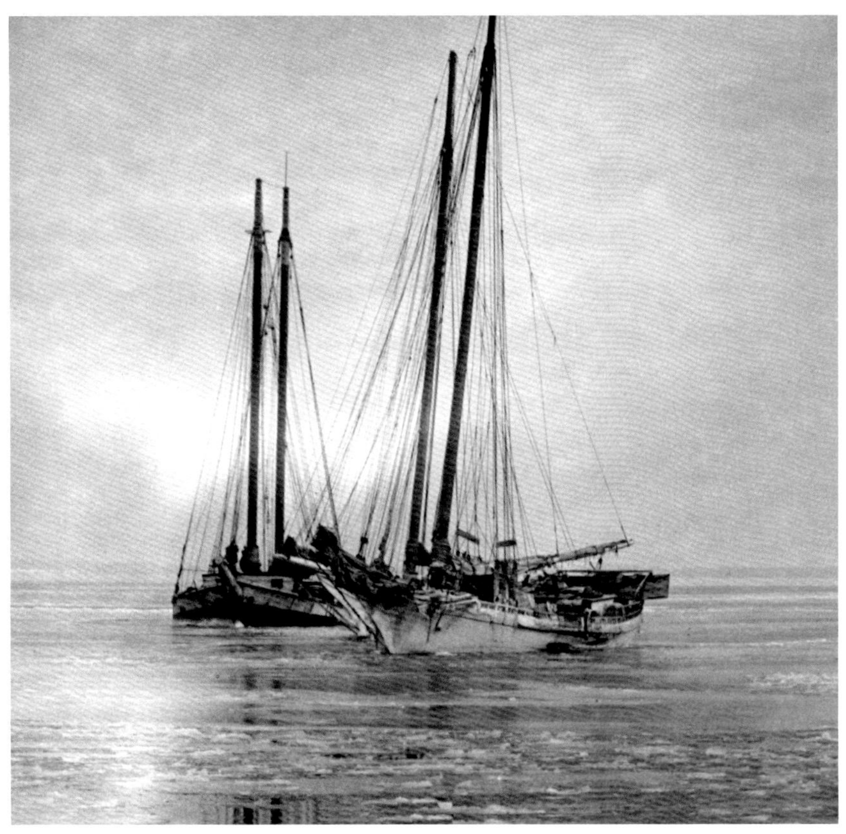

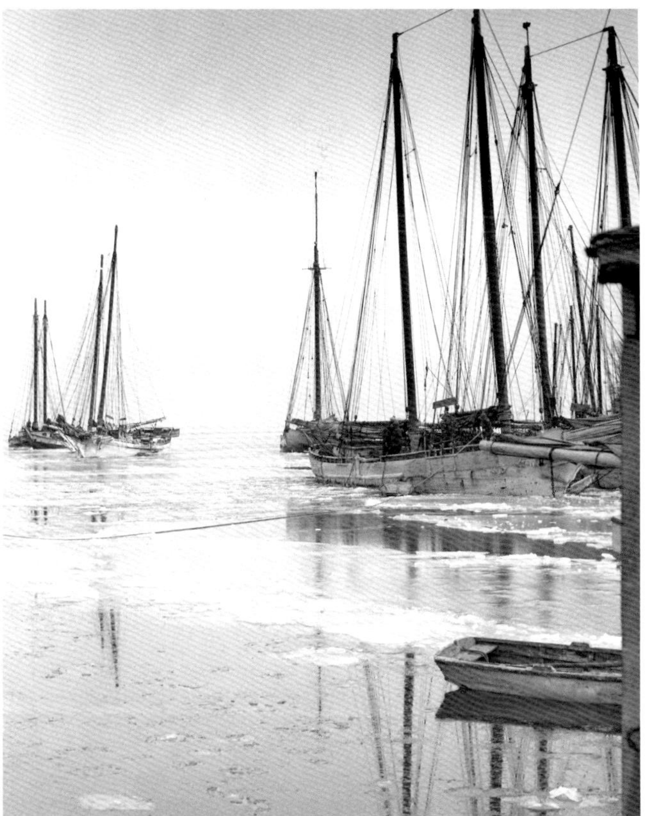

PLATE 093 The Big Freeze (1936)

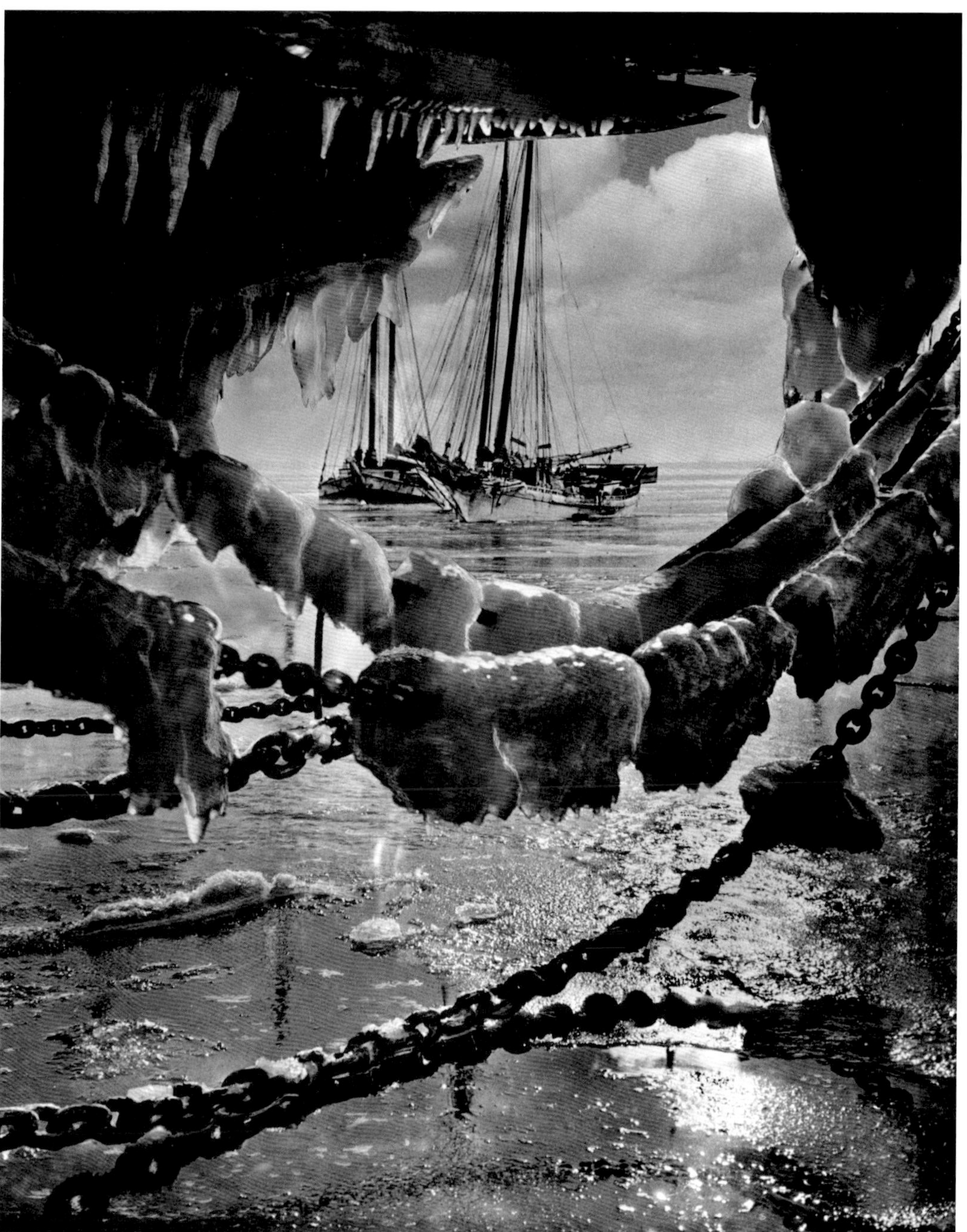

PLATE 104 Working on the Chesapeake Bay (1950)

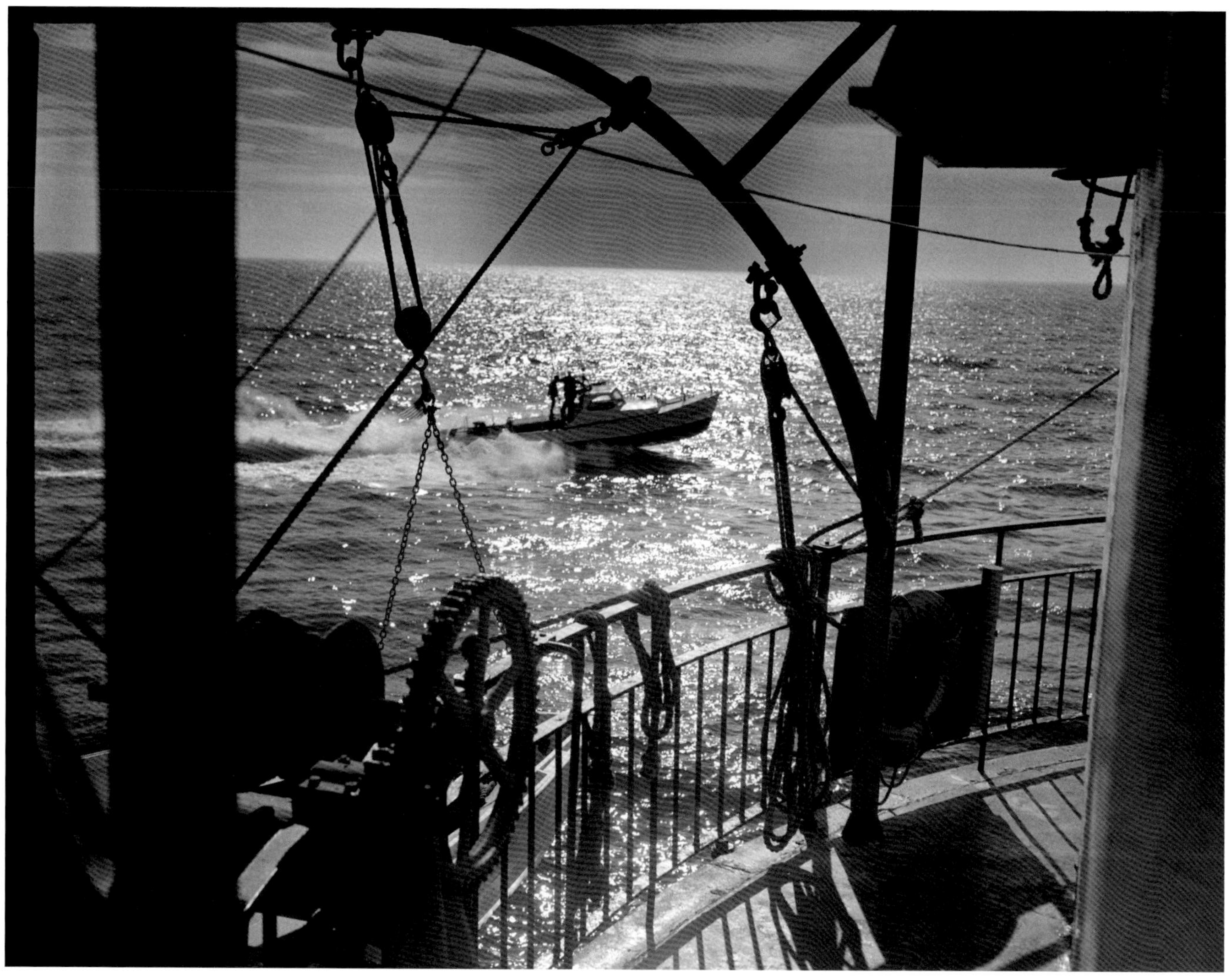

PLATE 105 *Edwin & Maud* (1953)

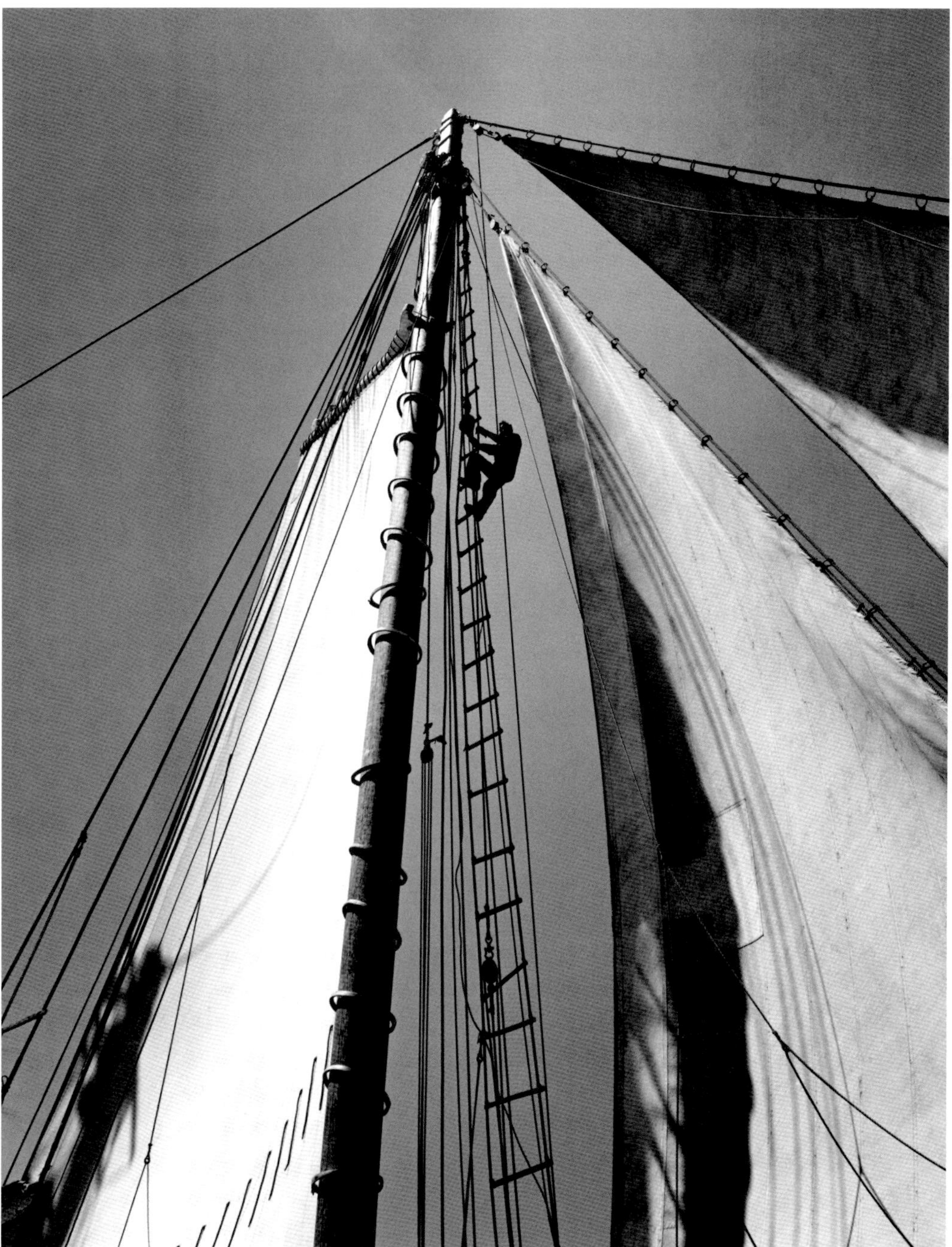

LEFT: PLATE 106 *Edwin & Maud* (1953)

RIGHT: PLATE 107 *Edwin & Maud* (1953)

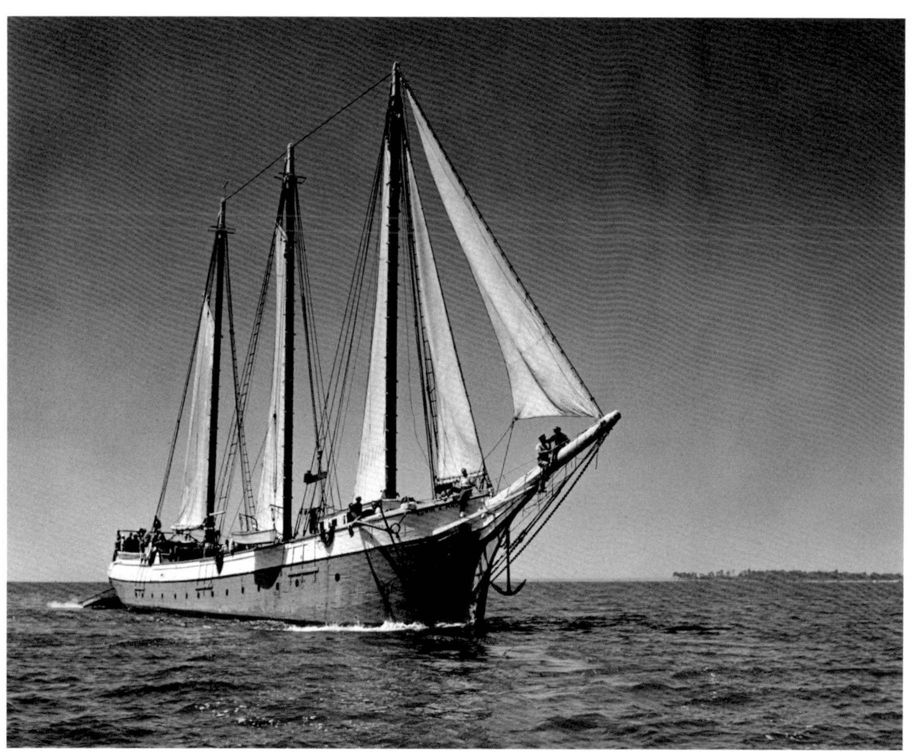

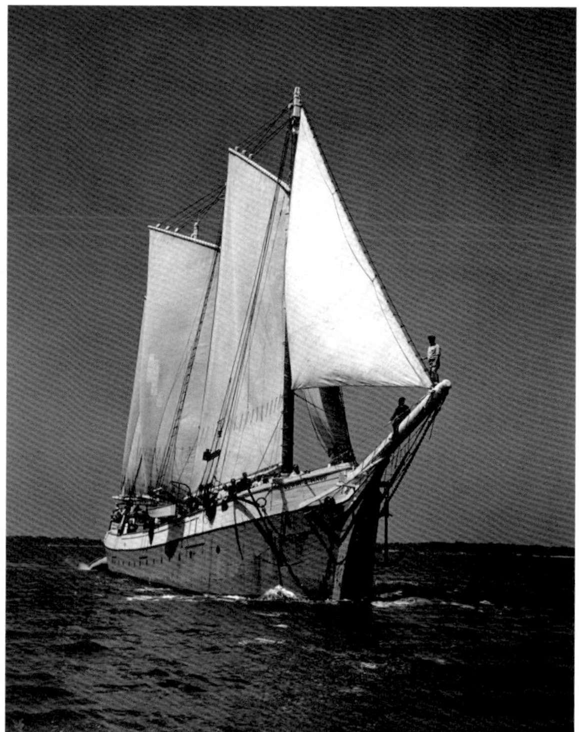

PLATE 108 *Levin J. Marvel* (1950)

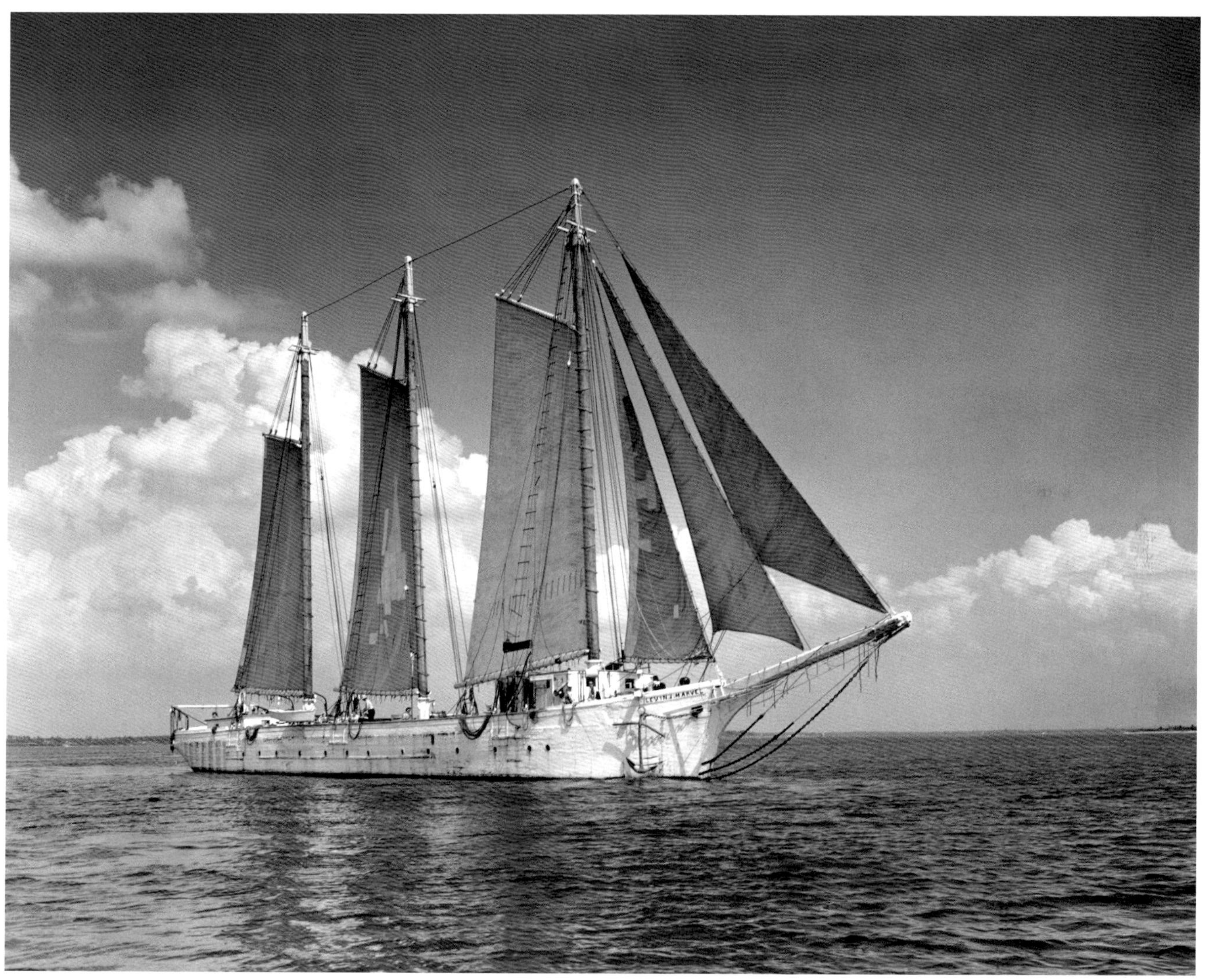

PLATE 117 Annapolis Yacht Club, Largest in America (ca. 1950)

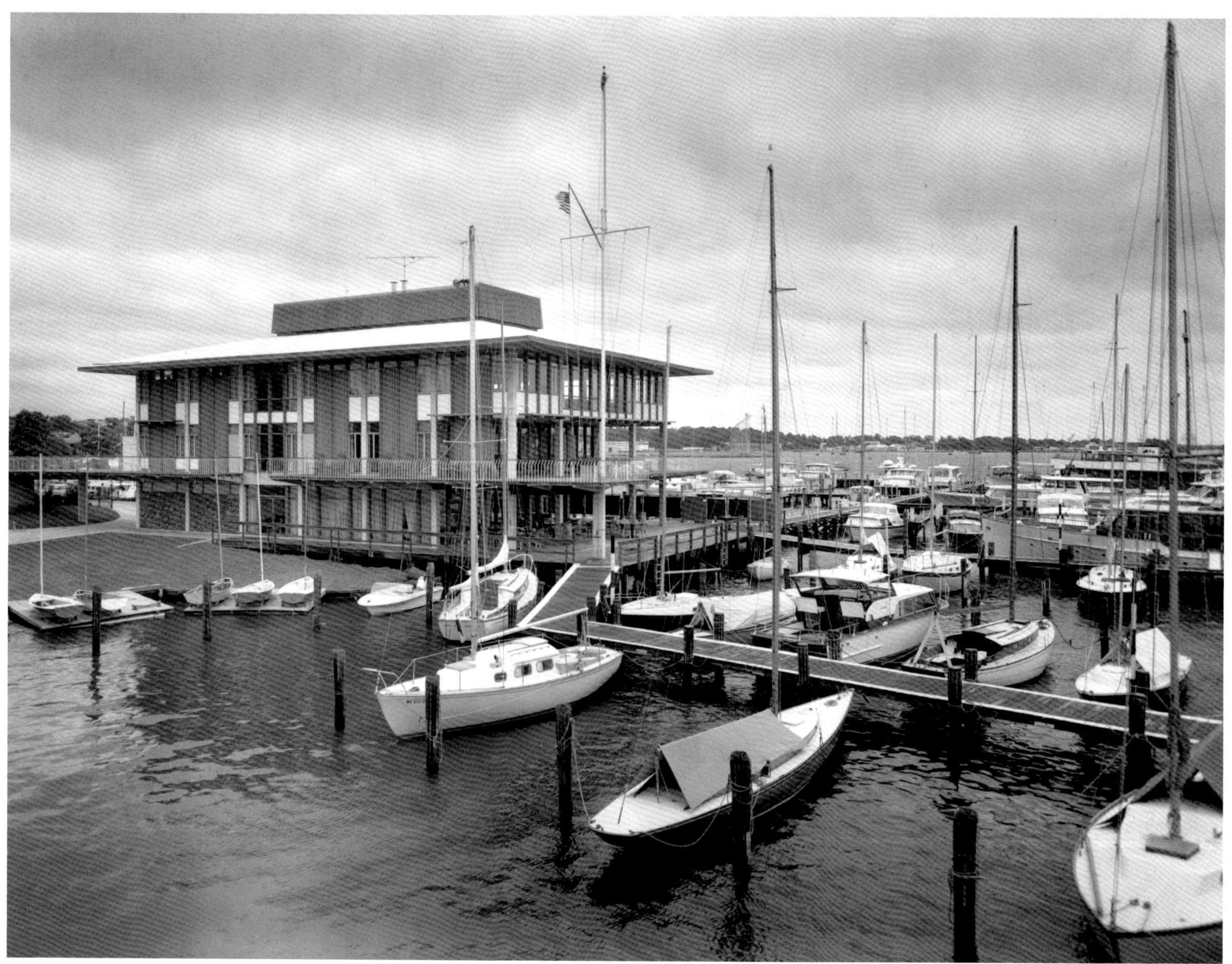

PLATE 118 Chesapeake Bay Racing (ca. 1950)

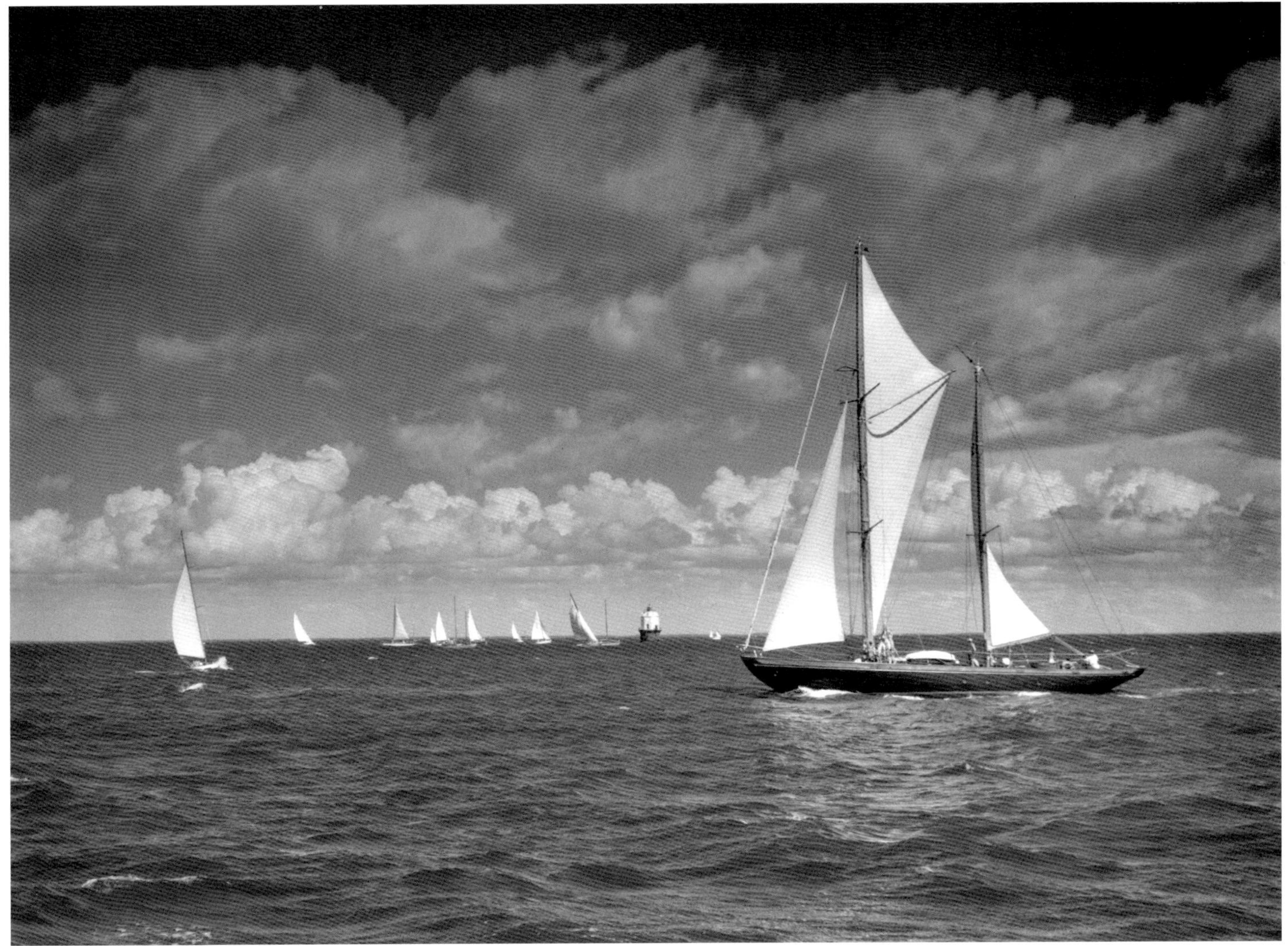

PLATE 119 Sailboats, Chesapeake Bay (1947)

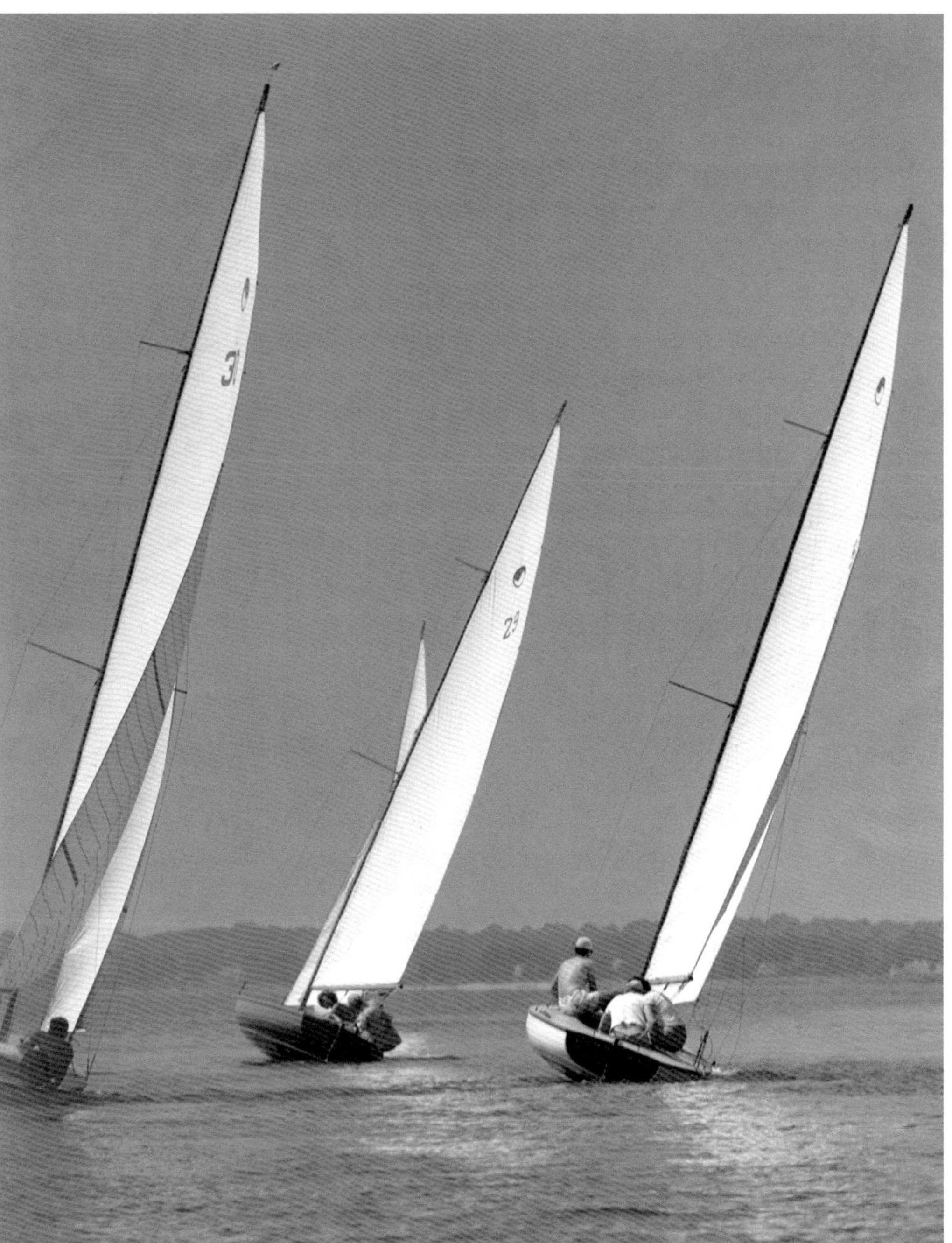

PLATE 120 Sailing off Naval Academy, Severn River (ca. 1950)

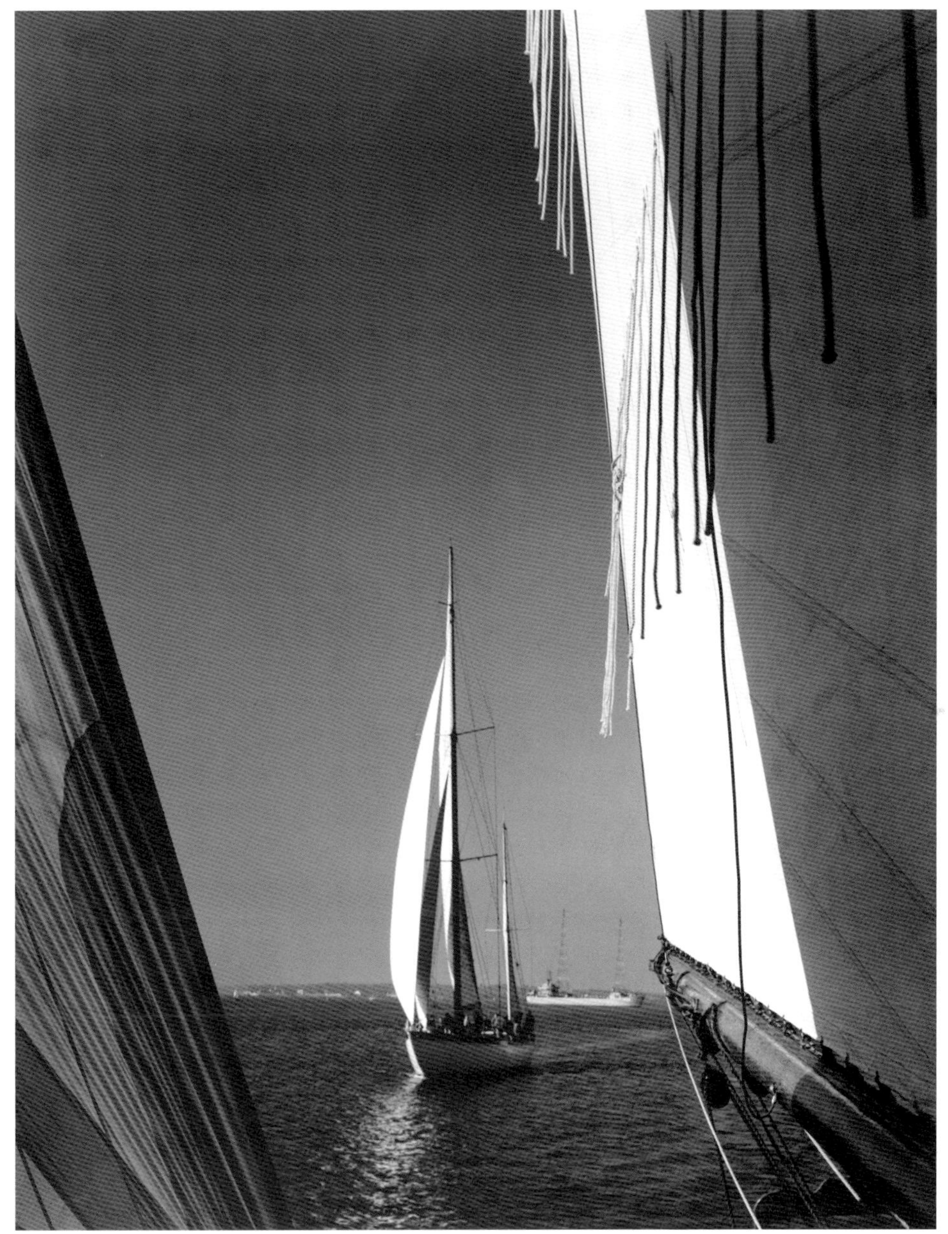

PLATE 121 Chesapeake Bay Championship Races (1932)

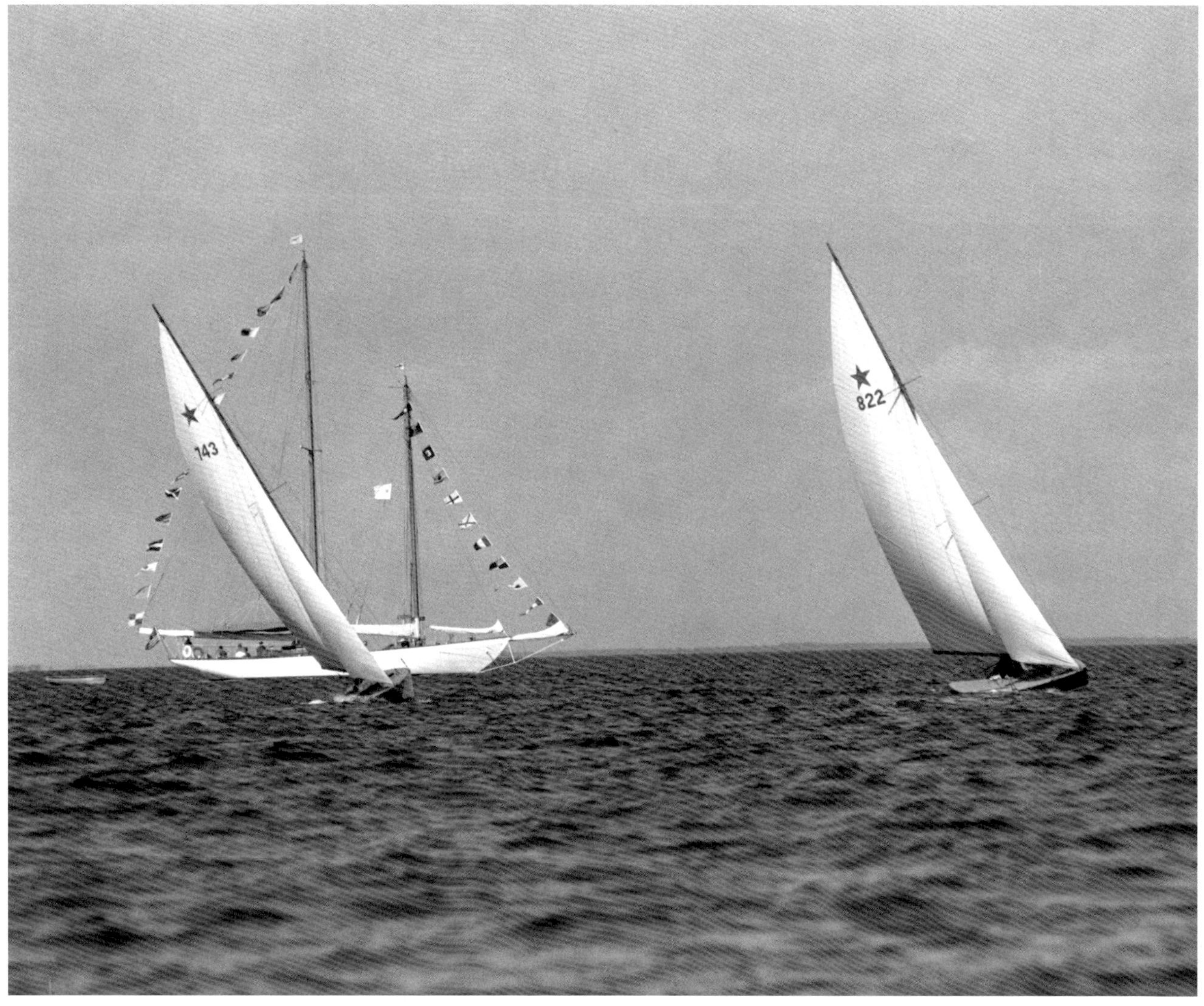

PLATE 122 Rounding the Mark (1947)

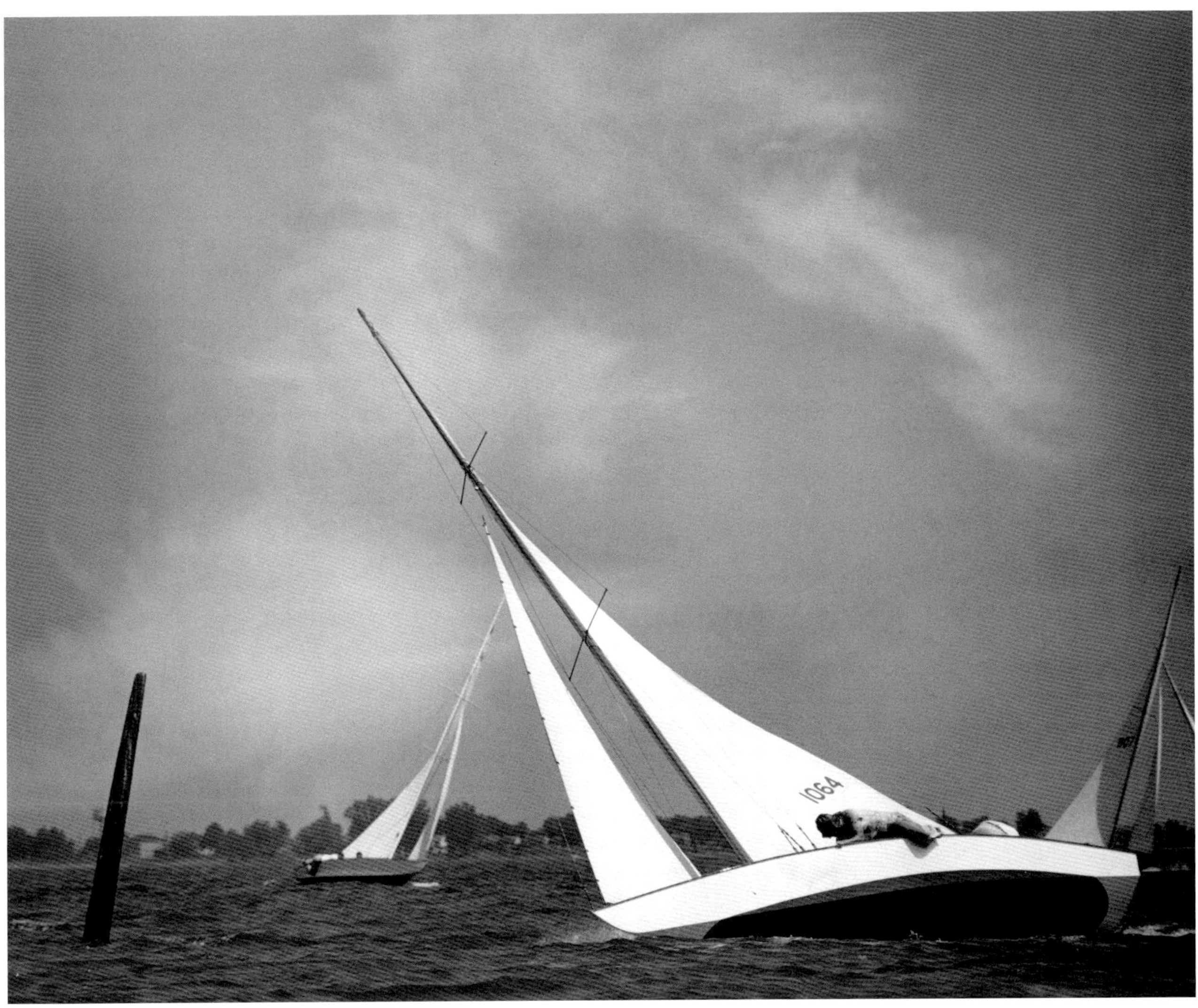

LEFT: PLATE 123 Sailing on the Severn (ca. 1950)
RIGHT: PLATE 124 Rounding the Mark (ca. 1950)

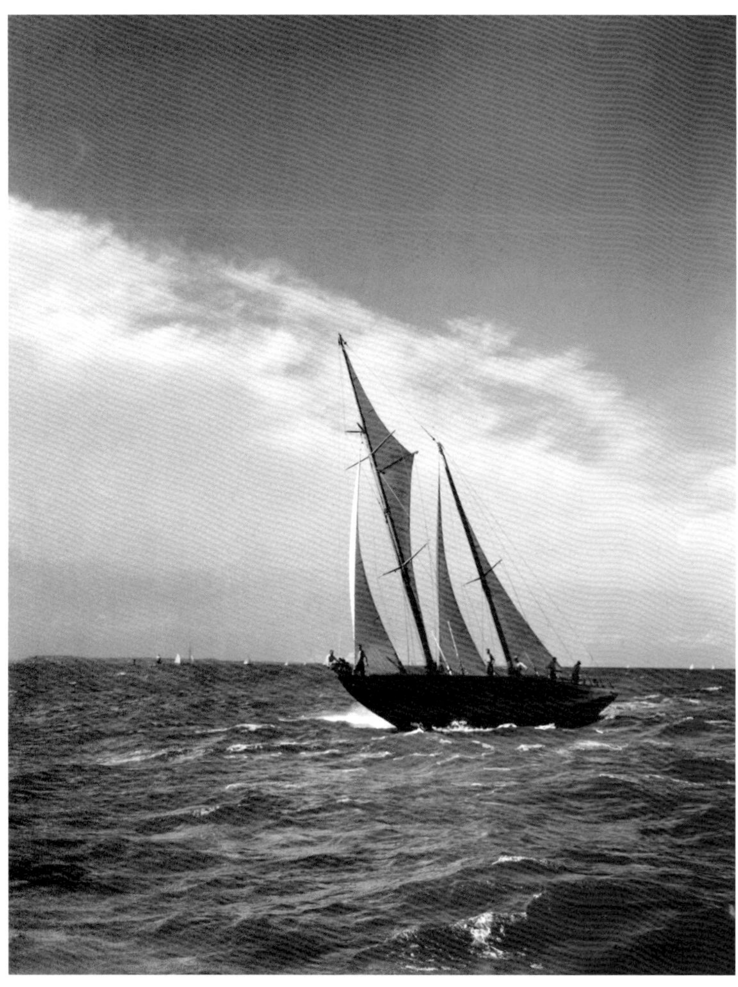

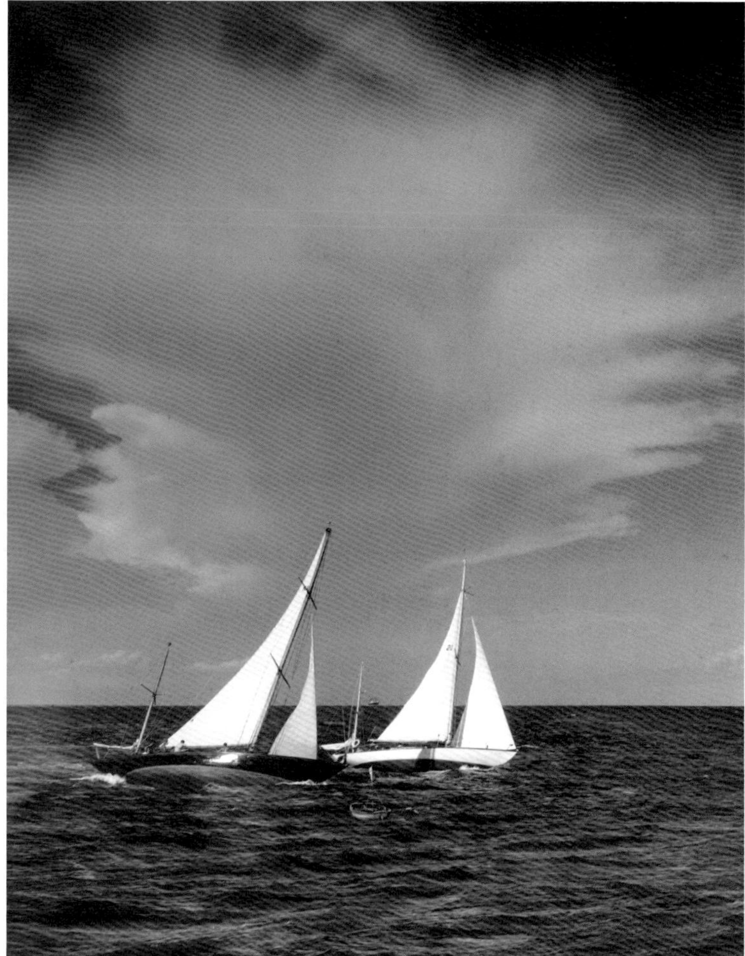

PLATE 125 *Royona*, Naval Academy (1952)

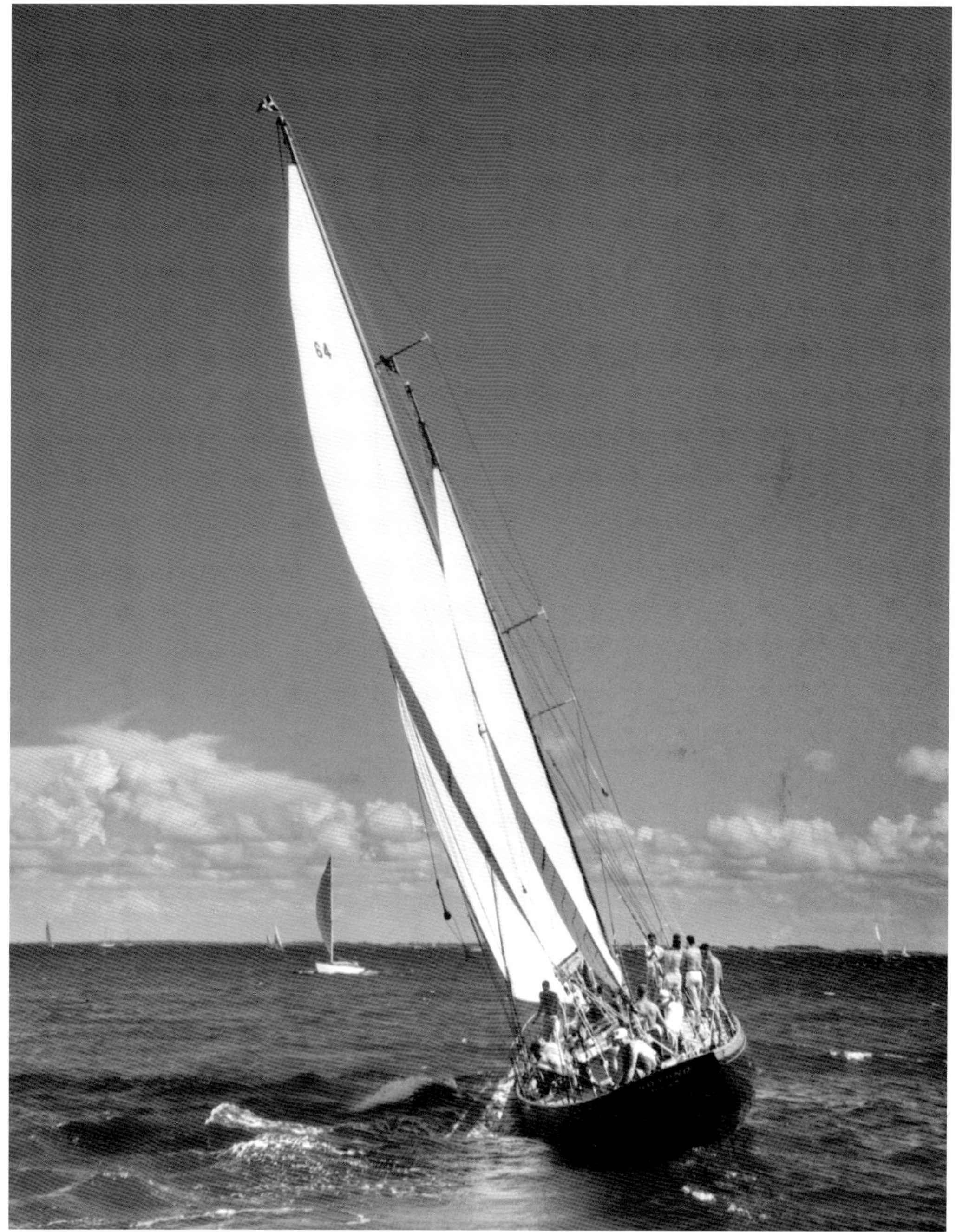

PLATE 126 Chesapeake Bay Championship Races (1932)

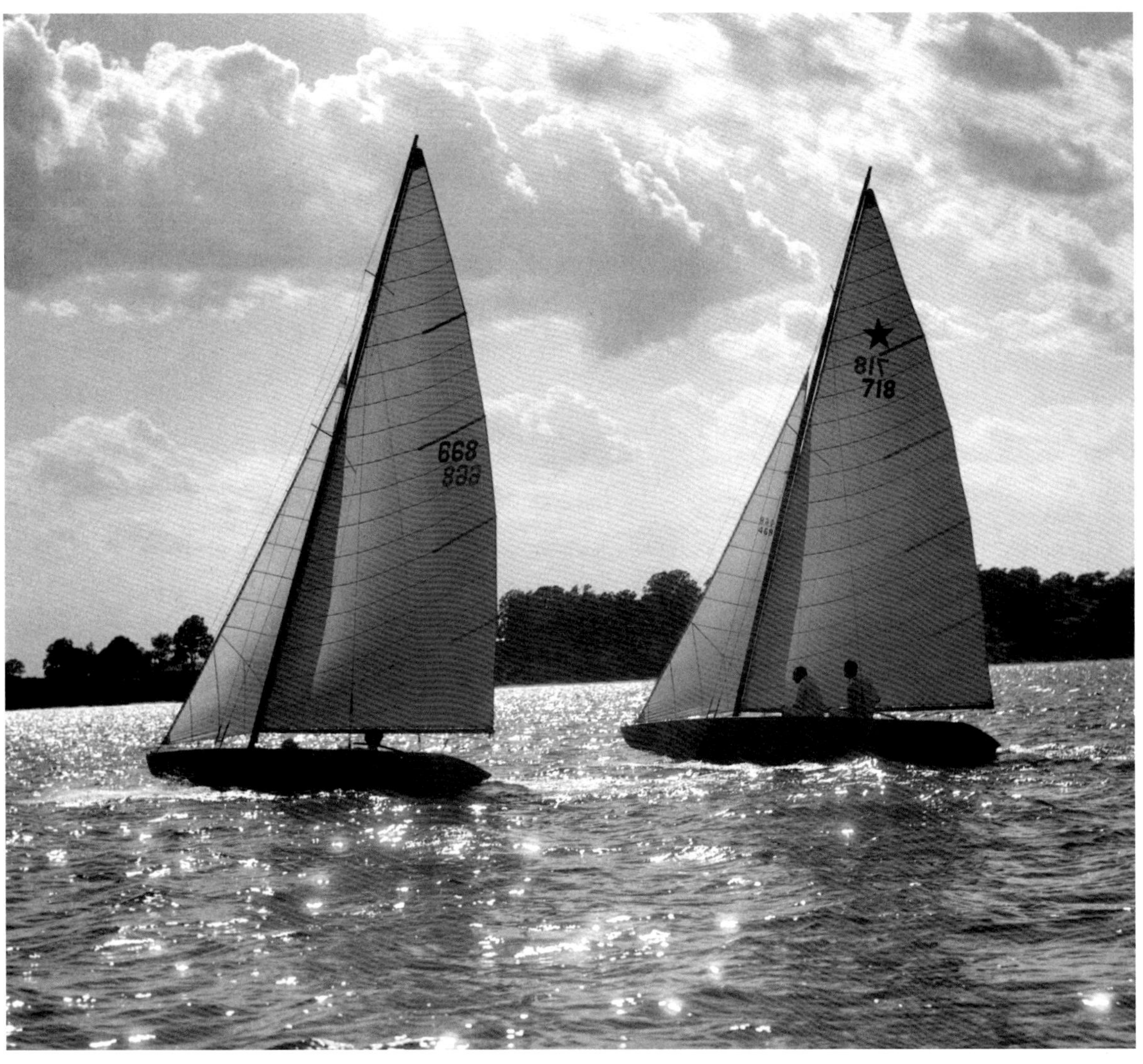

PLATE 127 Chesapeake Bay Sailboat Race (1955)

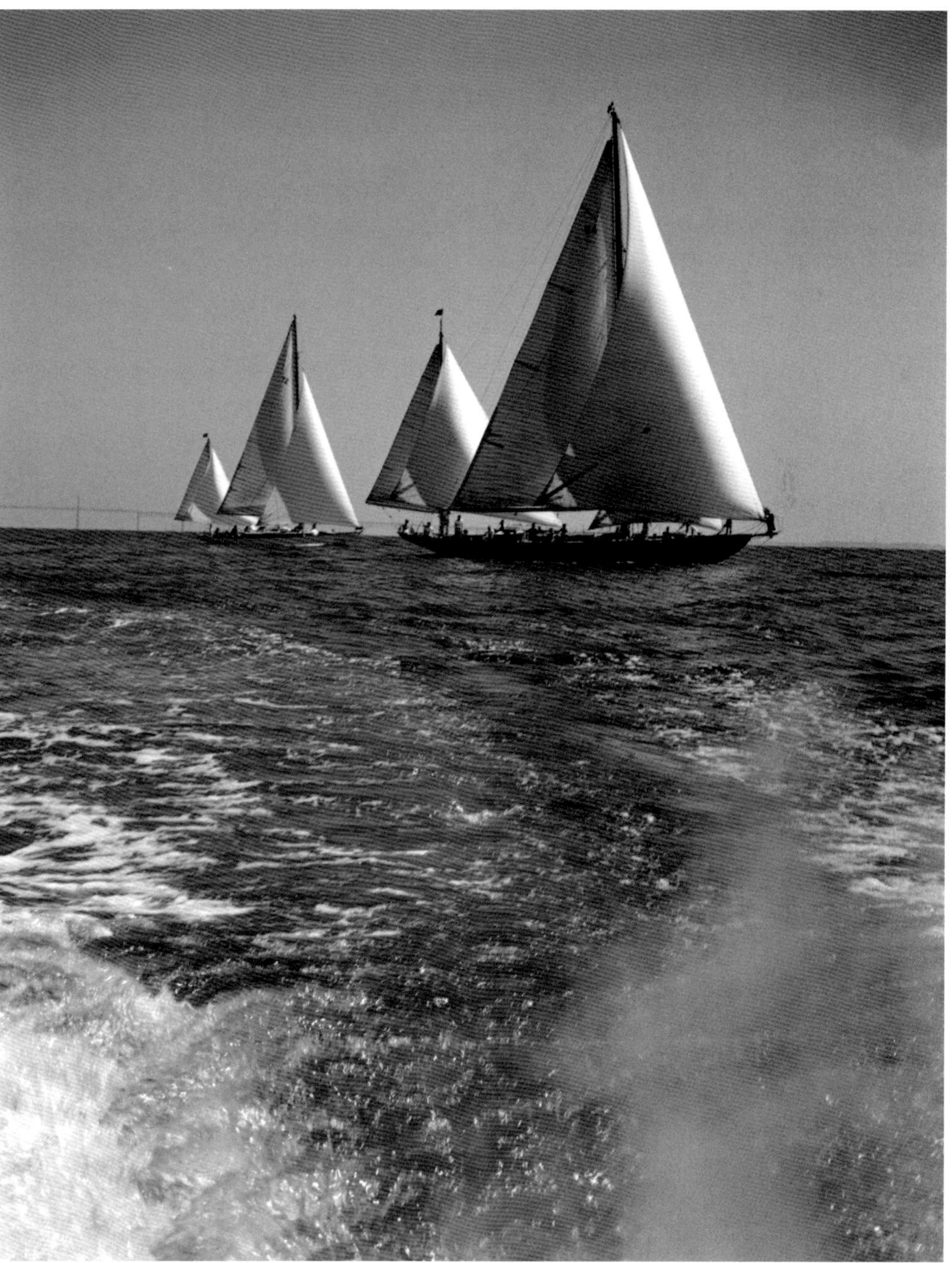

PLATE 130 Bancroft Hall, Naval Academy (1957)

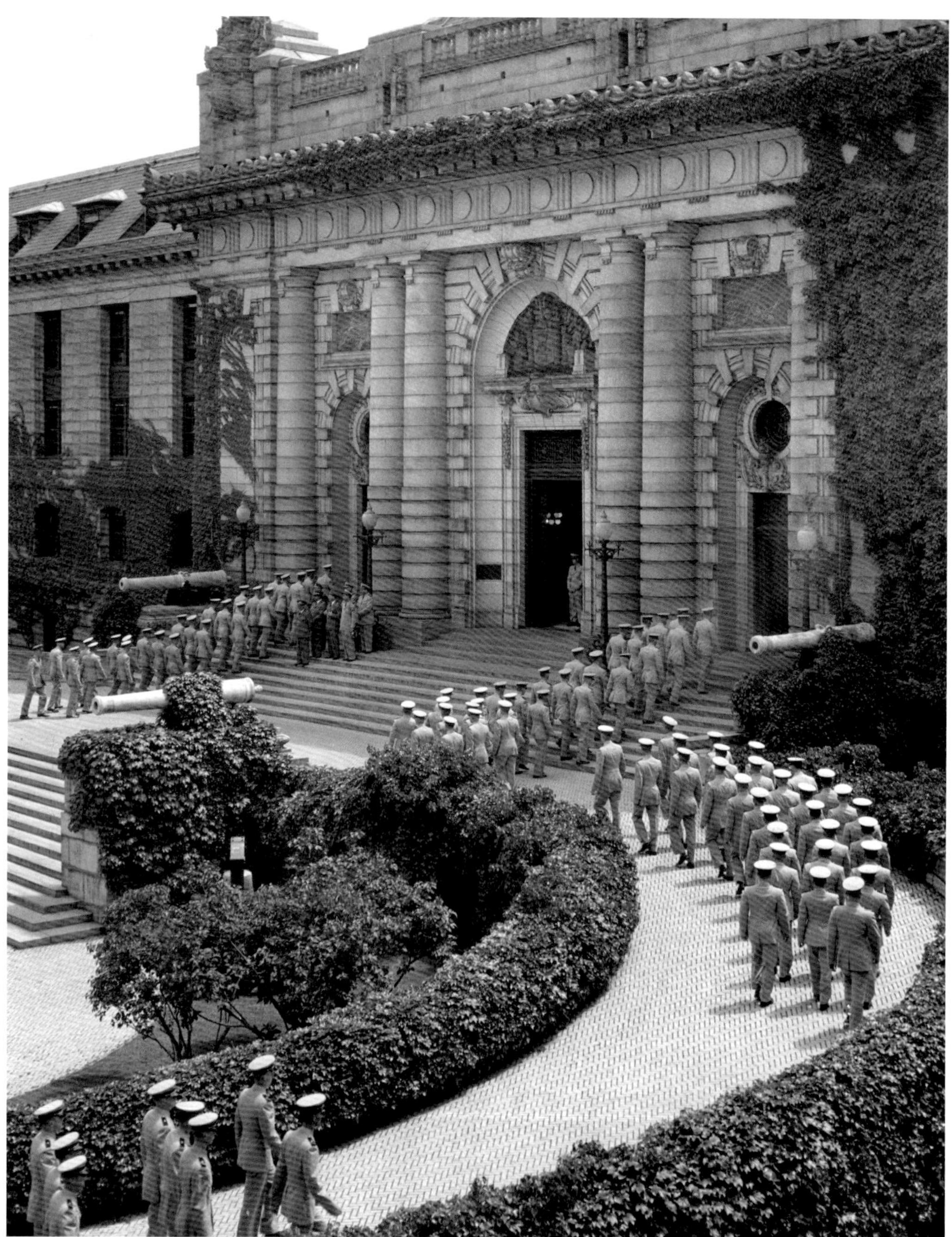

PLATE 131 Bancroft Hall, Naval Academy, Annapolis (1952)

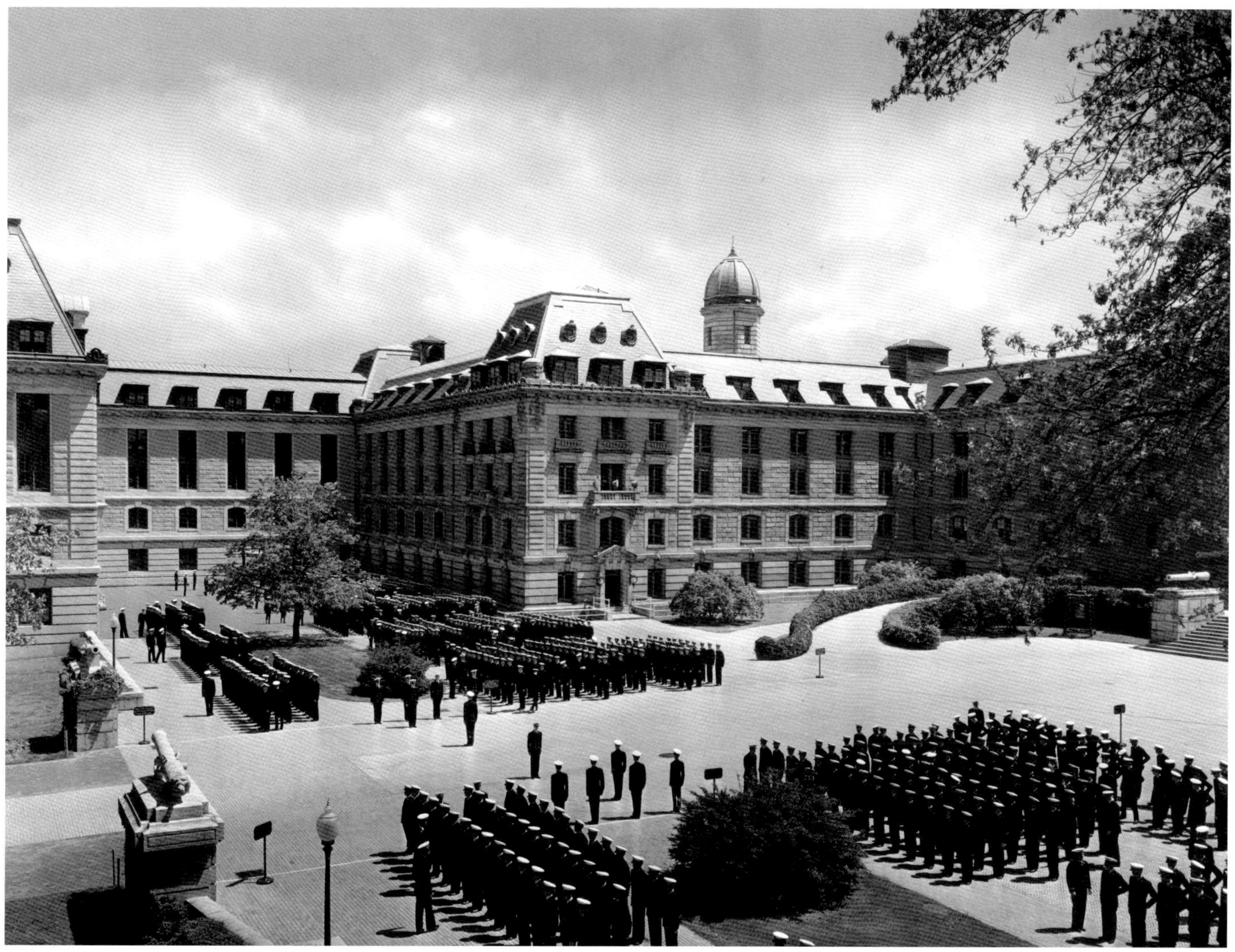

PLATE 132 Marching Stribling Walk (1929)

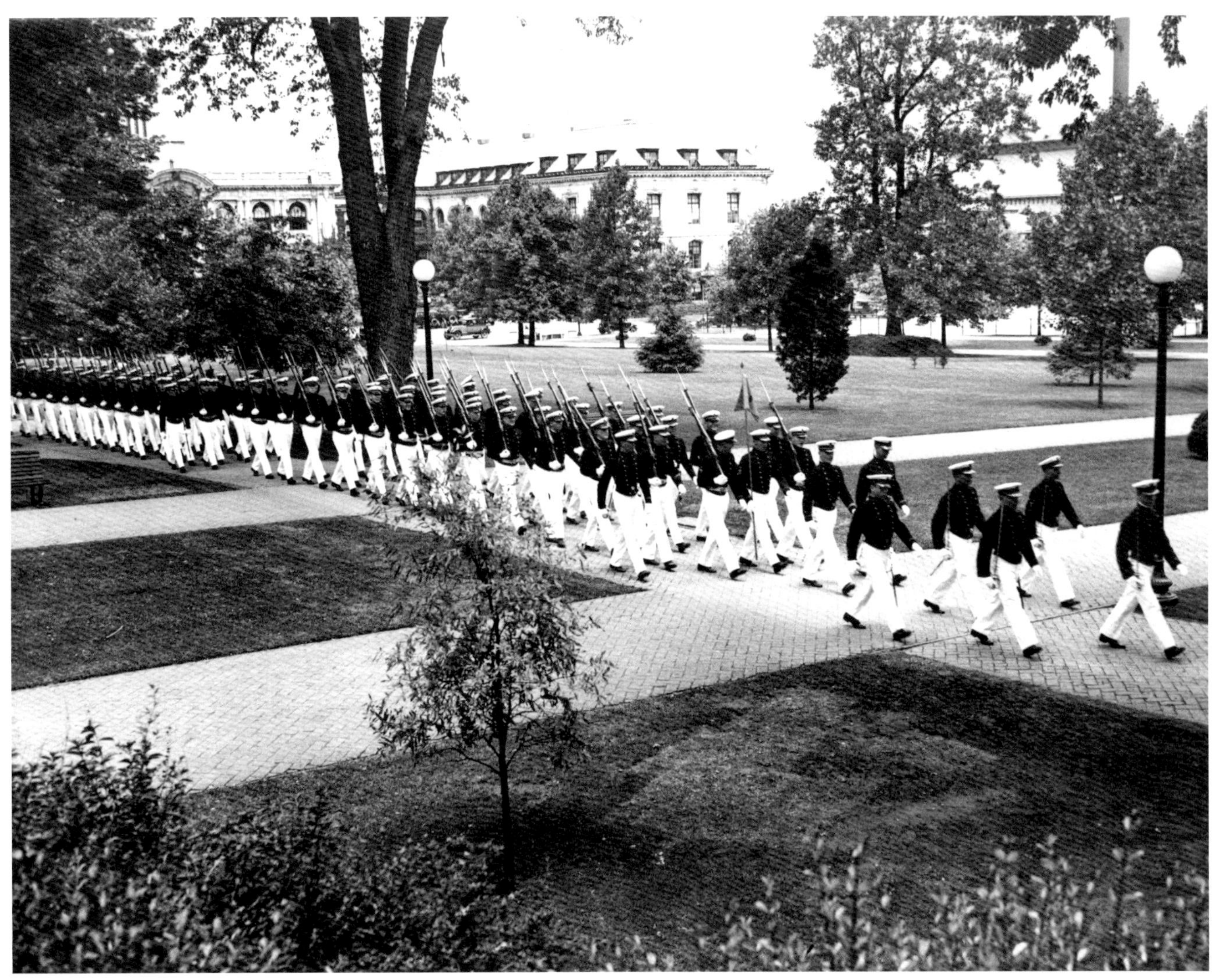

PLATE 133 Naval Academy, June Week (1956)

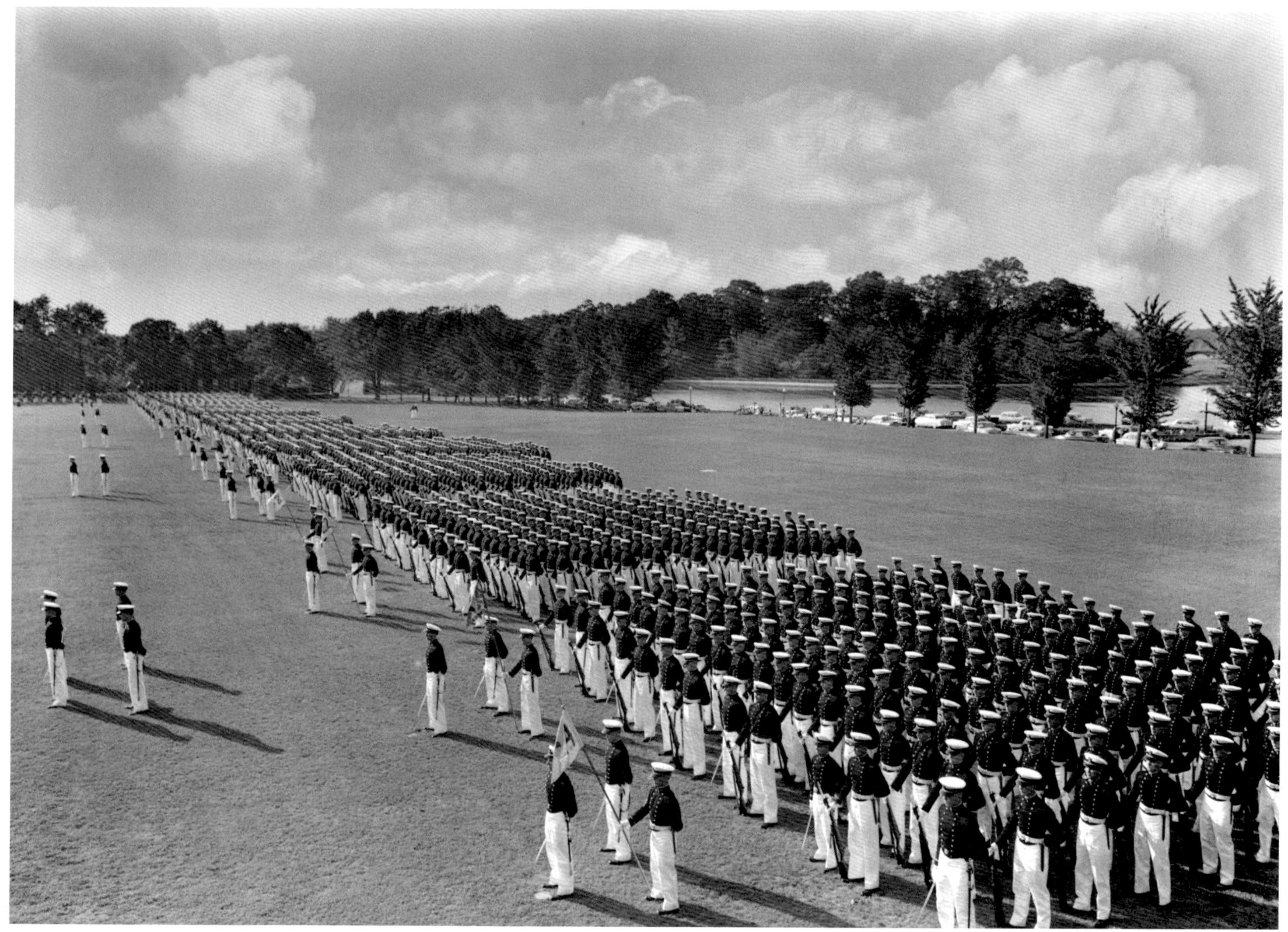

LEFT: PLATE 141 Naval Academy Midshipman (1947)
RIGHT: PLATE 142 Naval Academy Midshipman (1947)

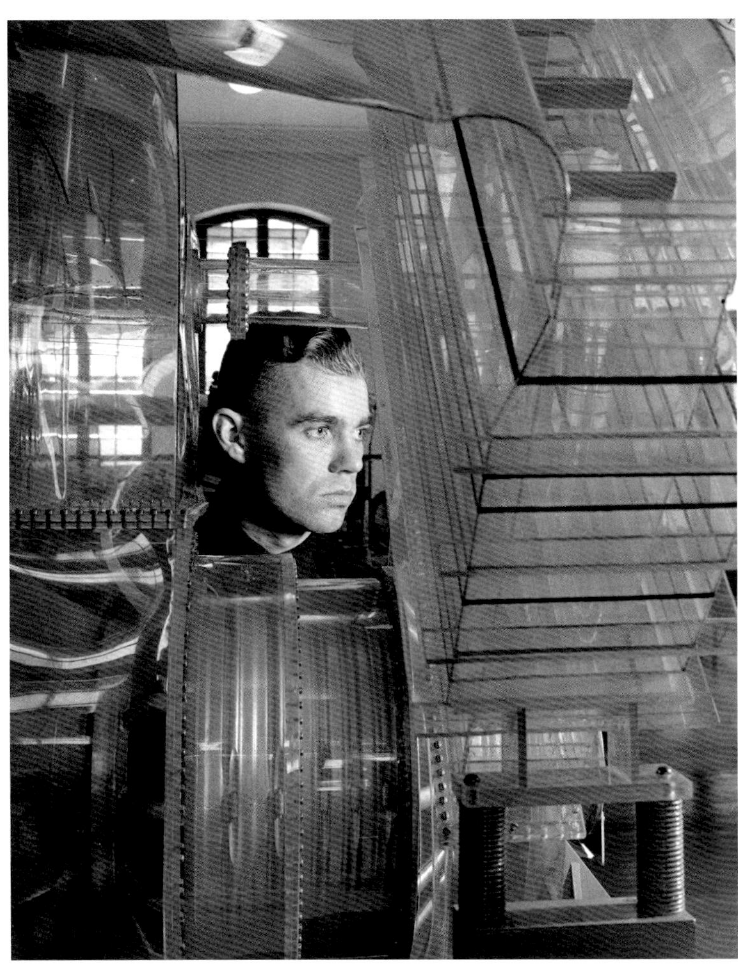

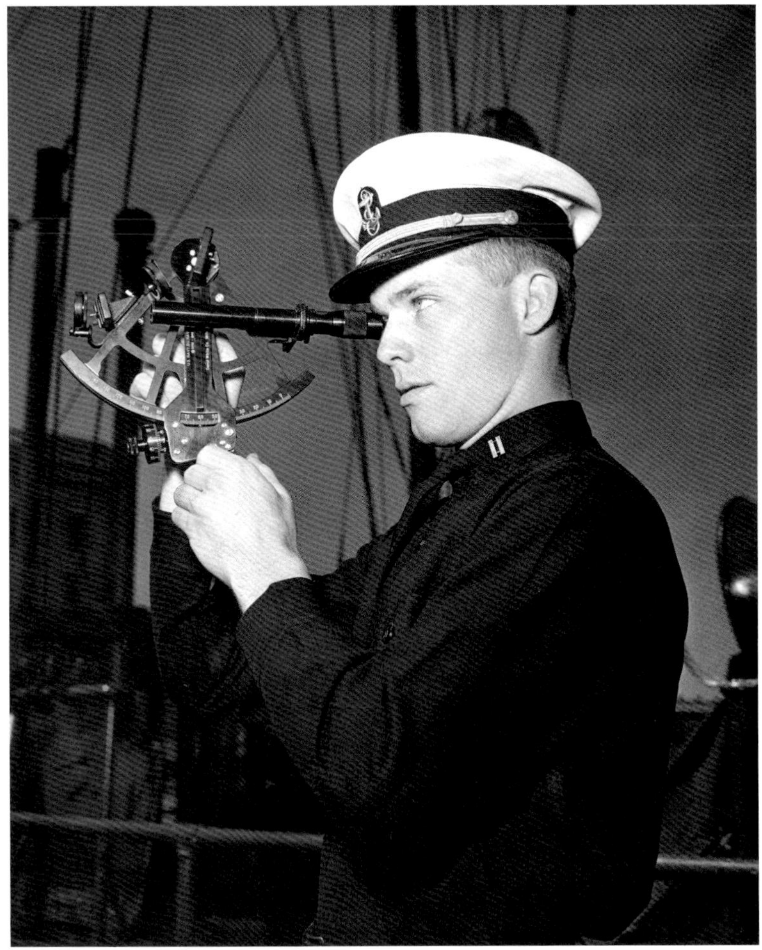

PLATE 143 Naval Academy Midshipman (1947)

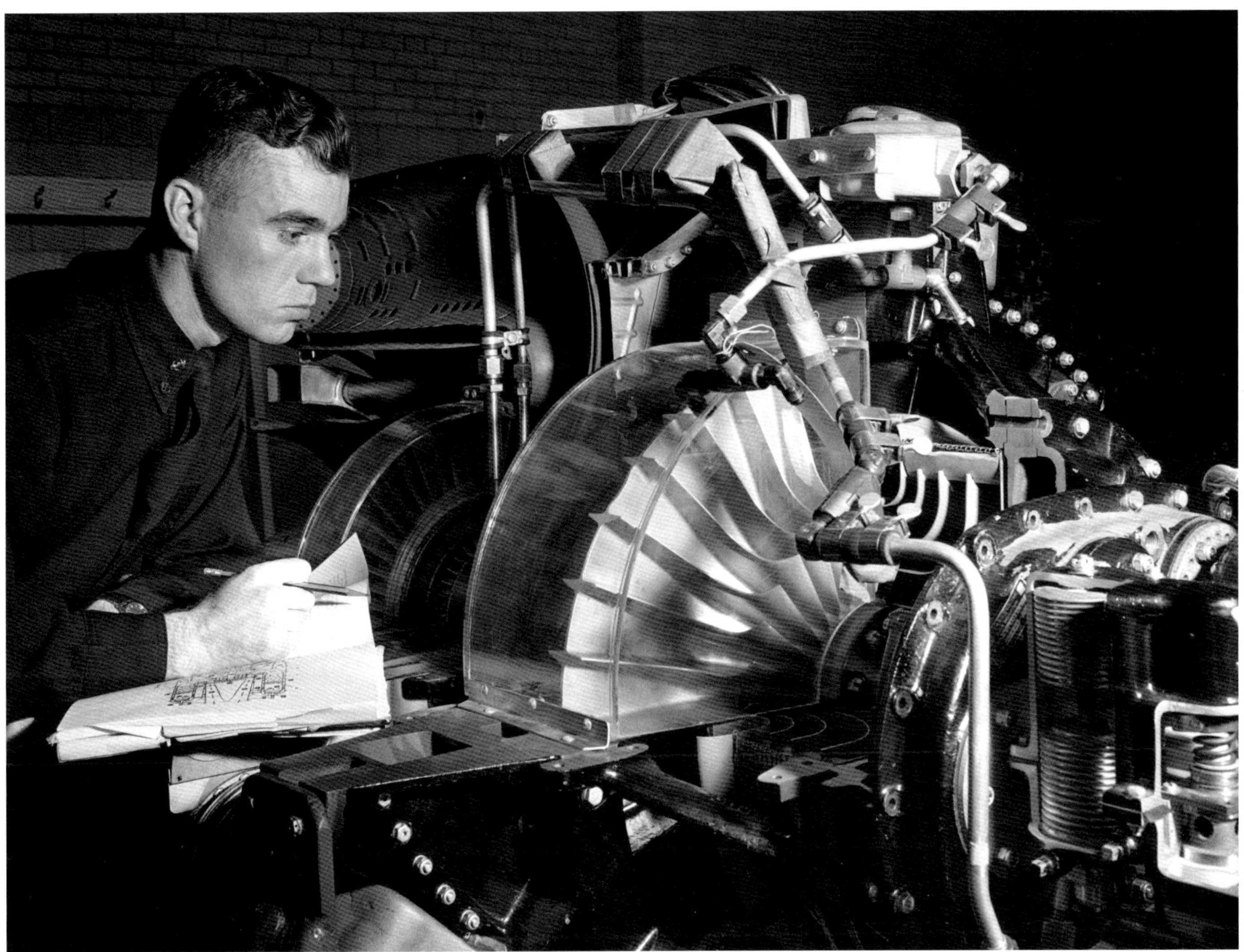

PLATE 144 Naval Academy Library (1957)

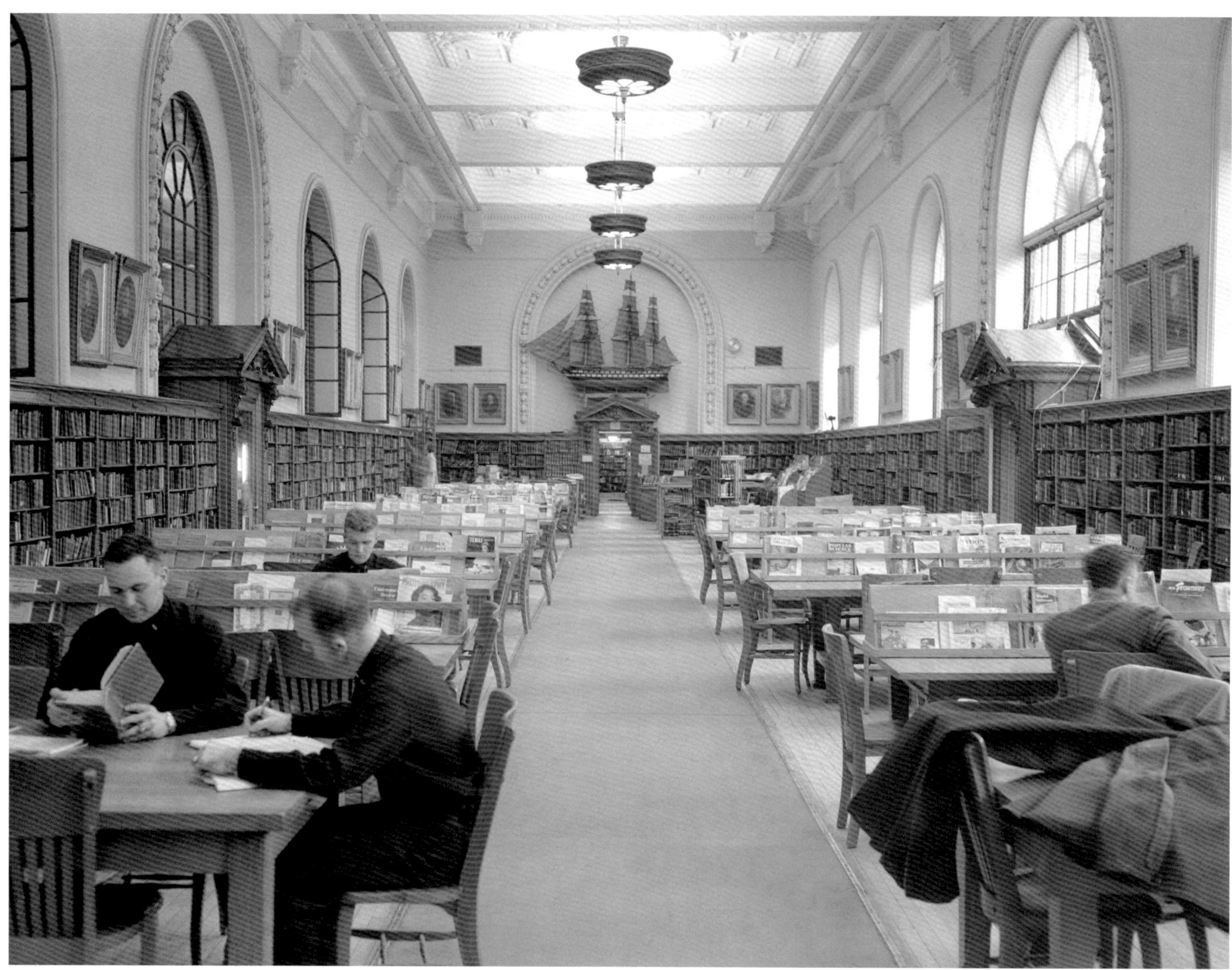

PLATE 145 Navy and Ohio State Football Game (1930)

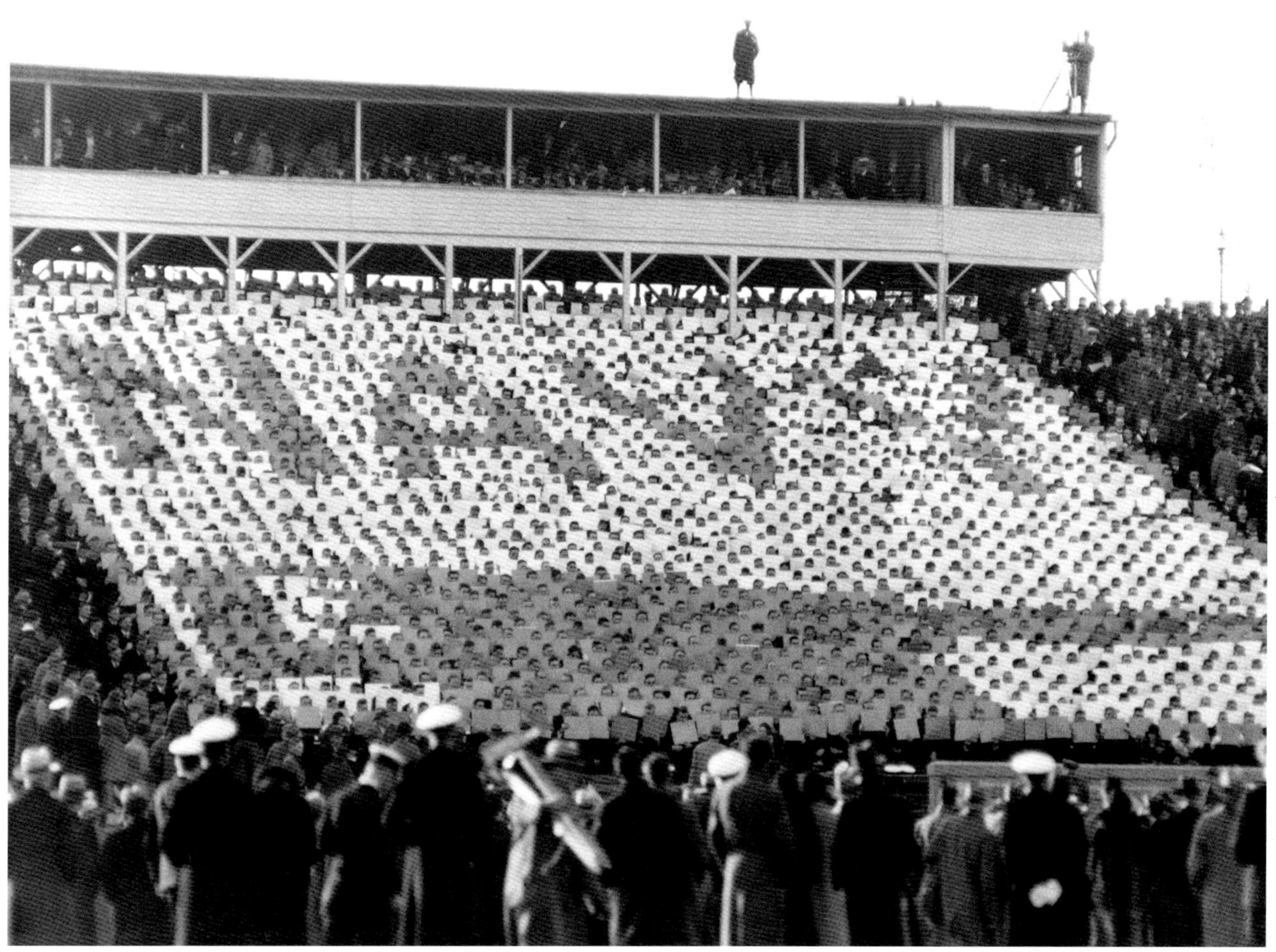

PLATE 146 Navya and Ohio State Football Game (1930)

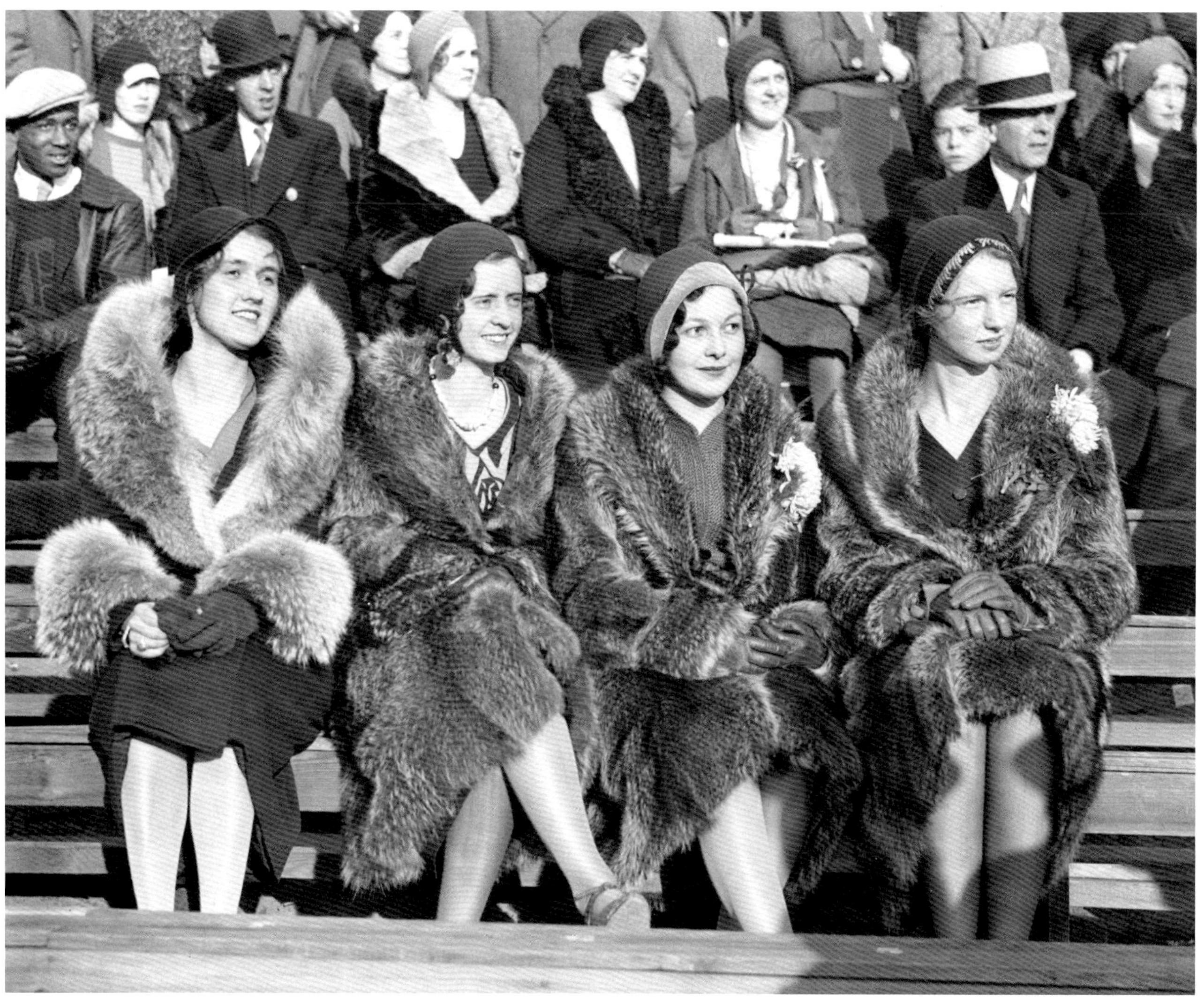

LEFT: PLATE 147 Worden Field: Presentation of Colors (1932)

RIGHT: PLATE 148 Bill the Goat (1928)

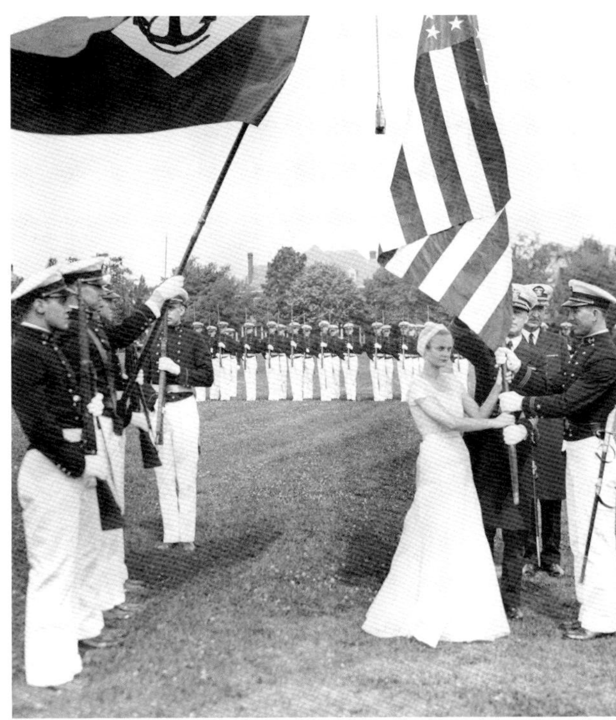

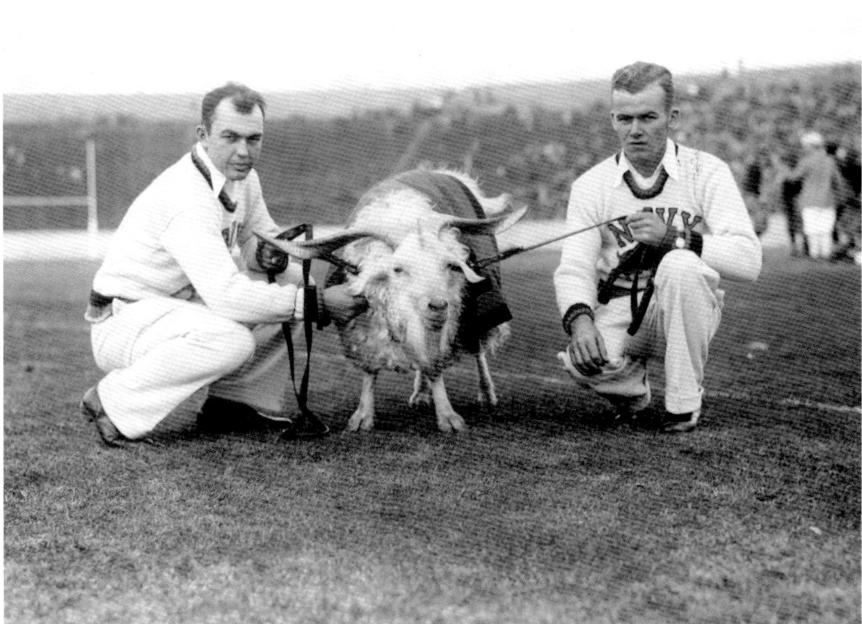

PLATE 149 *Highland Light* (1942)

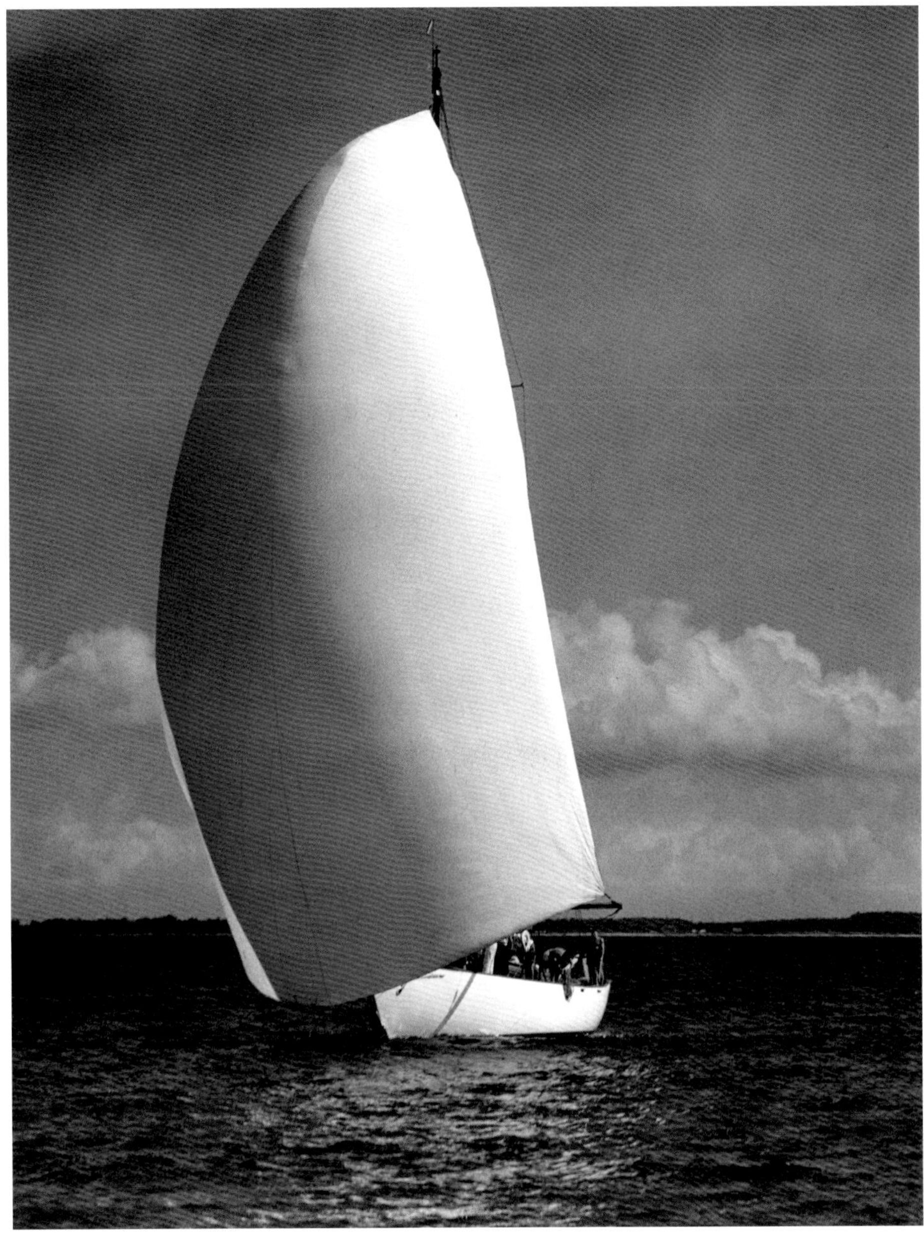

PLATE 150 Day at the Races (1927)

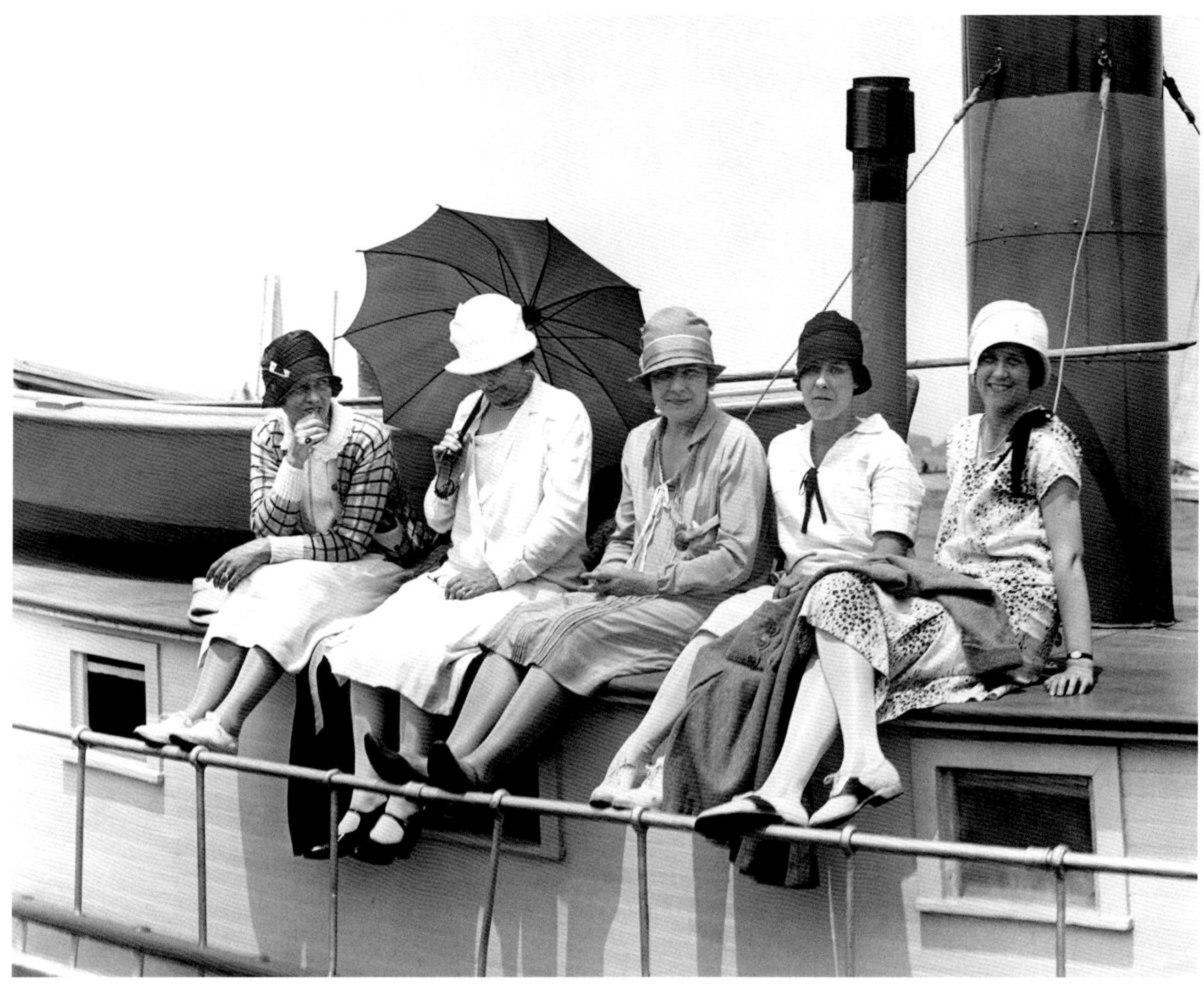

PLATE 153 USNA *Royona* (1952)

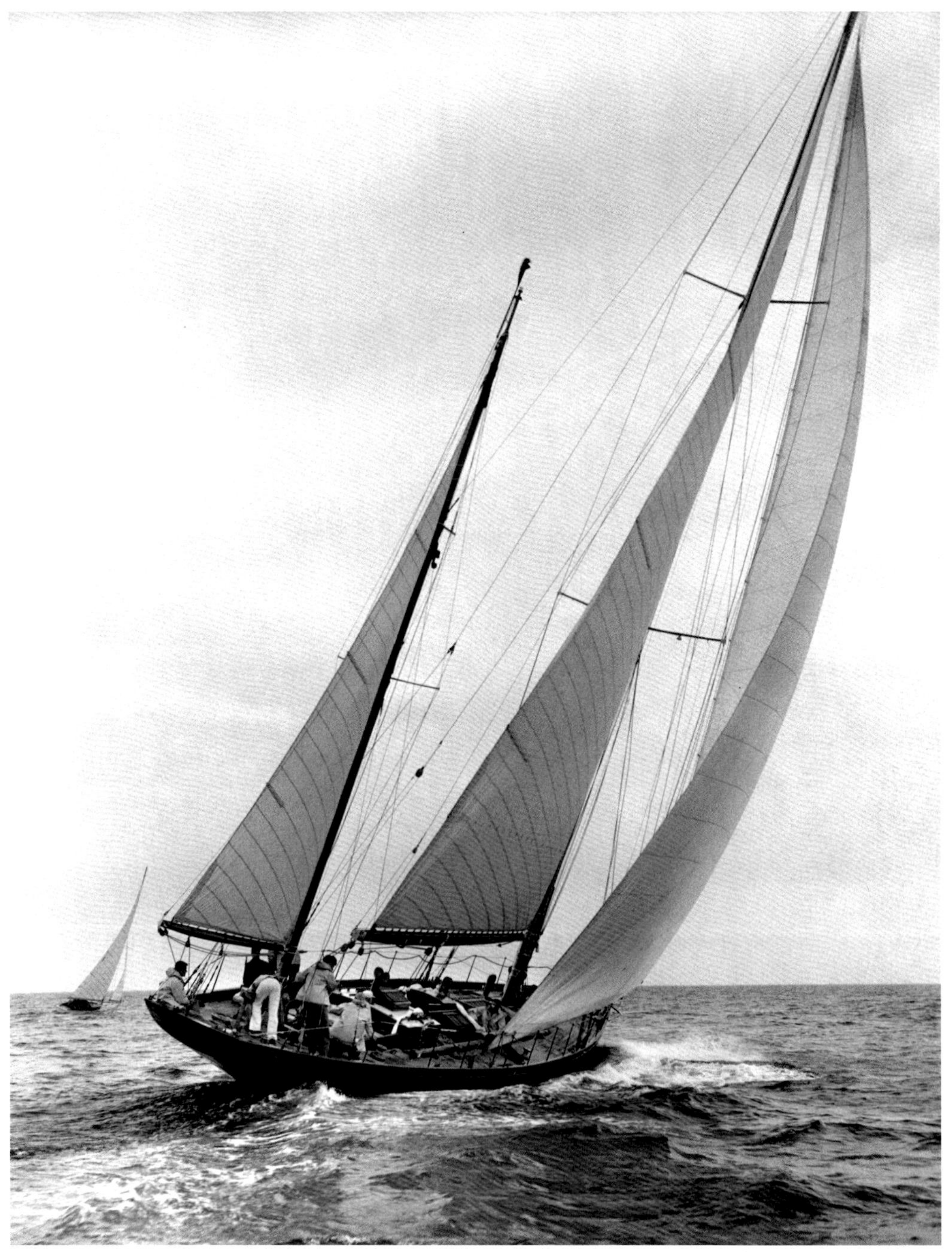

PLATE 154 Naval Academy from Eastport (1953)

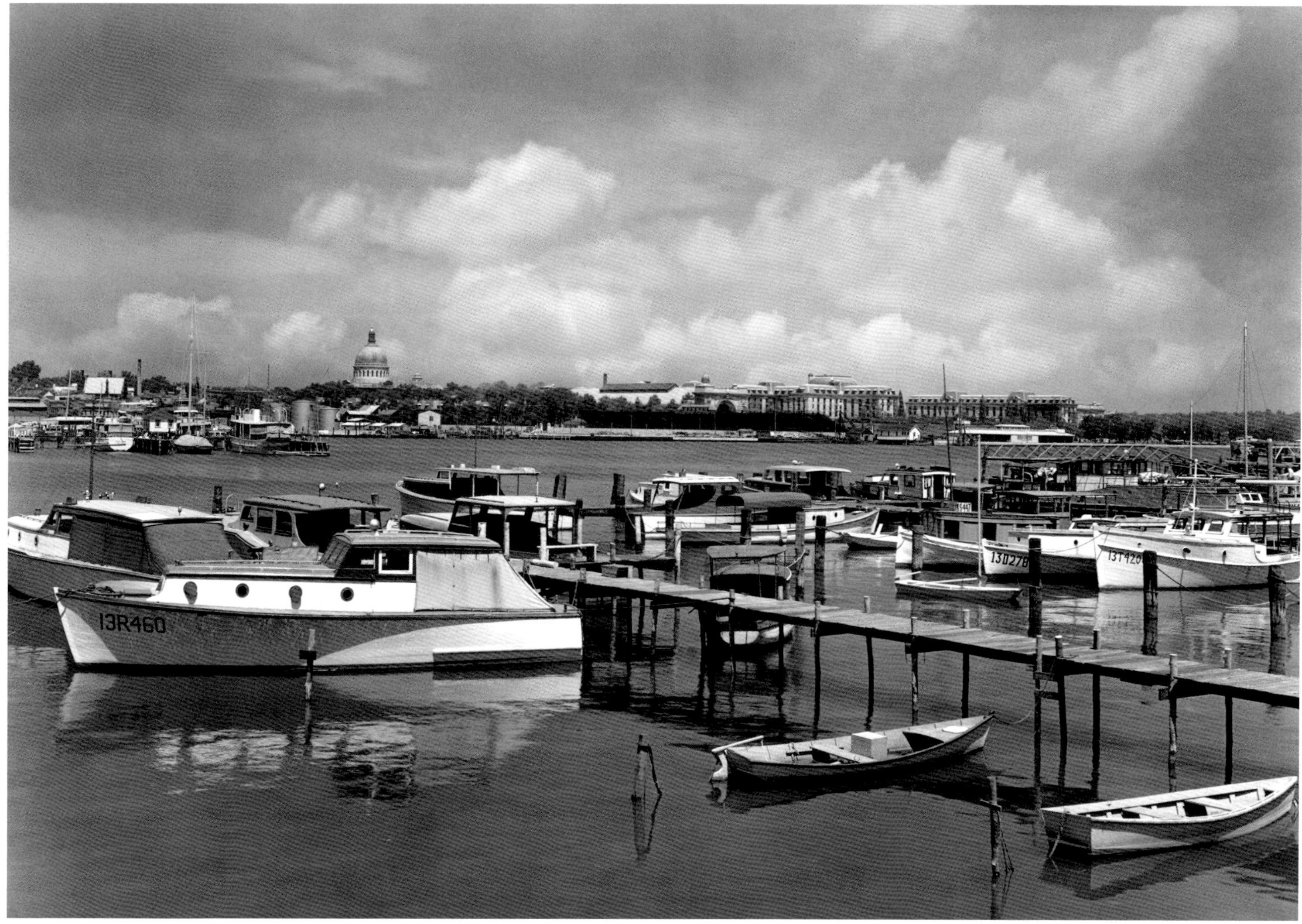

PLATE 155 Naval Academy from Eastport (1949)

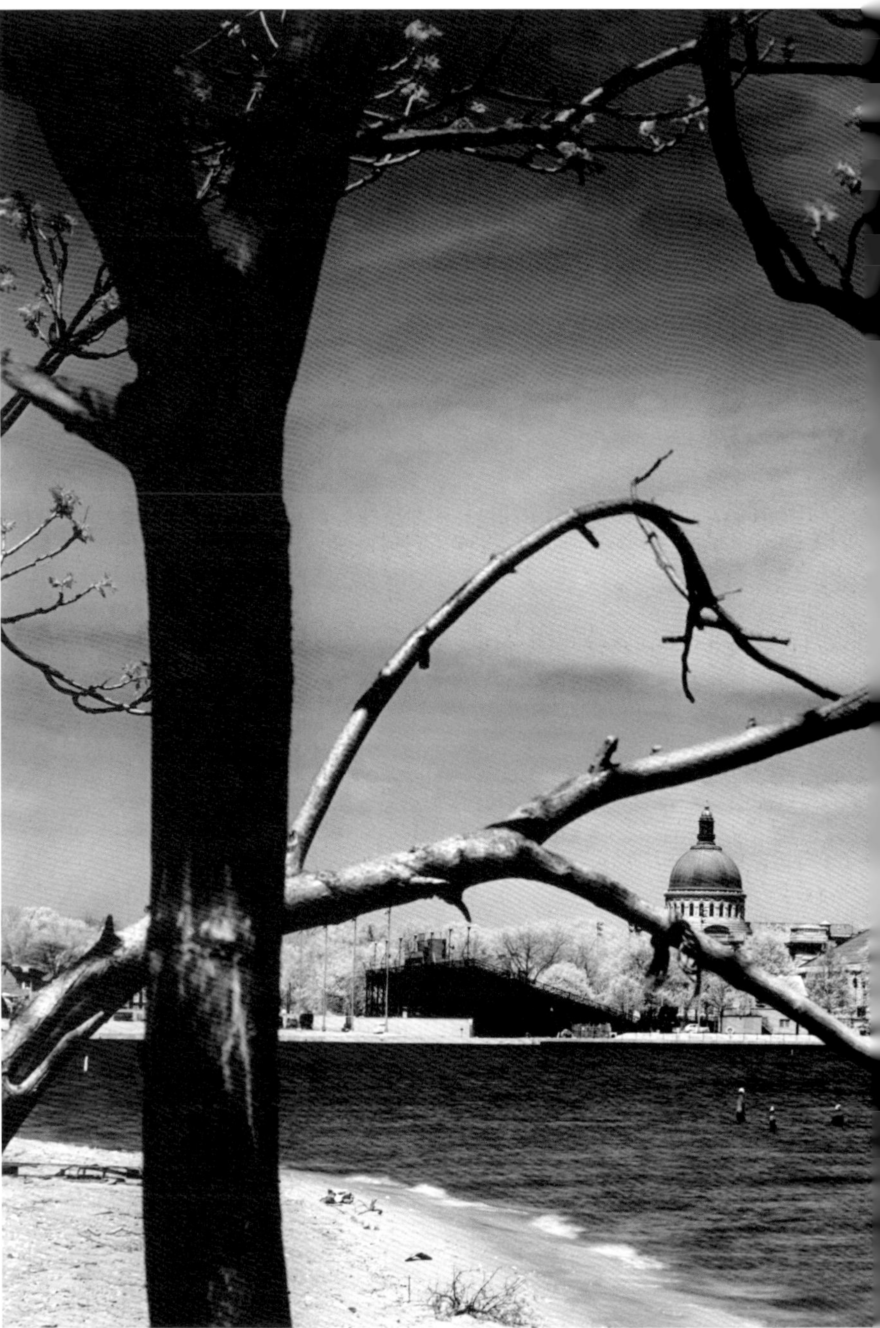

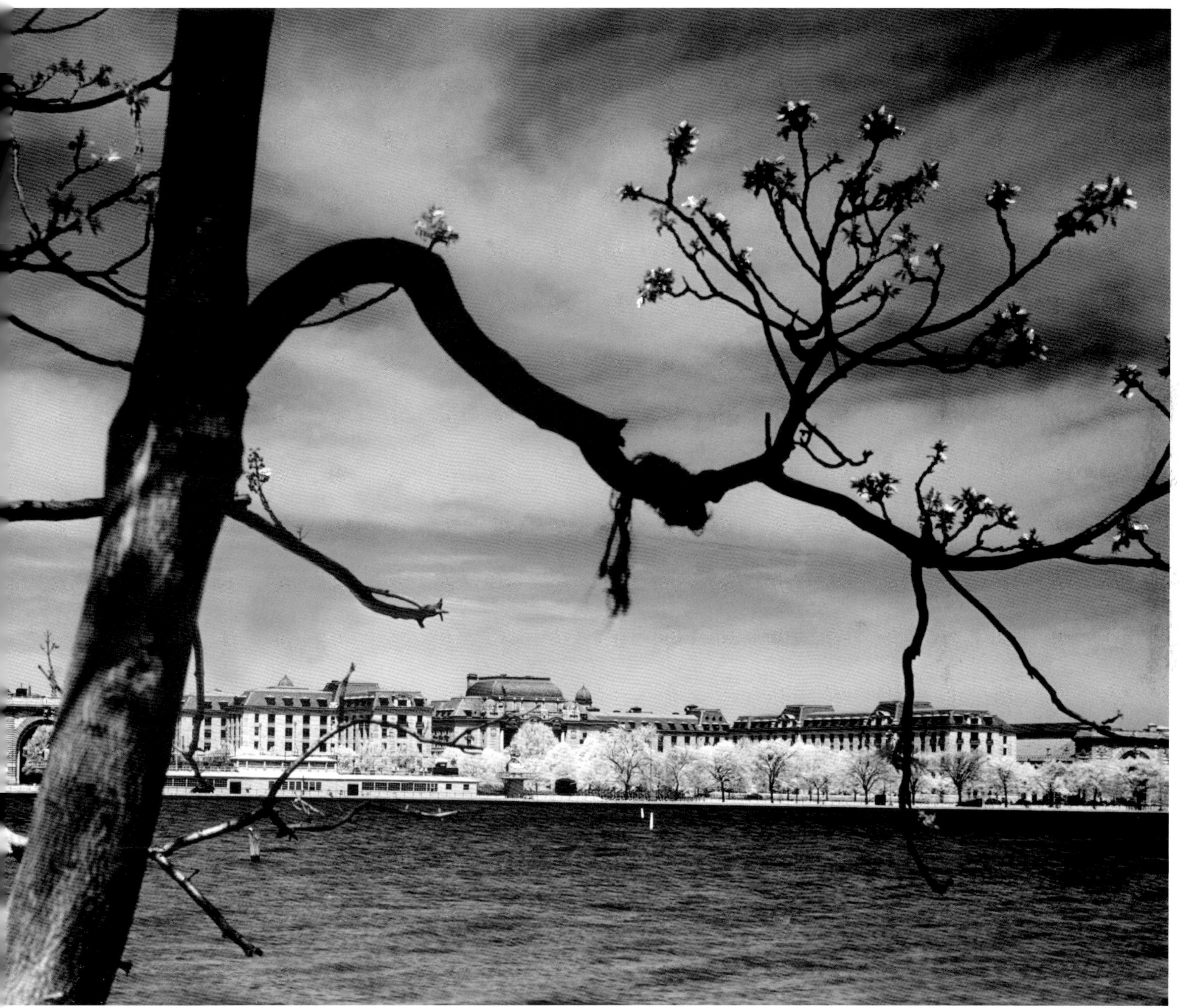

PLATE 156 Naval Academy (1951)

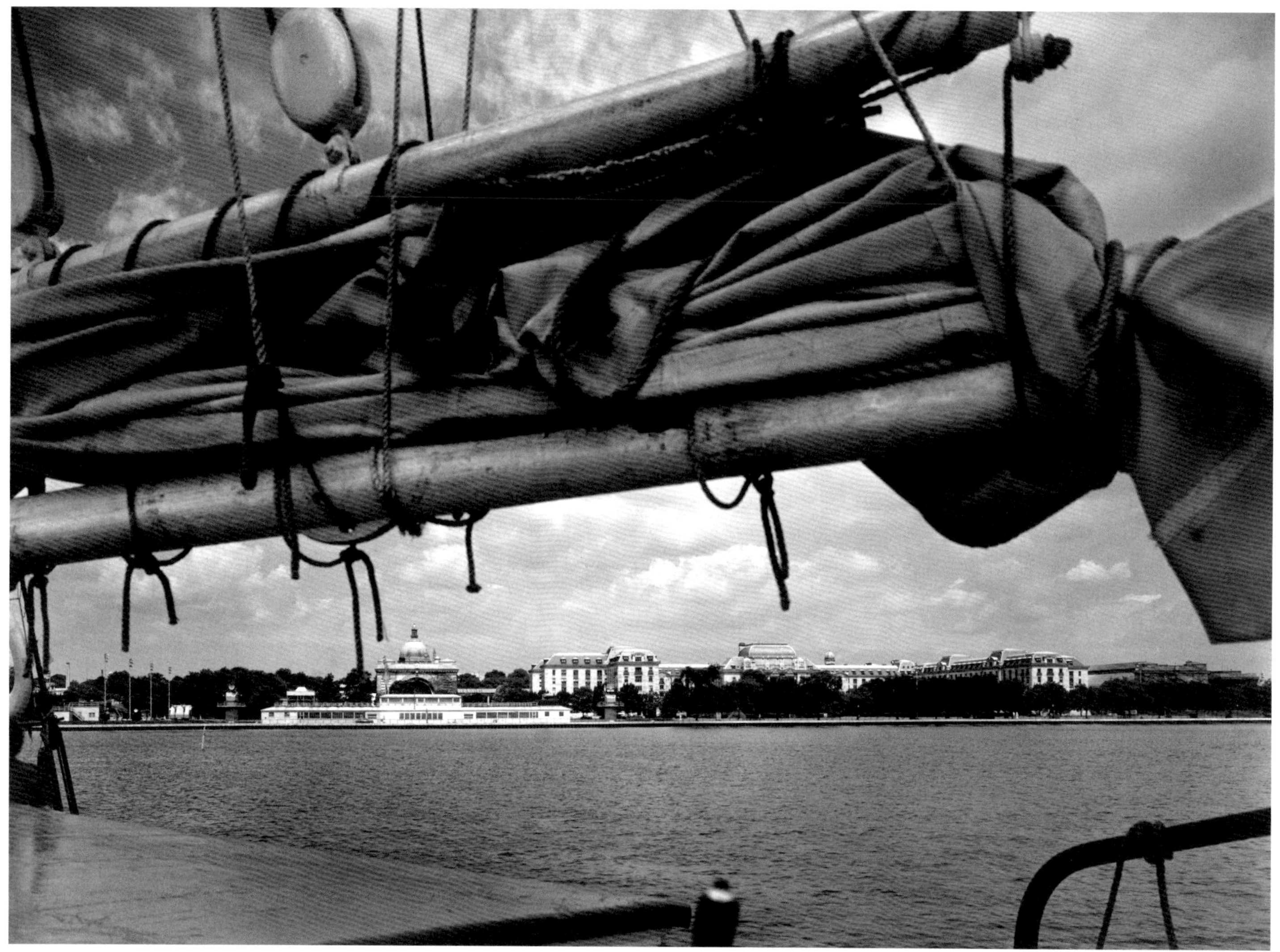

PLATE 157 Naval Academy from Westport (1949)

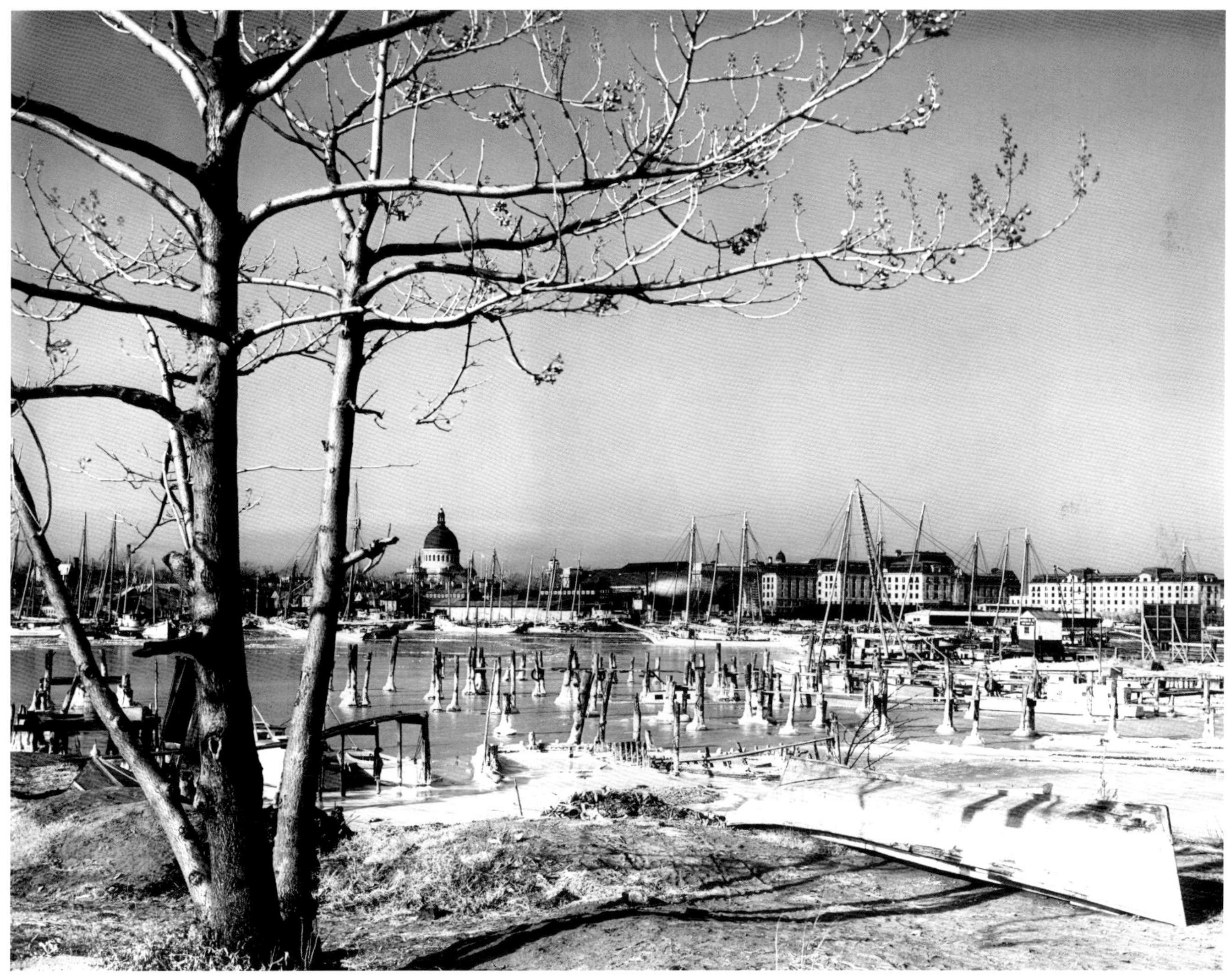

PLATE 158 Naval Academy (1949)

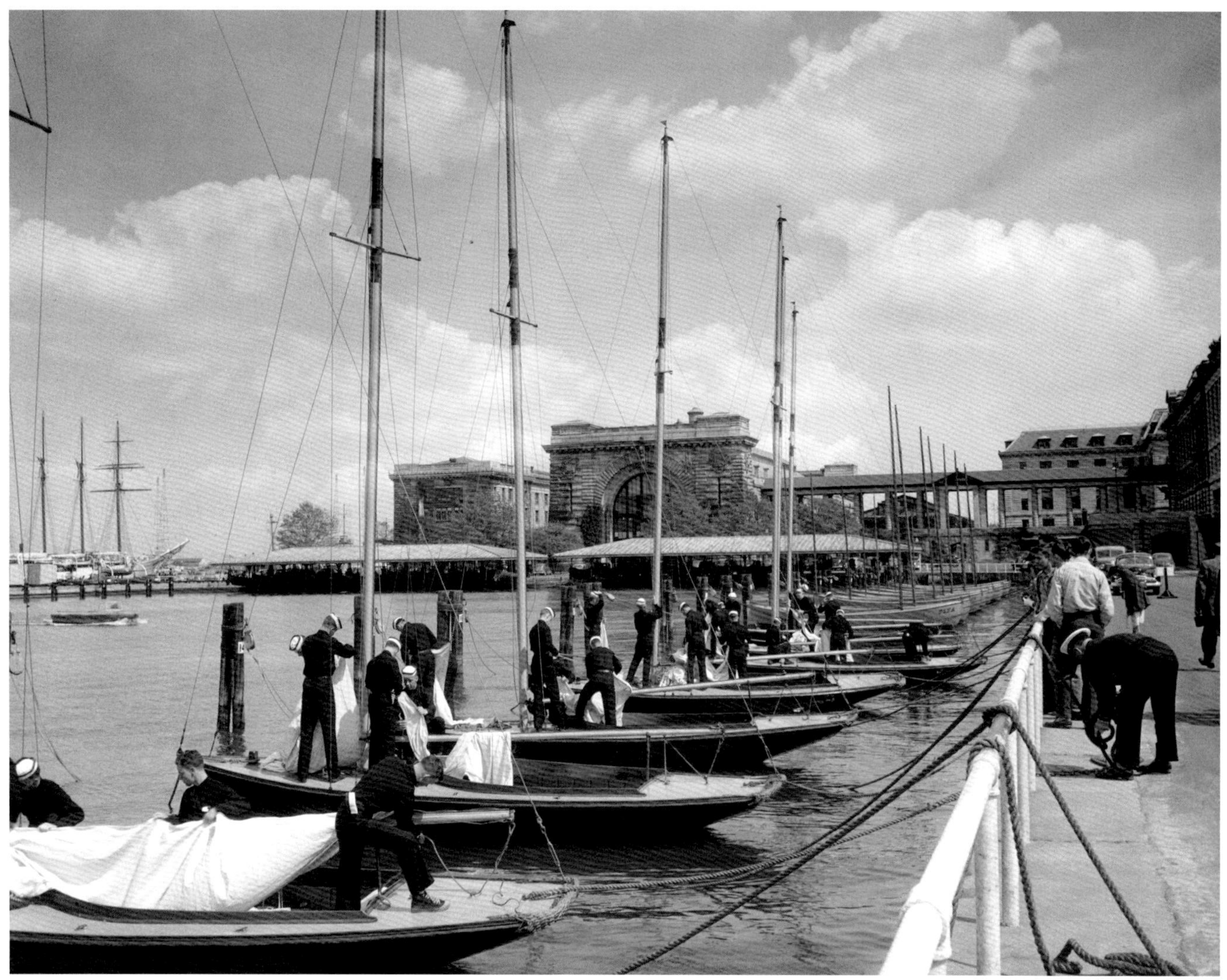

PLATE 159 Sailing on the Severn (ca. 1950)

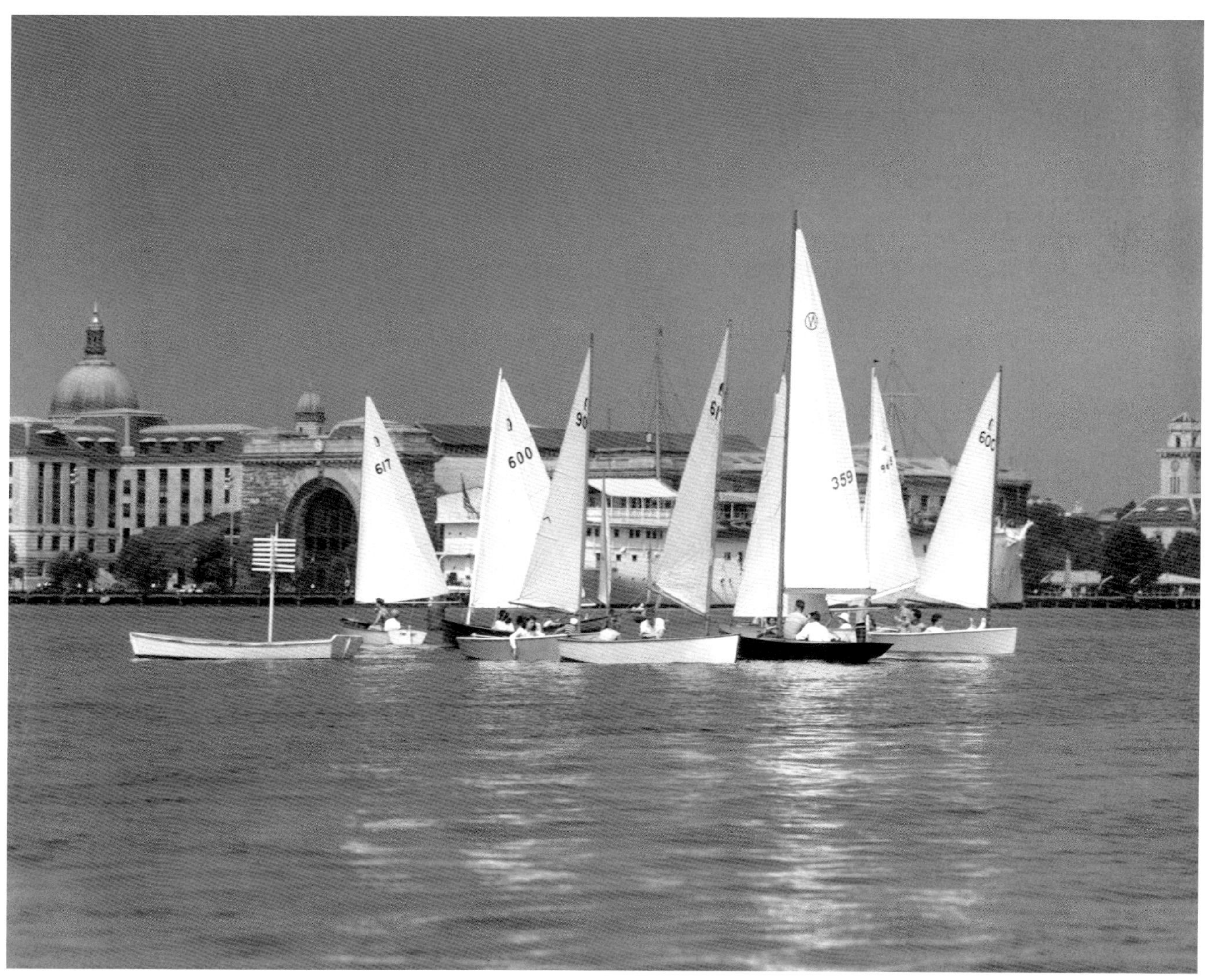

LEFT: PLATE 160 USS *Missouri* (1957)
RIGHT: PLATE 161 Off Annapolis (1954)

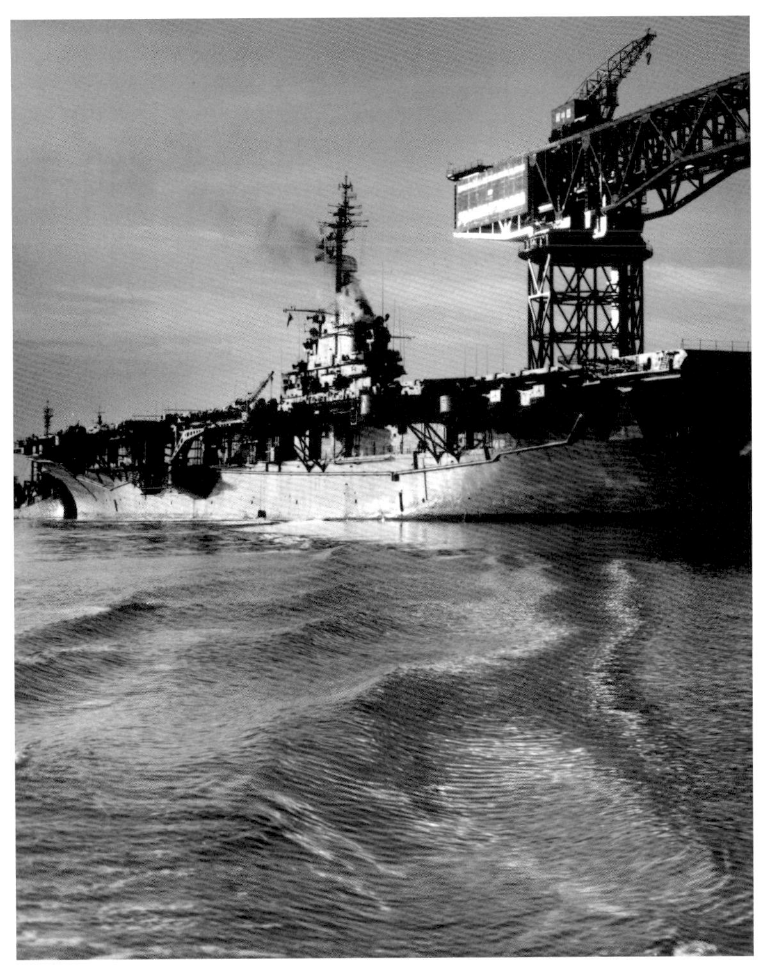

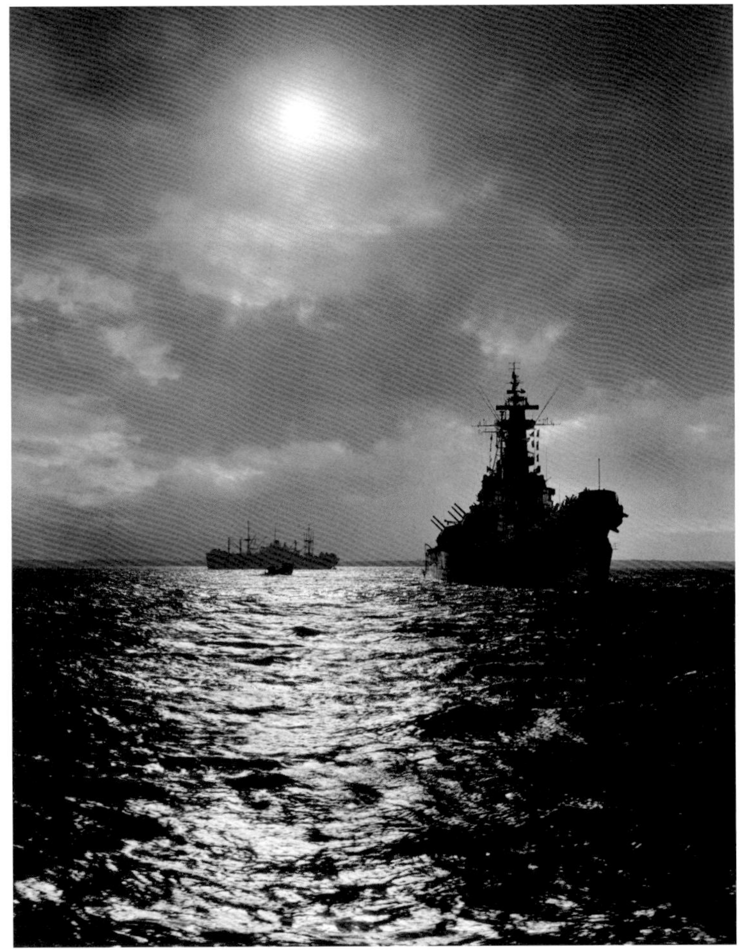

PLATE 162 USS *Missouri* off Annapolis for Middies (1954)

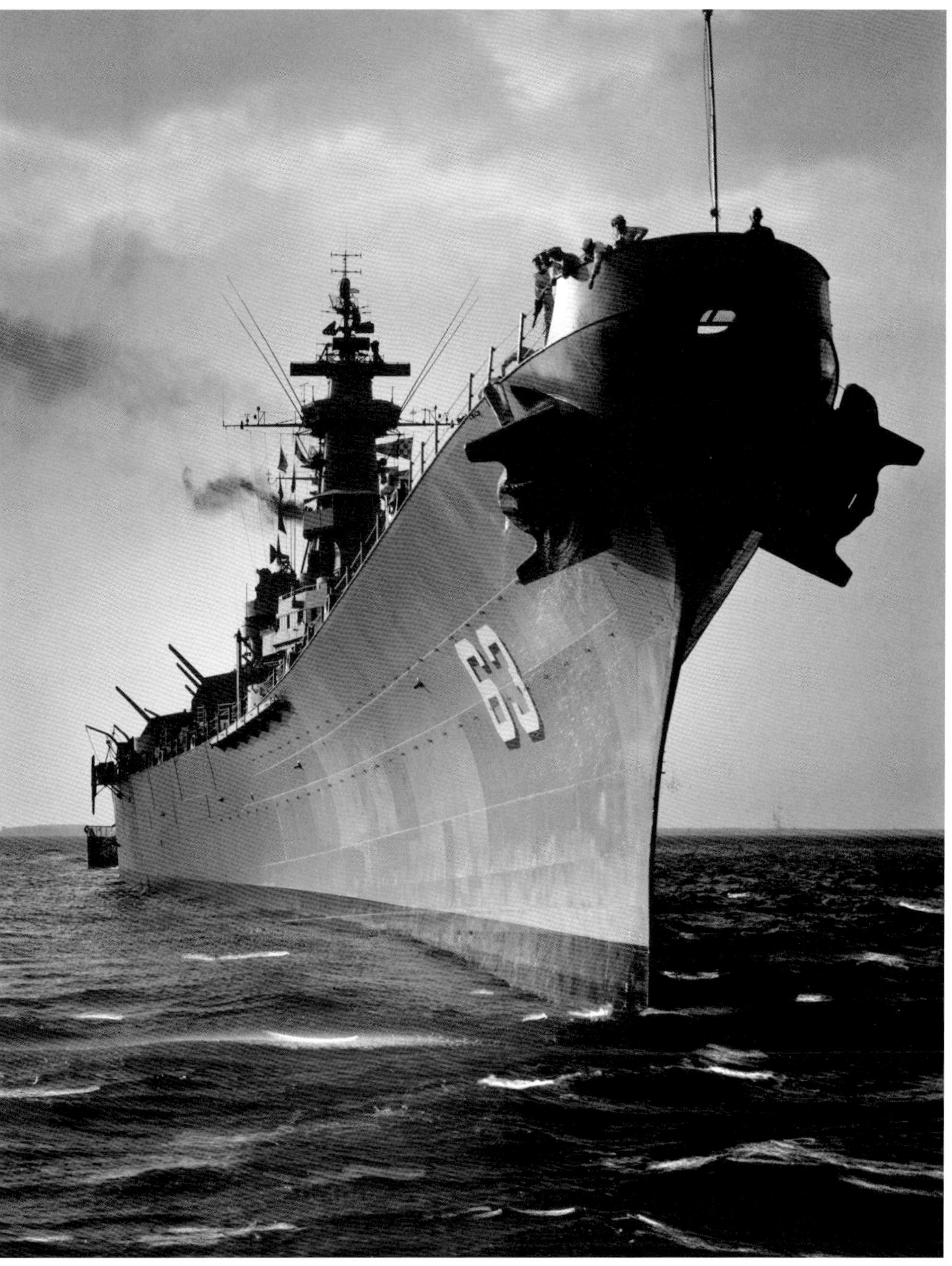

PLATE 163 Annapolis Eastport Bridge (1946).

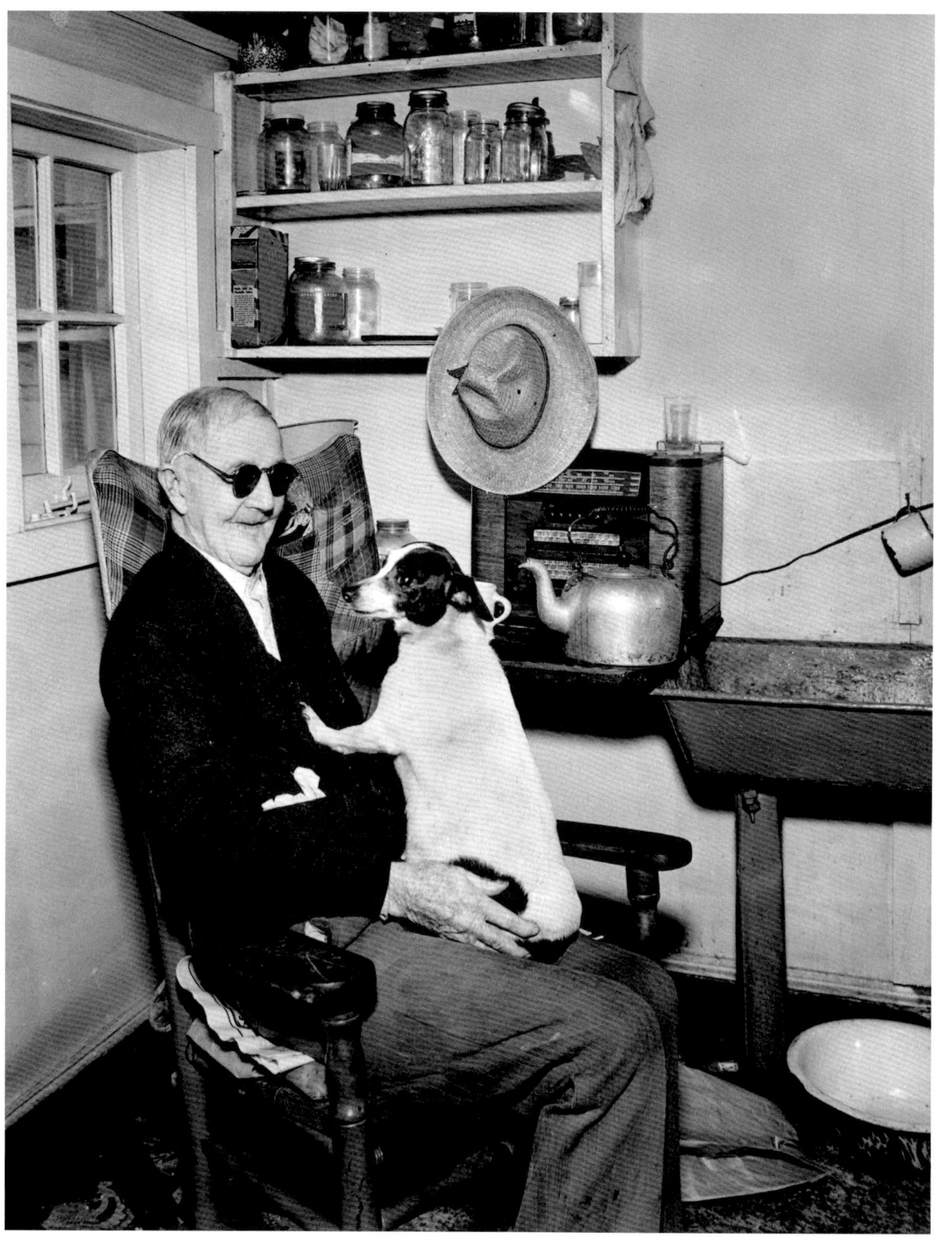

PLATE 164 Eastport Bridge, Annapolis (1938)

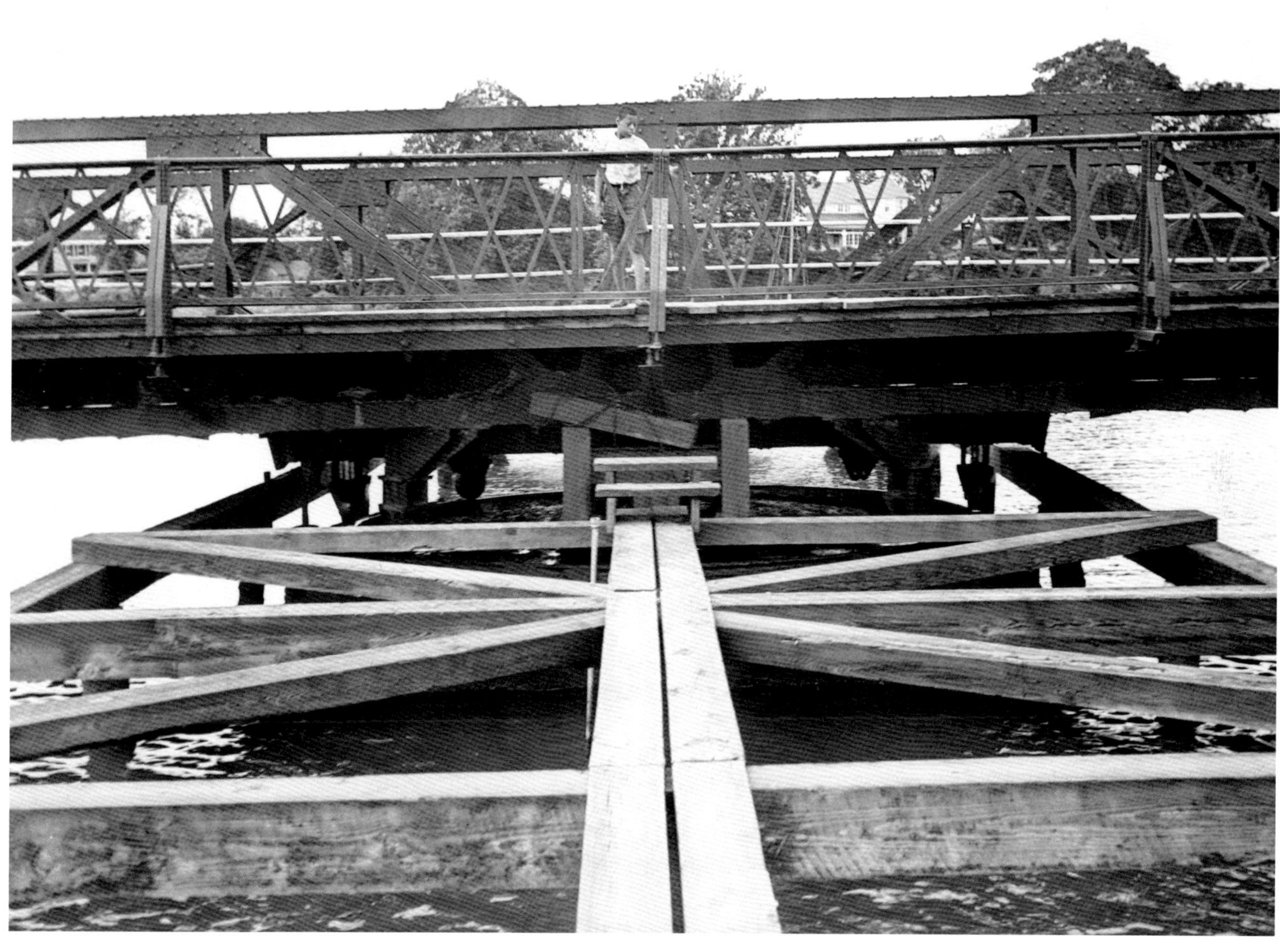

PLATE 165 Eastport Bridge, Annapolis (1938)

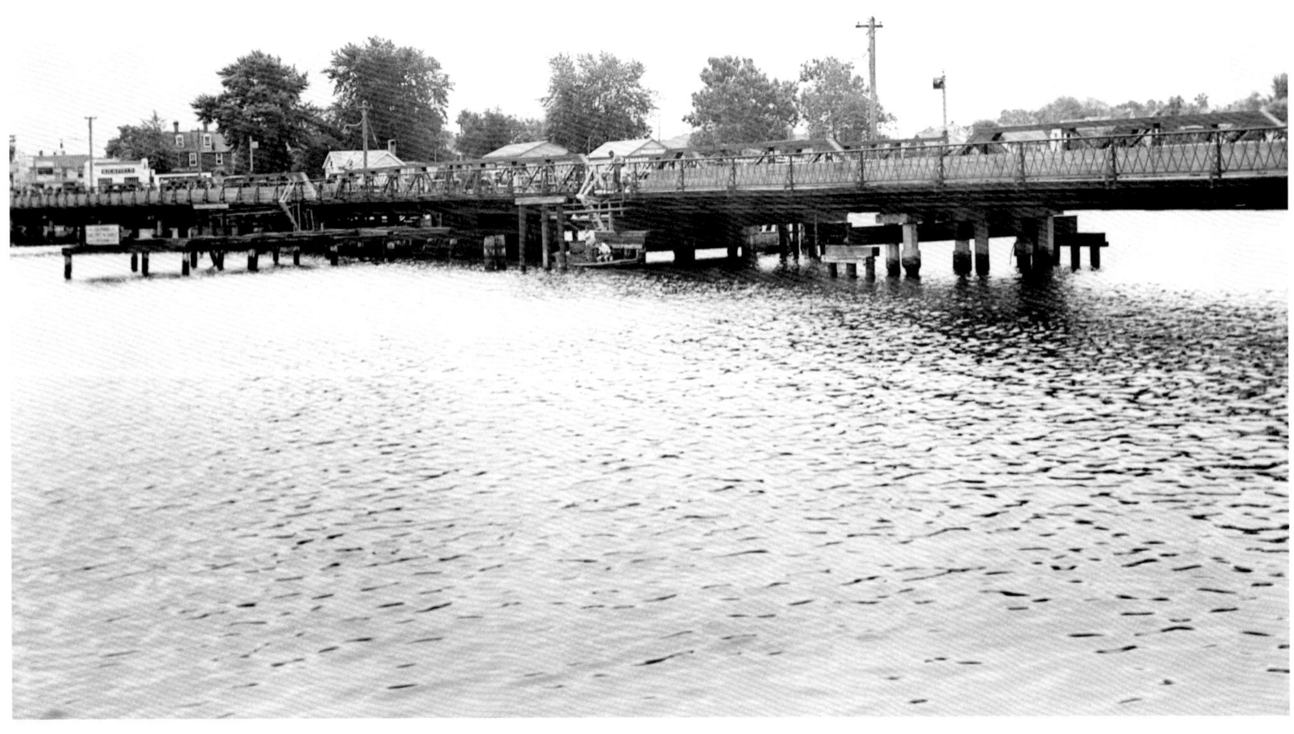

PLATE 166 Baltimore and Annapolis Railroad (1960)

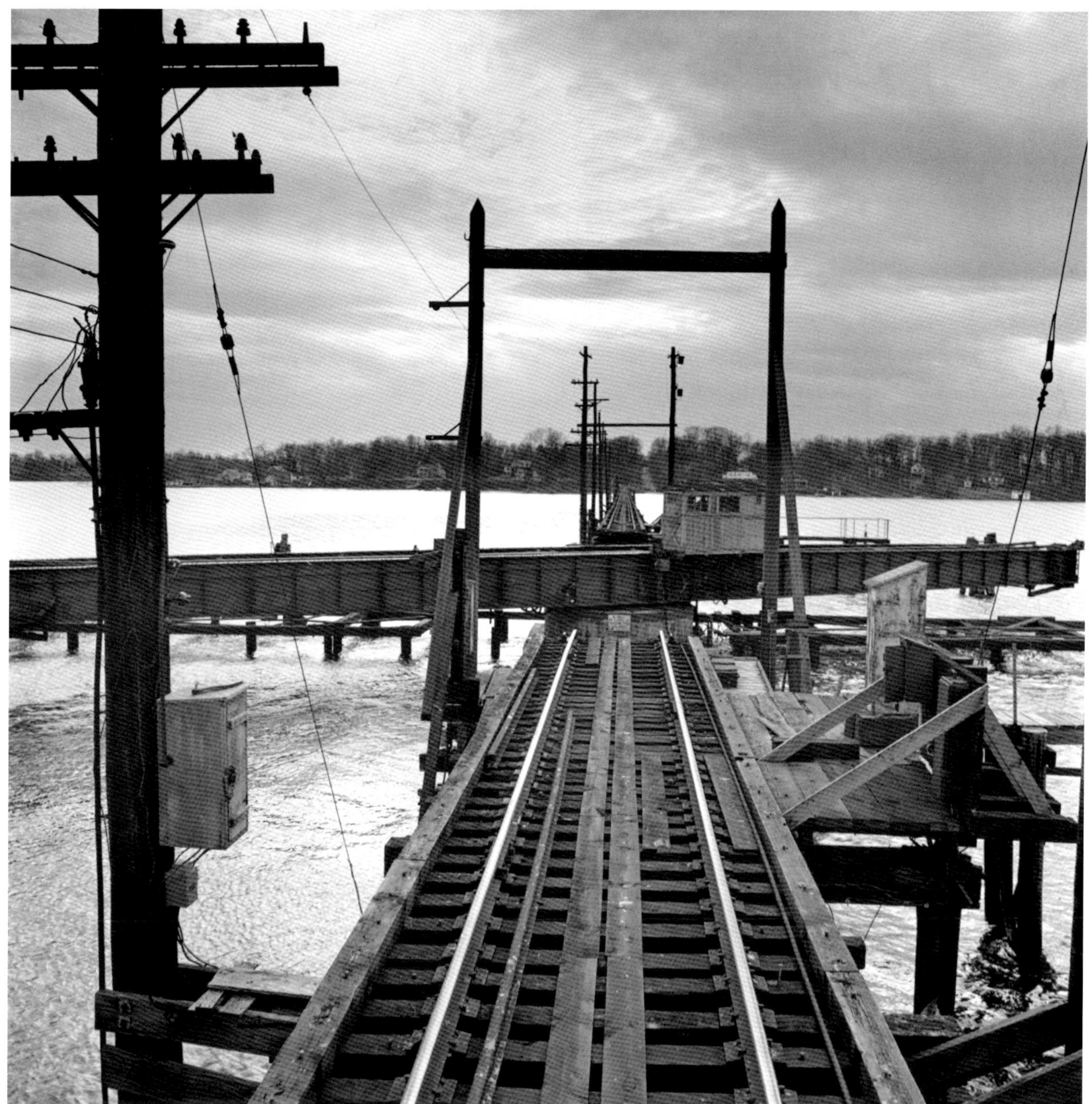

PLATE 167 Baltimore and Annapolis Railroad (1960)

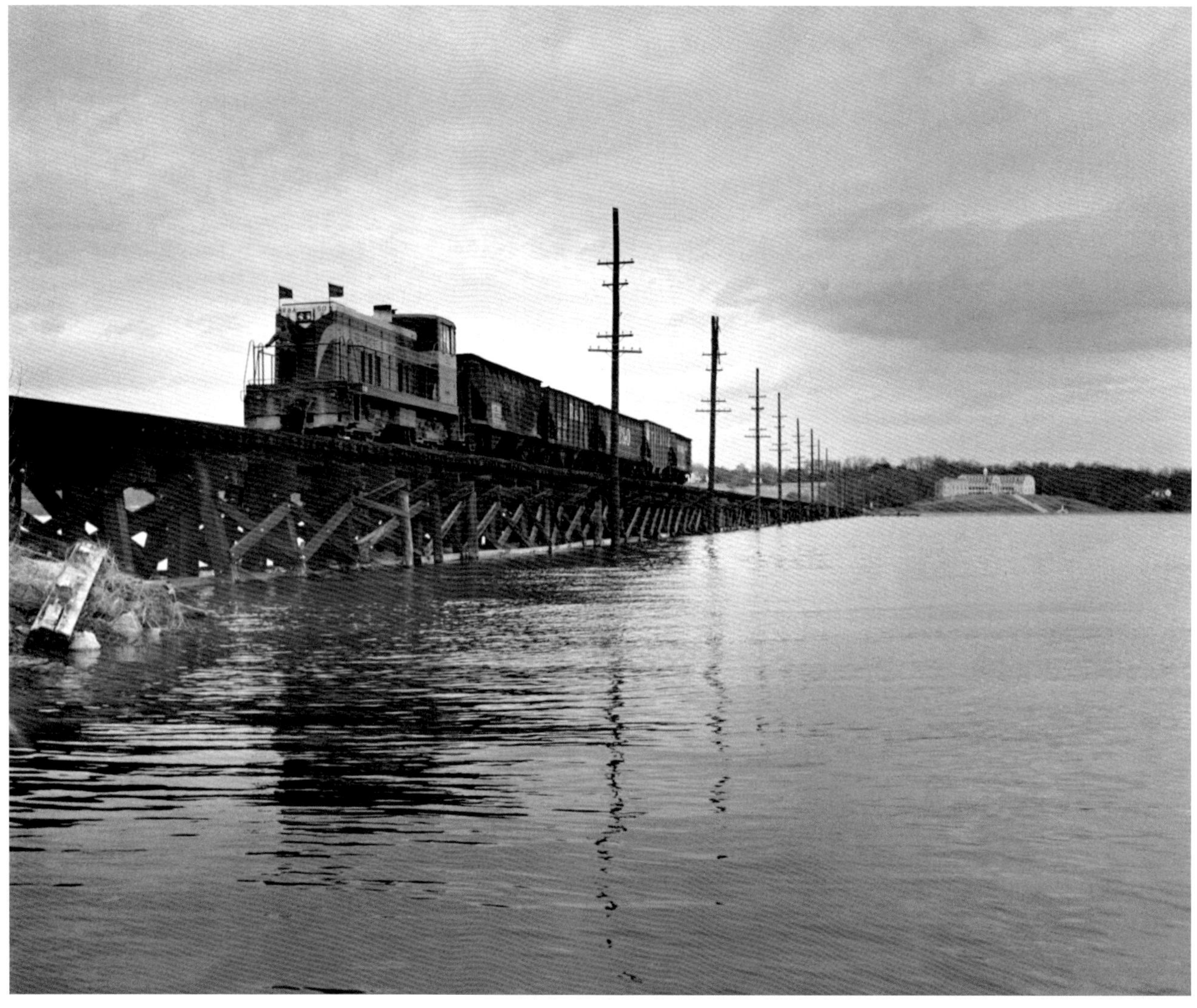

PLATE 168 End of the Line (1960)

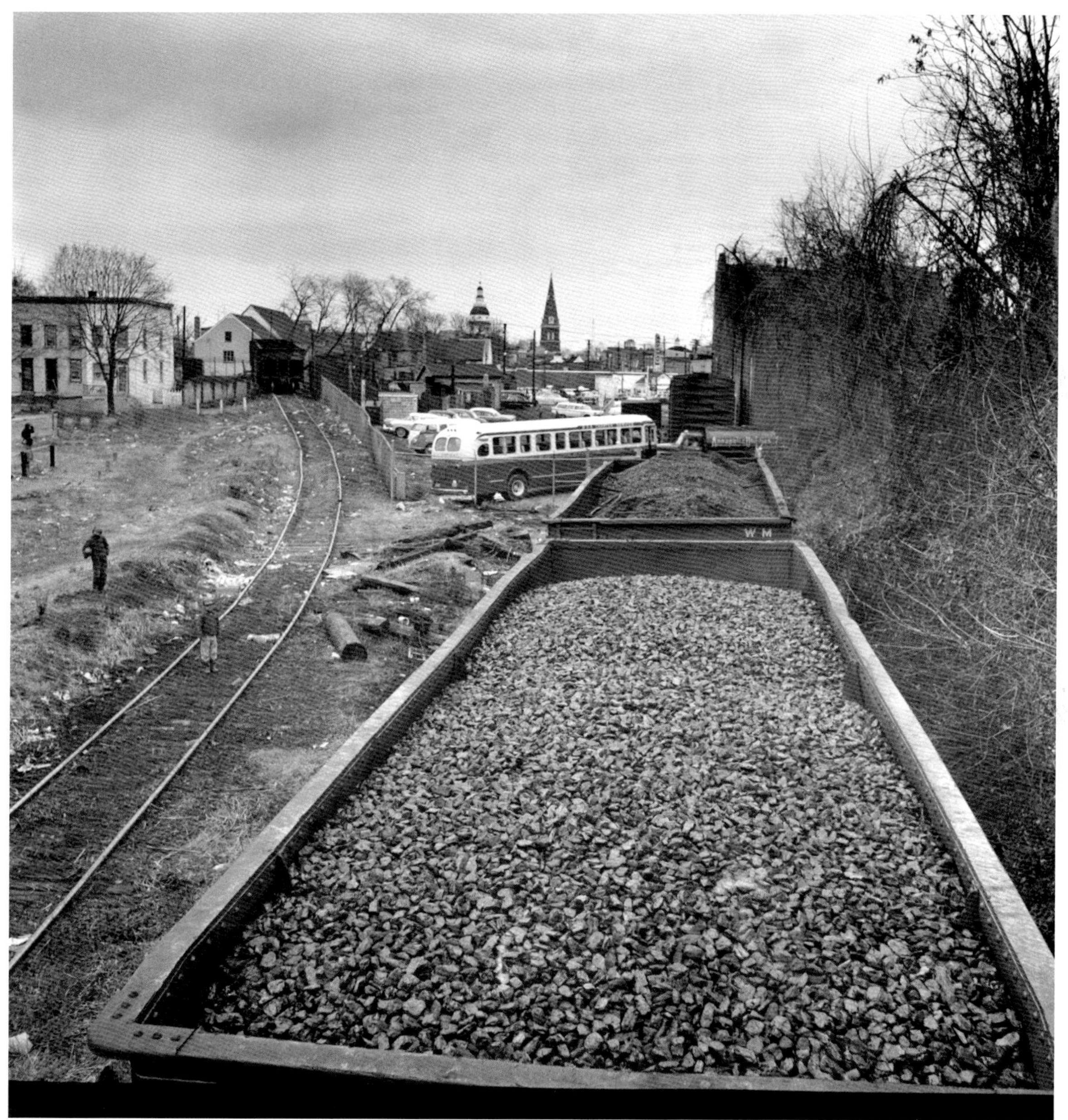

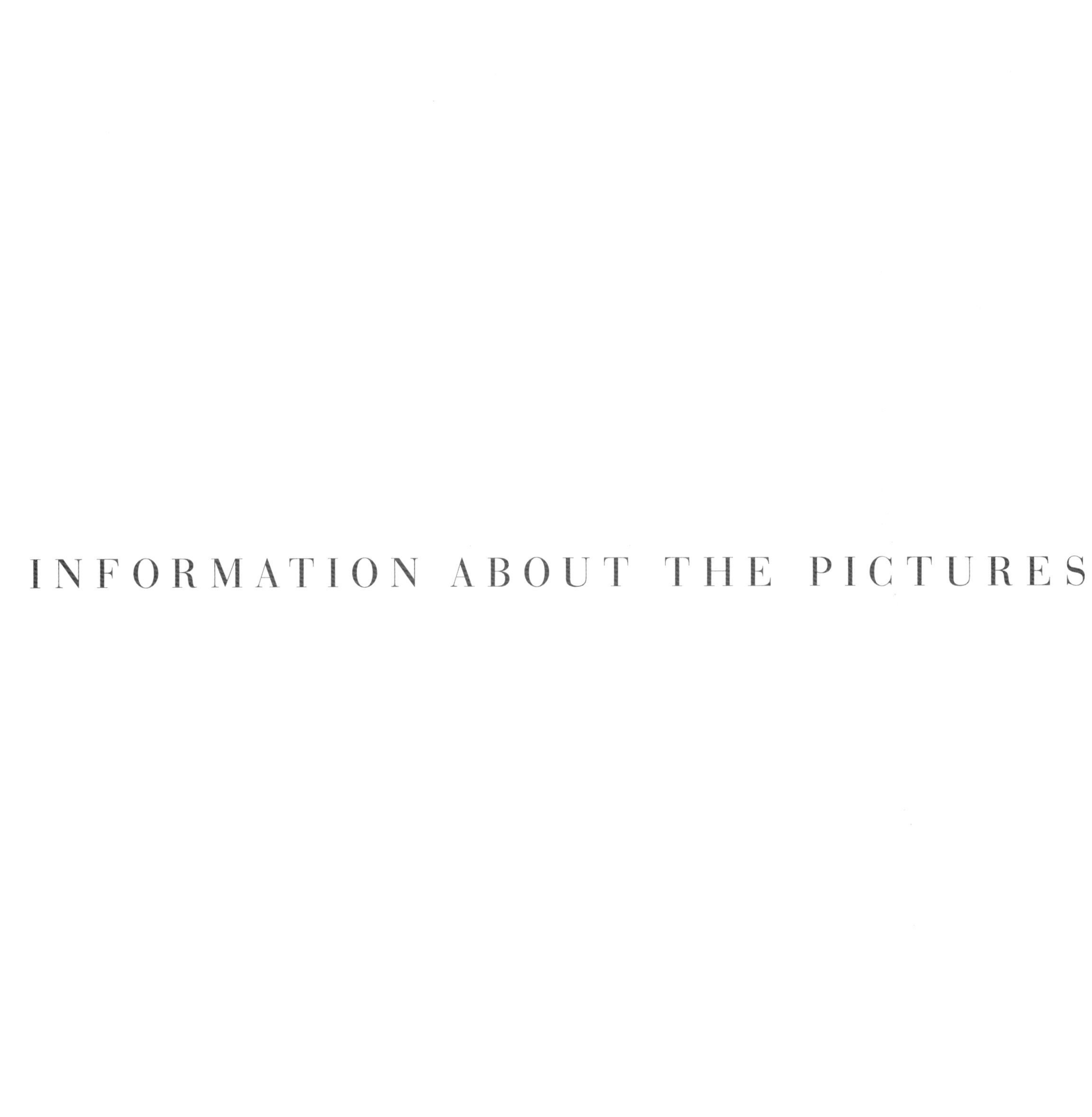

INFORMATION ABOUT THE PICTURES

PLATE 001. Annapolis, City Dock (1946). City Dock is off Spa Creek. Here is a view of the city and the State House dome. Small oyster, fishing, and crab boats tie up after a day in the bay and nearby rivers. Fishing parties find boats for hire.

PLATE 002. Shooting Stars (1953). Star boats, racing keel boats for two people, are sailing in Oxford. The first Star boat appeared in the Chesapeake after World War I. They are regulation 22 feet, 8 inches in length.

PLATE 003. Chesapeake Bay Races (1961). Sailboat racing on the Chesapeake Bay.

PLATE 004. Maryland State House, Annapolis (1962). This is the oldest state capitol in the United States still used for legislative purposes; construction began in 1772. This capitol has the distinction of being topped by the largest hand-hewn wooden dome in the United States constructed without nails; its white-painted dome is 116 feet high.

PLATE 005. June Week—Naval Academy Front of Bancroft Hall (1957). Midshipmen enter Bancroft Hall after noon formation. The entire brigade is housed in Bancroft Hall. Established on October 10, 1845, under Secretary of the Navy George Bancroft, the United States Naval Academy is the second oldest of the United States' five service academies. It educates officers for commissioning into the United States Navy and Marine Corps. The 338-acre campus is on the former grounds of Fort Severn, at the confluence of the Severn River and Chesapeake Bay, 33 miles east of Washington, DC, and 26 miles southeast of Baltimore. It replaced the Philadelphia Naval Asylum that served as the first United States Naval Academy from 1838 to 1845.

PLATE 006. *Highland Light* (1956). Dudley Wolfe raced her to the first under-three-day time in the Bermuda Race in 1932—a record that stood until 1974. Wolfe died in 1939 in a failed attempt to climb K2, and his sailboat was donated to the Navy for use at the Naval Academy. The craft was acquired in 1940 and remained in service at the academy until struck from the Naval Vessel Register in 1965. The *Highland Light* Trophy at the USNA is constructed from the ship's wheel. She was the winner of many races on the Chesapeake Bay.

PLATE 007. Annapolis, Brigade of Middies, Worden Field (1936). This photograph of the entire brigade of the United States Naval Academy—some 3,600 midshipmen—was taken from a helicopter. In autumn and spring the entire brigade drills at dress parades on Worden Field. In the background is the dome of the state capitol.

PLATE 008. Chesapeake Days (ca. 1950). A leisurely cruise on the Chesapeake Bay.

PLATE 009. Jonas Green House in Annapolis (ca. 1950). Jonas Green (d. 1767) was an American newspaper publisher during the colonial era in Maryland and a strong opponent of the Stamp Act. Green—a protégé of Benjamin Franklin—moved to Maryland in 1738 and became the province's official printer. He then became the publisher of the *Maryland Gazette*.

PLATE 010. Naval Academy (1931). Midshipmen leaving Dewey Basin for a sail.

PLATE 011. Government House, Annapolis (1967). Government House is the official residence of the governor of Maryland and is at State Circle. It has been the home of Maryland governors since 1870. In 1936, end chimneys, broad gables, Palladian windows, and flanking wings were added. In 1967 it underwent extensive renovation. St. Ann's Church is on the left.

PLATE 012. Government House Annapolis, (1954). Governor Theodore McKeldin with Jennifer Bodine—Bodine's daughter and editor of this book—standing by the mansion's reflecting pool.

PLATE 013. Annapolis Main Street (1965). This drawing illustrates a proposal for remodeling a section of Main Street. The aim is to retain the current buildings but bring them into conformity with the city's distinctive atmosphere.

PLATE 014. Chesapeake Bay Bridge (1955). Maryland's eastern and western shores are linked by one of the largest continuous entirely-over-water steel structures in the world. The bridge, shore to shore from Sandy Point to Kent Island, measures 4.35 miles. The entire project, including approach roads, is 7.727 miles long. About 6,500,000 man-hours of work and 60,000 tons of steel were needed to build it. Work began on November 3, 1949. The bridge opened on July 30, 1952. It cost about $45,000,000 and was to be paid for by tolls from this and other state bridges. The bridge was built in a graceful, sweeping curve to comply with regulations determined by the Corps of Engineers, US Army, and to land the structure on favorable terrain.

PLATE 015. City Dock Annapolis Harbor (1950). Annapolis "Crab Town" sunrise at City Dock.

PLATE 016. Annapolis Harbor (1957). Tongers and dredgers tied up at City Dock.

PLATE 017. Reflections of City Dock (1946). Fishing boats.

PLATE 018. City Dock, Annapolis (1946)

PLATE 019. City Dock, Annapolis (1946)

PLATE 020. City Dock, Annapolis (1946)

PLATE 021. City Dock, Annapolis (1957)

PLATE 022. City Dock, Annapolis (1959). View of Annapolis from the *Bay Belle* at City Dock.

PLATE 023. Annapolis Harbor (1947). Fishing boats are tied up at City Dock. The bows of fishing boats were used to create an interesting design; the central and most important object is the fishing boat about to depart.

PLATE 024. Annapolis Harbor (1942)

PLATE 025. St. Mary's and the Carroll House, Annapolis (1959). Charles Carroll of Carrollton (1737–1832)—the only Catholic signer of the Declaration of Independence—was born and raised in the house on the right. The original, smaller structure was built by his father, Charles Carroll, of Annapolis, in the 1720s. The house was substantially enlarged in the 1790s, and a wing added in 1856 gives it the appearance shown. The Victorian Gothic structure is St. Mary's Catholic Church on Duke of Gloucester Street; it was dedicated in 1860. For many years the Carroll House was used as a novitiate and a house of studies by the Congregation of the Most Holy Redeemer, a Catholic religious order whose members are known as Redemptorists.

PLATE 026. St. Mary's and the Carroll House, Annapolis (1943)

PLATE 027. Aerial view of Annapolis (1945). Aerial view of Annapolis looking toward City Dock and the Severn River.

PLATE 028. Aerial view of Annapolis (1945). Aerial view of Annapolis looking toward the Naval Academy (*left*); the eastern shore of Maryland is on the horizon in the background.

PLATE 029. Aerial view of Annapolis (1956). Streets in Annapolis radiate from State Circle and Church Circle. The stream is Spa Creek and across it is Eastport.

PLATE 030. Government House, Annapolis, Governor and Mrs. Millard Tawes (1964)

PLATE 031. Government House, Governor and Mrs. Spiro T. Agnew (1967)

PLATE 032. Government House (1967). See plate 011.

PLATE 033. Government House (1936). In 1935–36 the conversion of Government House to its current appearance took place; in 1947 more renovations were done, including cleaning, painting, and roof repairs.

PLATE 034. Government House Entrance Hall (1964). In the entrance hall are portraits of Queen Henrietta Maria, after whom Maryland was named, and Charles Calvert, Fifth Lord Baltimore. The portrait of Queen Henrietta Maria was painted in 1901 by Florence MacKubin after the original by Anthony Van Dyck, which hangs in Warwick Castle in England.

PLATE 035. Government House Drawing Room (1964). Charles Willson Peale's portrait of George Washington painted during the Revolutionary War decorates the drawing room.

PLATE 036. Governor J. Millard Tawes' office in Government House (1962)

PLATE 037. Governor's Mansion State Dining Room (1964). The Governor's Mansion state dining room has two fireplaces. The oval picture on the far wall is a portrait of Priscilla Downey Ridgely, wife of Gov. Charles Ridgely, and painted by Rembrandt Peale. It was presented by Mrs. Theodore McKeldin. The picture on the right wall is an eighteenth-century painting of Governor Sharpe's family by Gawen Hamilton. It was presented by Mrs. William Preston Lane.

PLATE 038. State House, Annapolis (ca. 1950). It houses the Maryland General Assembly and offices of the governor and lieutenant governor. Statue of Chief Justice of the United States Roger Brooke Taney (1777–1864) stands in front of the building. The statue was removed in 2017.

PLATE 039. Maryland State House Capitol Dome at Night (1962)

PLATE 040. Maryland State House Capitol Dome in Daytime (1962)

PLATE 041. Annapolis State House Dome Interior (1962). From ground floor looking up, the interior of the dome as it looks from the rotunda of the State House.

PLATE 042. Annapolis State House, Where Washington Resigned His Commission (1948). In the early days of the USA this room in the State House held its sessions from November 16, 1783, to June 3, 1784. During that time George Washington appeared before it and presented his resignation as commander in chief of the Continental army. It was here that the Treaty of Paris was ratified, whereby Great Britain formally recognized American independence.

PLATE 043. Ridout House, 120 Duke of Gloucester Street (1959). Built in 1765, Ridout House was the home of John Ridout, secretary to Governor Sharp. Ridout and his wife, Mary Ogle, were close friends of the George Washingtons and entertained them in this home until the revolution, when each man had to decide between king or country. The house faces east, with its garden extending down to the harbor. A portico extends from the main entrance and above are Palladian windows.

PLATE 044. Ridout House, 120 Duke of Gloucester Street (1959)

PLATE 045. Shiplap House (1960). Shiplap House (built c. 1715) is one of the oldest surviving houses in Annapolis. It served as a store and tavern in the eighteenth century. The house is named for its random-width flush siding (called shiplap).

PLATE 046. Carvel Hall (1970). The house was constructed between 1763 and 1765 by William Paca, a signatory of the Declaration of Independence. Its architecture was largely designed by Paca himself. The 2-acre walled garden, which included a two-story summer house, has been restored to its original state.

PLATE 047. Brice House (1937). The Brice House is a simplified Georgian-style mansion that relies on its elevated site along a narrow street. It is a five-part plantation house transplanted to an urban setting. The house remained in the Brice family until 1874. The house is substantially original in all respects, retaining its plasterwork, glass, woodwork, and flooring. Archeological excavations at the Brice House in 1998 uncovered hoodoo caches, spiritual offerings placed by slaves who were house servants at the mansion. Ghosts accredited to the house are said to be those of Mrs. Brice's son and a servant who clubbed him to death in the night.

PLATE 048. Brice House (1937)

PLATE 049. Brice House (1937)

PLATE 050. Brice House (1956)

PLATE 051. Brice House (1944)

PLATE 052. Hammond Harwood House (1950). Hammond Harwood house started construction in 1774 by Matthias Hammond, tobacco planter. This house is one of the premier colonial houses remaining in America from the British colonial period (1607–1776). It was designed by architect William Buckland in 1773–74. Harwood, whose name is attached to the home, was a Civil War-era schoolteacher whose loyalty to the south was such that he walked to Baltimore twice weekly rather than submit to a loyalty oath required of rail passengers.

PLATE 053. Hammond Harwood House (1952)

PLATE 054. Chase-Lloyd House (1944). The Chase-Lloyd House is a three-story brick Georgian mansion dating from 1769. Its construction was started for Samuel Chase, a signatory to the Declaration of Independence and associate justice of the Supreme Court. Chase sold the building unfinished to Edward Lloyd IV in 1771. Lloyd completed the house in 1774. The house remained in the Lloyd family until 1847, when it was sold to descendants of Chase. In 1888 the house was bequeathed for use as a home for elderly women. It continues in this use today.

PLATE 055. Chase-Lloyd House (1959)

PLATE 056. Chase-Lloyd House (1959)

PLATE 057. Whitehall (1952). Whitehall is a plantation house that was built starting in 1764, east of Annapolis, by Provincial Governor Horatio Sharpe. The house sits on a peninsula between Whitehall Creek and Meredith Creek, opposite Sharpe's Point on a branch of Chesapeake Bay. The site originally comprised about 1,000 acres. The house is a five-part Georgian mansion of great length, but only one room deep in the main section. It features elaborate original interior woodwork attributed to William Buckland and is one of only two pre–Revolutionary War houses in the thirteen colonies to have a temple portico. Tradition says George Washington danced and Benjamin Franklin played the musical glasses during one evening at Whitehall. It has been pronounced "one of America's truly great Colonial residences."

PLATE 058. Whitehall (1970)

PLATE 059. Tulip Hill (ca. 1950). Tulip Hill is a particularly fine example of an early Georgian mansion. The garden front overlooks the West River and the Chesapeake Bay. The house was erected in 1756, and was named for the tulip poplars that abounded on the property. In his diary George Washington recorded several visits here. It was built by Samuel Galloway for his wife, Ann (Chew) Galloway. The pierced chimneys were uncommon for the time.

PLATE 060. Oyster Tongers (1958). Hand-tonging for oysters from the slippery deck of a bobbing boat is one of the toughest jobs in Bay country. These watermen are working south of the Chesapeake Bay Bridge. Bodine wrote: "First of all, this particular area is my favorite hunting ground in the Chesapeake. Then the scene includes the Bay Bridge. And the oyster tongers provide some human interest."

PLATE 061. Bay Bridge Rising (1951)

PLATE 062. Chesapeake Bay Bridge Construction (1951). See plate 014.

PLATE 063. Chesapeake Bay Bridge Construction (1951)

PLATE 064. Moon Light Bay (1955)

PLATE 065. Ribbon of Light (1953)

PLATE 066. Jack Lewis, Annapolis Artist Sketching on Main Street (1946). A painter develops his vision of picturesque Main street just off City Dock.

PLATE 067. Annapolis: Main and Francis Streets (1965)

PLATE 068. Signs, Wires, and Concrete Veneer (1965). Signs, wires, and concrete veneer clutter Main Street as it appeared in 1965. One of the problems Annapolis faced was to modernize and yet preserve its colonial charm. The city council approved an ordinance requiring the removal of such signage.

PLATE 069. Cornhill Street, Annapolis (1953). Looking up Cornhill Street toward State Circle. Restoration of the old houses has given Cornhill Street a bright look. Once a private road leading to the governor's mansion, it was made into a street in 1720. The houses along it were occupied by small tradesmen and those engaged in importing and exporting.

PLATE 070. State House from Chancellor Court (1959). Costumed Heritage Week guides walk down Cornhill Street in Annapolis. The tall building in the background is the Old Treasury Building.

PLATE 071. Cornhill Street, Annapolis (1959). Costumed Heritage Week guides walk down Cornhill Street in Annapolis.

PLATE 072. Reynolds Tavern, St. Anne's Church (1940). In 1692 St. Anne's parish was established; it is the third church on this site, last rebuilt in 1859. An altar tomb contains the remains of Sir Robert Eden, the last provincial governor. To the left is the 1737 Reynolds Tavern. The tavern provided a meeting place for farmers, gentlemen, merchants, and soldiers. Here one could eat, drink, leave messages, buy theater tickets, conduct business and trade, stable horses, and have a game of cards, chess, or backgammon. The Corporation of the City of Annapolis and the Mayors Court met regularly at the tavern.

PLATE 073. Taylor Street—Helen's Lunchroom (1950). Taylor Street as seen from Legum's Corner in Annapolis. The curving thoroughfare is a favorite spot for photographers and artists who try to catch some of the charm of the old city, frequently called Crabtown.

PLATE 074. Taylor Street, Annapolis (ca. 1950)

PLATE 075. Taylor Street Annapolis (1952)

PLATE 076. Taylor Street Annapolis (1952)

PLATE 077. Cornhill Street (1953). 56 Cornhill Street, Annapolis.

PLATE 078. Cornhill Street (1953). All four houses were originally the same height; about 1900 the house on the left had a roof raising.

PLATE 079. Rock Fishing on the Ice, Spa Creek, Annapolis (1945)

PLATE 080. St. John's College (1952). St. John's College is a private liberal arts college. St. John's is one of the oldest institutions of higher learning in the United States as the successor institution of King William's School, a preparatory school founded in 1696. The current institution received a collegiate charter in 1784. Early alumni included two of Washington's nephews, as well as notable Marylanders Reverdy Johnson and Francis Scott Key.

PLATE 081. St. John's, McDowell Hall (1952). McDowell Hall is named for the first president of the college.

PLATE 082. Liberty Tree, St. John's College, Woodward Hall (1952). Revolutionary meetings held beneath it gained this name for the huge tulip poplar, believed to be more than 600 years old and 29 feet around. A treaty with Susquehannock Indians is said to have been signed under it in 1652. The tree stands in front of Woodward Hall, the library building of St. John's College. It reached a height of 120 feet. In the years preceding the American Revolution, liberty trees were meeting places for local patriots throughout the colonies. Prior to the Annapolis Tea Party in 1774, rebellious colonists met under the Liberty Tree before marching down to the harbor to burn the tea-laden brig *Peggy Stewart*. French soldiers under Lafayette camped under this tree en route to the battle of Yorktown in 1781. Lafayette was honored on a return trip to Annapolis in 1824. The stories this tree could tell. The tree was struck by lightning in 1999 and had to be removed for safety reasons. Roughly half of the Liberty Tree wood was purchased by Taylor Guitars in 2000.

PLATE 083. St. Johns College, Annapolis (1949). Shaded lawns and walks are hugged by ivy. McDowell Hall is on the left.

PLATE 084. Hall of Records, Annapolis (1958). The St. John's College library is on the southwest corner of the campus and is housed in the renovated building once known as the Maryland Hall of Records.

PLATE 085. Old Treasury Building (1956). The Old Treasury Building at State Circle is the oldest public building in the state. It was erected in 1735–37 for the issuance of paper money; it later became a council chamber.

PLATE 086. Sandy Point Light (ca. 1950). Sandy Point light is a three-story brick lighthouse on a caisson foundation erected in 1883. It lies 0.6 mi off Sandy Point, north of the Chesapeake Bay Bridge. The whole gamut of light sources ran from oil wicks, to incandescent oil vapor (1913), to electricity (1929). After automation in 1963, the light became subject to vandalism due to its visibility and accessibility. The original lens was destroyed in 1979. The Coast Guard made efforts to maintain and restore the structure from 1988 to 1990, but it continued to deteriorate. In 2006 it was sold at auction to a private bidder after an unsuccessful attempt to find a nonprofit group to take responsibility for the light.

PLATE 087. Thomas Point Light (ca. 1950). At the South River entrance to the Chesapeake Bay, Thomas Point Light was built in 1825 and is still in operation. The last manned lighthouse on the Chesapeake, it was automated in 1986.

PLATE 088. Bay Bridge, *Danmark*: "The Old and the New" (1958). The full-rigged ship that is about to pass under the modern Chesapeake Bay Bridge is the *Danmark*, on which for many years Danish merchant marine officers received their training. During World War II, thousands of American seamen were trained on her. She visited Baltimore on her last ocean voyage before the Danish government retired her from service.

PLATE 089. *Danmark*, "The Old and the New" (1958)

PLATE 090. Galesville (1952). Galesville is an unincorporated town in Anne Arundel County. It is along the western shore of the West River, an arm of the Chesapeake Bay. The area was an early center of Quaker settlement in America and, through the West River Friends meeting, is considered the birthplace of organized Quakerism in Maryland. The town was once the terminus of a steamship line connecting Annapolis and Baltimore. Once a thriving community of Chesapeake Bay watermen and their families, the town has developed an industry around pleasure boating.

PLATE 091. Oyster Boat and Buy Boat (1936)

PLATE 092. Oyster Boats (1936)

PLATE 093. The Big Freeze (1936). Normally the Chesapeake Bay is free from ice, but occasionally a severe winter belies its location below the Mason-Dixon Line; this happened in 1936. The bay iced over completely for 80 of its 195 miles, almost down to the Patuxent River. Its tributaries right on down to the James River froze. Fields of ice drift lay between the Virginia Capes. These dredge boats, framed by a necklace of icicles, sought shelter in Spa Creek in Annapolis; they were immobilized for weeks. The boats in this picture are in plates 091 and 092.

PLATE 094. Annapolis Ice Boat (1936)

PLATE 095. Great Freeze in Bay (1936). *Solarina* following the *Peter Kerr*. Ice breakers open the bay for freighter traffic during the big freeze of 1936.

PLATE 096. Chesapeake Bay (ca. 1963). The bay is an immensely rich protein source for Maryland, yielding millions of dollars commercially and providing superb recreational opportunities. Its future usefulness rests primarily on the care that is taken now. This crab potter is working his traps; 300 million crabs will be caught in Virginia and Maryland waters.

PLATE 097. Oyster Dredgers (1953). Dredging at the mouth of the Choptank River in Talbot County.

PLATE 098. Clams—Bay (1961). Thousands of bushels of Chesapeake softshell clams are sold in New England for its clambakes. Blown out of the mud and onto a conveyor belt by jets of water, the clams are brought up to the boat. Cullers earn 75 cents to $1 a bushel. Wives help many clammers.

PLATE 099. Clams (1961)

PLATE 100. Kent Narrows (ca. 1950). Kent Island is the largest island in the Chesapeake Bay and a historic place in Maryland. To the east, a narrow channel known as Kent Narrows barely separates the island from the Delmarva Peninsula, and on the other side the island is separated from Sandy Point, near Annapolis, by roughly 4 miles of water. The main waterway of the bay is at its narrowest at this point and is spanned here by the Chesapeake Bay Bridge. The Chester River runs to the north of the island and empties into the Chesapeake Bay at Kent Island's Love Point. To the south of the island lies Eastern Bay.

PLATE 101. Skipjacks, Kent Narrows (ca. 1950)

PLATE 102. Watermen by Bay Bridge (1953)

PLATE 103. Working on the Chesapeake Bay (1950)

PLATE 104. Chesapeake Bay (1962). Chesapeake Bay off Point No Point.

PLATE 105. *Edwin & Maud* (1953). The ram is built with a narrow beam, enabling it to pass through the C&D Canal. The schooner—a three-mast ram built in Bethel, Delaware—was christened the *Edwin & Maud* after her captain's two children. During the first half of the twentieth century she carried lumber and fertilizer along the Eastern Seaboard. *Edwin & Maud* served as a merchant vessel during both world wars. Because she was constructed of wood, she was assigned duty during WWII to check the antisubmarine mine fields of the Chesapeake Bay, making sure magnetic mines were still on station. After WWII she was converted to the passenger trade, sailing for several years out of Annapolis.

PLATE 106. *Edwin & Maud* (1953)

PLATE 107. *Edwin & Maud* (1953)

PLATE 108. *Levin J. Marvel* (1950). The *Levin J. Marvel*—one of the last five rams to sail the bay—sank off North Beach Park, Holland Point, in 1955, with a loss of fourteen lives. Rams, none of which are to be found on the Chesapeake today, are three masted, bald headed (without topmasts), and schooner rigged. They were designed to carry heavy cargoes of lumber from the Carolina sounds. On Monday, August 8, 1955, the *Marvel* left Annapolis with four crew members and 23 passengers anticipating a week long bay journey. The loss of the 125-ft. *Levin J. Marvel* remains one of the worst maritime calamities in the history of tidewater Maryland. This loss resulted in a change in Coast Guard regulations regarding passenger carrying vessels. The following year Congress passed a law giving the Coast Guard authority to regularly inspect all commercial vessels carrying more than six passengers.

PLATE 109. *Levin J. Marvel* (1950)

PLATE 110. Claiborne to Annapolis Ferry (1941). The Claiborne-Annapolis Ferry Company ran both passenger and automobile ferry service across the Chesapeake Bay from 1919 to 1952. Cars are waiting to cross the bay aboard the *Dennis*.

PLATE 111. Annapolis Matapeake Ferry (1940). Ferries ran from Matapeake to Annapolis beginning in July 1930, as the connecting link between the Eastern and Western Shores of Maryland. The clubhouse, built in 1936, served as a place to have a meal or get a drink while waiting to board the ferry. Prior to the opening of the Chesapeake Bay bridge in 1952, a 3-mile-long line of cars often waited on peak summer weekends to board the small Matapeake ferry.

PLATE 112. *Gov. Harry W. Nice* Ferry (1941). The keel was laid September 15, 1937, at Maryland Drydock Co. She launched December 11, 1937, and was delivered April 30, 1938. The dimensions were 208' × 62' × 9' and six lanes across; she was placed in service on May 4, 1938, under Capt. Thomas Woolford. The capacity was 65 vehicles, 730 passengers, accommodation for a crew of 22, and staterooms for four officers. She was purchased by Washington State Ferries in 1951 for use on the Puget Sound and renamed the *Olympic*.

PLATE 113. Schooner *J. A. Chelton* (1930). The schooner *J. A. Chelton* and the steamer *Annapolis* in the background.

PLATE 114. Sailing (ca. 1950)

PLATE 115. *Gov. Emerson C. Harrington* (1940). The *Gov. Emerson C. Harrington* was retired in 1937 and replaced by the *Gov. Harry W. Nice*, a double ender that could hold up to 68 cars. It was sold in 1938 to C. K. Duncan, who brought the vessel to Pocomoke City, Maryland, and made it into a floating restaurant, nightclub, and hotel. In 1949, the superstructure was stripped off and her furnishings were purchased by a VFW for its new post home.

PLATE 116. Annapolis Boatyard (1928). Spa Creek is on the Eastport side of the bridge. The large shed may be the current Chart House Restaurant. The yard became Trumpy's Boatyard in 1947.

PLATE 117. Annapolis Yacht Club, Largest in America (ca. 1950). Once known as the Severn Boat Club, the Annapolis Yacht Club is one of the oldest in the country and traces its origin to 1886. This building, which some members refer to as "Japanese Colonial" in style, was completed in 1963 at a cost of $500,000. The club is the starting point in alternate years for the classic yacht race between Annapolis and Newport. It suffered a catastrophic fire in 2015; the club was rebuilt and has been restored to its former glory.

PLATE 118. Chesapeake Bay Racing (ca. 1950). A fleet of racing sailboats stretches out during a race in perfect sailing weather. The Chesapeake Bay is one of the best sailing areas in the United States. Along its shores are hundreds of yacht clubs, boat clubs, and marinas. Bay waters are used just about the year round by a variety of craft, ranging from ancient log canoes to sleek ocean-racing yachts.

PLATE 119. Sailboats, Chesapeake Bay (1947)

PLATE 120. Sailing off Naval Academy—Severn River (ca. 1950)

PLATE 121. Chesapeake Bay Championship Races (1932). The Star boats make time. Two racing Stars off Gibson Island are racing with the committee boat *Water Gypsy* in the background.

PLATE 122. Rounding the Mark (1947)

PLATE 123. Sailing on the Severn (ca. 1950)

PLATE 124. Rounding the Mark (ca. 1950). Two racing yawls heel hard to port as they round the course mark in a Chesapeake Bay race from Gibson Island to Cedar Point.

PLATE 125. *Royona*, Naval Academy (1952). *Royona* was designed in 1935 and built for D. Spencer Berger in 1936. In 1948 she was offered to the Naval Academy. John F Kennedy and Marilyn Monroe are believed to have had a rendezvous onboard.

PLATE 126. Chesapeake Bay Championship Races (1932). The *Sole* wins the Chesapeake Bay Championship.

PLATE 127. Chesapeake Bay Sailboat Race (1955). Three racing yachts streak down the bay in the Chesapeake Skipper invitation 100-mile, which is from the Severn River to Point-No-Point Lighthouse and return. The trip has been made in seventeen hours. One year it took almost thirty hours.

PLATE 128. Go Navy! (1936). This photograph of the entire brigade of the United States Naval Academy—some 3,600 midshipmen—was taken from a helicopter.

PLATE 129. Naval Academy Midshipmen (1947)

PLATE 130. Bancroft Hall—Naval Academy (1957). June Week—the Naval Academy front of Bancroft Hall.

PLATE 131. Bancroft Hall, Naval Academy, Annapolis (1952). The United States Naval Academy is a four-year coeducational federal service academy in Annapolis, Maryland.

PLATE 132. Marching Stribling Walk (1929). Company #7, winner of competitive drills.

PLATE 133. Naval Academy June Week (1956). A dress parade on Worden Field officially opens the June Week ceremonies. During fall and spring of the academic year, the midshipmen brigade drills here weekly.

PLATE 134. Eyes Right! (1932). Dress parade on Worden Field.

PLATE 135. June Week, Dress Parade (1949). Dress Parade on Worden Field.

PLATE 136. June Week (1936). 1936 Dress Parade on Worden Field.

PLATE 137. Naval Academy Chapel (1940). The midshipmen attend nondenominational services every Sunday. The dome towers more than 200 ft. In a crypt beneath the chapel are the sarcophagus of John Paul Jones and other historic relics.

PLATE 138. Tecumseh, Naval Academy (1940). This bronze replica of the USS *Delaware*'s figurehead is Tecumseh, the god of 2.5—the academy's passing grade (perfect is 4.0). Tamanend was honored as the figurehead of USS *Delaware* in a carving by William Luke. The *Delaware* burned in 1861 at the Gosport Navy Yard to prevent Confederate capture at the start of the Civil War. In 1868 the saved figurehead, officially titled *Tamanend, Chief of Delaware Indians*, was transferred to the Naval Academy. It was placed on a pedestal outdoors and simply labeled as the "figurehead of the *Delaware*." It was replaced with a bronze depiction in 1930, presented by the class of 1891. The bronze was cast at the US Naval Gun Factory in 1929–30. Tamanend—a pacifist and friend to William Penn—did not inspire the midshipmen of the academy. They eventually took to calling the figurehead Tecumseh, after the Shawnee warrior chief and ally of the British who was killed in the Battle of the Thames during the War of 1812. The statue is positioned on a base of Vermont marble immediately in front of Bancroft Hall and measures 96 × 59 × 46 in. The area between the figurehead and Bancroft Hall is called Tecumseh Court.

PLATE 139. Chapel, Naval Academy (1940)

PLATE 140. Tecumseh, US Naval Academy (1947)

PLATE 141. Naval Academy Midshipman (1947). Marine engineering class with a plastic experimental model of a gas turbine.

PLATE 142. Naval Academy Midshipman (1947)

PLATE 143. Naval Academy Midshipman (1947). A midshipman is inspecting a jet motor.

PLATE 144. Naval Academy Library (1957). Reading room of the US Naval Academy library in Mahan Hall.

PLATE 145. Navy–Ohio State Football Game (1930). Ohio State 27, Navy 0. Midshipmen (1,800) spell "Navy" with their programs during halftime.

PLATE 146. Navy–Ohio State Football Game (1930). Ladies from the Women's College of Maryland are in attendance.

PLATE 147. Worden Field: Presentation of Colors (1932). June Week.

PLATE 148. Bill the Goat (1928). The navy mascot did his share of parading up and down the field.

PLATE 149. *Highland Light* (1942). This tremendous sail, resembling a half section of a blimp, is the parachute spinnaker the Naval Academy's yacht *Highland Light* carried as it finished first in the Chesapeake Bay Yacht Club race from Gibson Island to Town Point, Oxford. The yacht's speed won it the "Poker Bowl." The occasion was the fiftieth annual sailing races sponsored by the Chesapeake Bay Yacht Club.

PLATE 150. Day at the Races (1927). A group of interested spectators from Annapolis watching the races from aboard the Maryland Conservation Commission boat *Kent*.

PLATE 151. *Highland Light* (1942)

PLATE 152. *Valmarie* (1952). A ketch-rigged ocean racing yacht donated to the Regiment of Midshipmen at the United States Naval Academy in 1936. The *Valmarie* was the US Navy's racing yacht in local races on the Chesapeake Bay during the racing season in 1937. She was struck from the Navy list in 1955 and was broken up in December of the same year.

PLATE 153. *USNA Royona* (1952). See plate 125

PLATE 154. Naval Academy from Eastport (1953). Annapolis from Eastport, overlooking Spa Creek.

PLATE 155. Naval Academy from Eastport (1949)

PLATE 156. Naval Academy (1951). The Naval Academy grounds stretch along the Severn River, and a view of the buildings may be had from the shore opposite as shown. This picture was taken from the three-mast ram *Levin Marvel*.

PLATE 157. Naval Academy from Westport (1949)

PLATE 158. Naval Academy (1949). Small boat basin.

PLATE 159. Sailing on the Severn (ca. 1950). Small pleasure boats sailing in the Severn in front of the Naval Academy.

PLATE 160. USS *Missouri* (1957). *Big Mo*—every June a task force of battleships, heavy cruisers, escort carriers, and destroyer vessels move up the bay to Annapolis, where midshipmen board the ships for the summer cruise. The USS *Missouri* is often the flagship of the force. Early in 1950, the 45,000-ton ship spent fifteen ignominious days off Old Point Comfort aground on a Chesapeake Bay mudbank. The battleship is best known for its role in Tokyo Bay. On September 2, 1945, Japanese leaders boarded the ship to sign the instrument of format surrender to the Allied powers, ending World War II.

PLATE 161. Off Annapolis (1954)

PLATE 162. USS *Missouri* off Annapolis for Middies (1954)

PLATE 163. Annapolis Eastport Bridge (1946). William T. Branzell, the 86-year-old bridge tender on the Annapolis Eastport Bridge over Spa Creek, relaxes with his best friend. For the past twenty-six years he has lived in a little house on the bridge which is being replaced with a modern structure.

PLATE 164. Eastport Bridge, Annapolis (1938). Center of Eastport Bridge.

PLATE 165. Eastport Bridge, Annapolis (1938)

PLATE 166. Baltimore and Annapolis Railroad (1960). The Severn River drawbridge in its usual position (open). Normally the Severn bridge's draw stands open like this to let boats pass. The train's brakeman must close it to cross.

PLATE 167. Baltimore and Annapolis Railroad (1960)

PLATE 168. End of the Line (1960). The Baltimore and Annapolis Railroad at the southern end of the line on West Street. The B&A hauls much of the coal for the Naval Academy.

PLATE 169. A. Aubrey Bodine Portrait (ca. 1950)

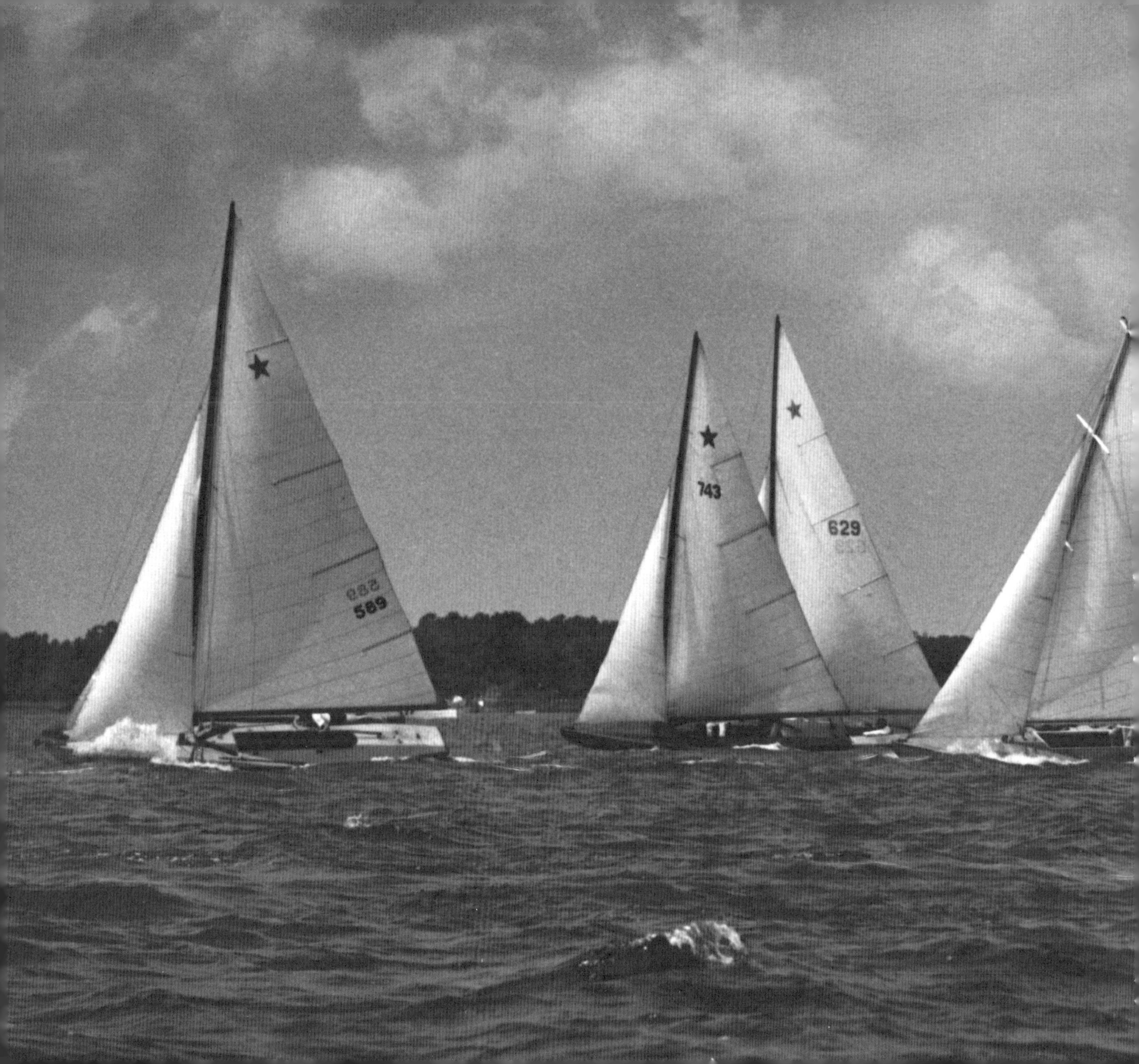
589
743
629